A CAMPER'S GUIDE TO OREGON & WASHINGTON

The Only Complete Guide to the Region's Non-membership RV Parks and Improved Tent Campgrounds

Third Edition

A CAMPER'S GUIDE TO OREGON & WASHINGTON

The Only Complete Guide to the Region's Non-membership RV Parks and Improved Tent Campgrounds

Third Edition

By KiKi Canniff

Ki² Enterprises
P.O. Box 186
Willamina, OR 97396

Library of Congress Cataloging-in-Publication Data

Canniff, KiKi
A camper's guide to Oregon & Washington: the only complete
guide to the region's non-membership RV parks and improved
tent campgrounds / by KiKi Canniff. -- 3rd ed.
p.   cm.
Includes index.
ISBN 0-941361-07-1
1. Camp sites, facilities, etc. -- Oregon -- Directories. 2. Camp
sites, facilities, etc. -- Washington (State) -- Directories.
I. Title.   II. Title: Camper's guide to Oregon and Washington.
GV191.42.07C36   1995
647'.94795 --dc20   95-2136

ISBN #0-941361-07-1

Ki² Enterprises
P.O. Box 186
Willamina, Oregon 97396

TABLE OF CONTENTS

Introduction 7
   What you will find in this book 7
   What to expect from a campground operator 7
      Private Campground Operators 7
      National Forest Service 8
      National Park Service 8
      Bureau of Land Management 9
      Oregon State Parks 9
      Washington State Parks 9
      Other Operators 10
   How the campground listings are arranged 10
   How to figure overnight fees 11
   Campground directions and abbreviations 12
   Choosing the right campground for your RV 12
   Tips for tent campers 12
   Tips for bicycle, horse and boat campers 13
   Accessibility for disabled campers 13
   Finding a group campground 14
   Camping with pets 14
Oregon's campgrounds 15
   Campgrounds along the Oregon Coast 17
   Campgrounds along the Oregon I-5 Corridor 49
   Campgrounds in Central Oregon 85
   Campgrounds in Eastern Oregon 115
Washington's campgrounds 127
   Campgrounds along the Washington Coast 129
   Campgrounds along the Washington I-5 Corridor .149
   Campgrounds in Central Washington 189
   Campgrounds in Eastern Washington 211
Index – by campground name, cities, and facilities 237
   Alphabetical index of Oregon campgrounds 238
   Alphabetical index of Washington campgrounds ...246

INTRODUCTION

WHAT YOU WILL FIND IN THIS BOOK

There are more than 1500 improved non-membership campgrounds in Oregon and Washington. These range from deluxe parks with sewer, electrical and water hookups, flush toilets, showers, heated pools, hot tubs, and cable tv, to barely civilized camps offering little more than picnic tables, fire rings and pit toilets.

You may already be aware that many State Parks and National Forests offer campgrounds, but this is the only source available that includes all of these, plus every private park, company, city, county, and other campground where an overnight fee is charged. It provides an easy way to compare costs and facilities without visiting each park.

In order to provide the best information available, this book carries no advertisements. This guarantees that every campground receives equal treatment, regardless of its budget.

Because individual campers are not all looking for the same camping experience, the campgrounds are also not rated. After reading this introduction you will be able to tell if a campground is right for your needs based on the campground operator, its location, and the facilities available.

Every effort has been made to insure that the information provided is accurate and up-to-date. If you visit a campground and find the facilities differ, please let us know. You can send update information to Ki² Enterprises, P.O. Box 186, Willamina, Oregon 97396.

WHAT TO EXPECT FROM A CAMPGROUND OPERATOR

Campground operators are, for the most part, people who enjoy the outdoors. Most cater to people on vacation.

Private Campground Operators
Private campgrounds are operated by individuals, families and businesses. They are perfect for campers who want hookups and the security of on-site caretakers. Some provide swimming pools, hot tubs, saunas, game rooms, cable tv hookups and laundry facilities; others cater to

boaters, those who fish, bicyclists or other activity orientated campers. Most accommodate RVs, but many also have grassy areas set aside for tents.

The majority of private campgrounds are open year round, have no restrictions on how long you can stay, and take reservations. Because these campgrounds are less publicized than government owned sites, many are half empty, even during peak vacation seasons.

National Forest Service
There are nineteen separate National Forests in Oregon and Washington. No matter where you plan to go, there will probably be at least one within a few hours drive. This land offers prime recreational space for camping, hiking, picnics, boating, fishing, swimming, mountain climbing, skiing and other outdoor fun.

A stop at any ranger station will provide you with current information on local trails, impending weather and special features. There are currently no entrance fees to National Forest lands. The Forest Service regional office is at 319 SW Pine St., Portland, OR - (503)221-2877.

Most improved forest service campgrounds have drinking water, picnic tables, firepits, toilets and a maximum stay limit of 14 days. Many are accessible to the physically challenged, and some offer group campsites.

National Park Service
The National Park Service provides campgrounds at Washington's Mount Rainier, Olympic and North Cascades National Parks, as well as Oregon's Crater Lake. These parks were established to regulate the use of the land to promote the conservation of wildlife, scenery, natural and historic features for current and future generations.

Entrance fees are charged at most National Parks. Golden Eagle and Golden Age Passports are available, providing discounted fees to disabled visitors, and those over the age of 62. These can be obtained at any National Park location.

Improved Park campgrounds offer drinking water, flush toilets, picnic tables, firepits and have a 14 day limit. No firearms are allowed in some national parks, and pets and motorized vehicles are prohibited on many trails. Pack and saddle horses, however, are allowed on most trails.

Bureau of Land Management (BLM)

The BLM manages nearly 16 million acres in Oregon. Several white water rivers flow through this land, including the Deschutes, John Day, Grande Ronde, Owyhee and Rogue Rivers. The BLM also provides several good areas for off-road vehicle recreation.

Unless posted otherwise, the maximum stay in BLM campgrounds is 14 days. Facilities generally include drinking water, picnic tables, toilets and firepits. National Park Golden Eagle and Golden Age Passport holders receive a discount on overnight fees.

The gathering of rocks, minerals, gemstones, berries, nuts and flowers on BLM land for personal use is allowed, but permits are required for large collections. All historic and related artifacts must be left undisturbed. The region's BLM headquarters are located at 825 NE Multnomah St., Portland, OR - (503)231-6274.

Oregon State Parks

Most of Oregon's Pacific Ocean beaches are state owned. Some of this land is strictly for day-use, other park lands include campgrounds. You will also find state park campgrounds near many of Oregon's most spectacular rivers, lakes, scenic and natural attractions.

A number of state campgrounds are open year round; others only from mid-April to late October. Most offer flush toilets, hot showers, picnic tables and firepits; many have RV hookups and other amenities. Special campsites for disabled campers and groups are available.

Reservations are taken by mail for some of the state's high-use camps. For further information, contact Oregon State Parks, 525 Trade St. SE, Salem, OR - (503)378-6305. March thru August you can also call (800)452-5687 or (503)238-7488.

Washington State Parks

Lots of Washington State Parks offer camping too. Most provide flush toilets, hot showers, picnic tables, firepits, utility hookups, and have a 10 day maximum stay. Parks with picnic areas include piped water, fireplace stoves and shelters; some offer kitchens. Many state parks have interpretive displays focusing on the area's historical or geological events.

A great number of Washington State Park campgrounds are open year round; the rest April 1 thru September 30. Most offer facilities that meet barrier-free guidelines for accessibility, and some have group facilities.

Campers who come from states where an out-of-state surcharge is levied on visitors are required to pay that same surcharge on top of the overnight fee. For further information contact Washington State Parks, 7150 Cleanwater Ln., Olympia, WA - (206)753-2027.

Other Operators
Other campground operators in Oregon and Washington include the Corps of Engineers, various Indian tribes, timber and power companies, and county and city parks departments. Although most only operate campgrounds in one or two areas, they are an important piece to the complete campground picture. For example, the Coulee Dam National Recreation Area provides campgrounds along Washington's 660-mile-long Roosevelt Lake, Pacific Power & Light on several Lewis River reservoirs and Josephine County along the scenic Rogue River.

HOW THE CAMPGROUND LISTINGS ARE ARRANGED

Each state has been divided into four sections: coast, I-5 corridor, central and eastern. These divisions are clearly marked on the state map found at the beginning of each state's listings. (Oregon - page 15, Washington - page 127)

There is also a map at the beginning of each of the state's four sections. These section maps include page numbers to help you quickly locate the listings for the area you will be visiting. Within each section, the cities are arranged north to south. These maps are not intended for navigation; you can get a full-size highway map free by contacting the state's tourism office.

All campground listings begin with the name, followed by its operating agency. Next, you will find a brief, but complete, listing of facilities. **All campgrounds have toilet facilities and drinking water unless otherwise noted.** Most also have picnic tables and firepits at each site.

If flush toilets are not mentioned, assume that the campground has pit or vault toilets. Established operating seasons, and elevations for isolated campgrounds over

500', have been included. General fee information and exact directions complete the listing.

An alphabetical listing of all campgrounds can be found in the index at the back of the book, providing a quick way to locate any campgrounds you know by name. The index is also a good way to locate areas which offer desireable facilities such as group or horse camps. It also contains an alphabetical list of cities.

HOW TO FIGURE OVERNIGHT FEES

The cost of an overnight stay in one of the region's improved campgrounds ranges from less than $5.00 to over $25.00 a night. Some operators levy an additional $2.00 per person charge for more than two people, and $5.00 for additional tents or vehicles.

At the end of each campground's facilities listing you will find one or more dollar signs. You can quickly calculate the cost of an overnight stay by multiplying each dollar sign by $5.00. This method of reporting fees was established to keep your book current for a longer time period. The exact fee breakdown is as follows:

$	=	$5.00 or less
$$	=	$5.01 to $10.00
$$$	=	$10.01 to $15.00
$$$$	=	$15.01 to $20.00
$$$$$	=	$20.01 to $25.00

Campground listings that show more than one grouping of dollar signs generally indicate that the operator charges more for a campsite with hookups than a tent site. Occasionally it is because they have a few premium sites overlooking the ocean, or other body of water, for which they charge a little more.

Exact amounts are given for group campsites, unless the charge is determined by the size of the group. In that case you will need to call the number listed for exact rates.

This region also has hundreds of cost-free campgrounds. Free campgrounds do not have hookups, showers or other luxuries. You can find complete information on these unimproved sites in *Free Campgrounds of Washington & Oregon* by the same author.

11

CAMPGROUND DIRECTIONS AND ABBREVIATIONS

The final block of information in each campground listing consists of simply stated directions. FSR has been substituted for Forest Service Road and CR for County Road. When exploring unpopulated lands, such as those managed by the forest service, it is helpful to have a detailed map of the area.

CHOOSING THE RIGHT CAMPGROUND FOR YOUR RV

When the RV symbol appears, it means that campground can accommodate trailers and RVs. This symbol does not necessarily mean hookups are available. That information is stated within the listing along with other limitations such as maximum length. If you have a very long RV, check the index listing for RVs 40' and over.

Whenever the term full hookups is used, you can expect to find appropriate fittings for water, electricity, sewer and cable or satellite tv. Some of the mobile home and RV parks also offer phone hookups.

Most of the parks that have trailer waste disposal provide that service without additional charge to overnighters. Many will also allow others to pump out their RV for a fee.

The terms maximum site and trailer length are given to help you to decide whether or not you will be able to comfortably park your RV or trailer. If your vehicle is too long for most spots, or you require a pull-thru site, reservations are adviseable.

TIPS FOR TENT CAMPERS

When the tent symbol appears after a campground name, that campground has non-paved, non-gravel sites where tents can be pitched. These sites are the same ones available to RVs unless otherwise stated.

Tent campsites are plentiful in Oregon and Washington. Most of the tent sites listed in this book include a parking space for your vehicle. If the term walk-in site is used, expect to be far enough away from your car to have to carry all of your equipment to your tent site, but near enough to run back for overlooked items.

A hike-in campsite can mean anything from a 30 minute walk to a couple of hours. The approximate distance is included at the end of the campground directions. A good rule of thumb for hike-in campsites is that unless you can carry all of your supplies in one trip, don't chose a hike-in camp.

TIPS FOR BICYCLE, HORSE AND BOAT CAMPERS

Many state parks, and other campgrounds, have special areas set aside for campers traveling by bicycle. Most offer shared facilities, providing lone bicyclists with an opportunity to meet others. The charge is generally small, and based on the number of people.

There are also numerous horse campgrounds with corrals, hitchracks, loading ramps and watering facilities. Check the index, under horse trails or facilities, for a list of page numbers where these can be found. When taking your horse into a wilderness area, or National Park, call well in advance to acquaint yourself with any feeding or other restrictions.

Lots of Pacific Northwest campgrounds are located at lakes and along rivers, many include boat ramps. These too are listed in the index. If a lake or reservoir has predictable periodic changes in water levels, this information has been included. Changes in water level are not always predictable, so if it is not included or the season has been drier than usual, call the operating agency and ask about the water level.

Every effort has been made to mention any boating restrictions on a campground lake. If motors are not allowed, or there is a speed limit, this information was included to help motor boaters, water skiers and canoeists select a site where they can enjoy their sport. The index also has a listing for boat-in campgrounds.

ACCESSIBILITY FOR DISABLED CAMPERS

Wheelchair accessible restrooms are found at over half of all Pacific Northwest campgrounds. A few even offer sites with modified hookups. If your limitations require more than barrier-free restrooms, call the campground operator and discuss your needs. We have taken each operators word on accessibility; let us know if you have problems.

Sites that have been modified for people with accessibility limitations can often be reserved, even when all other sites are on a first-come basis. The phone number has been included within the campground listing. The National Forest Service also provides a special TTD phone number for the hearing impaired - (800)879-4496.

FINDING A GROUP CAMPGROUND

Hundreds of group campsites are available in Oregon and Washington. A few are strictly for tents, most can accommodate RVs. Check the index for a list of page numbers where these can be found.

Nearly all group camps are available only by reservation. Call the phone number included in the listing for complete details on group facilities, fees and requirements.

CAMPING WITH PETS

Pets are welcome in most Pacific Northwest campgrounds, as long as you follow three simple rules of courtesy.

1) Dogs should never be allowed to disturb others by barking or running loose.

2) Pets should not be permitted to chase wildlife.

3) Your pet's feces should be picked up and properly disposed of when on trails and in camp.

Private campground operators may have additional rules. If there is a restriction on size or extra charge, it is noted within the listing.

When tying your dog up in camp, be sure the chain will not damage the site or plant life. Dogs are permitted on nearly all national forest trails, but banned from some wilderness area and National Park trails. You will find this fact posted on signs at the trailhead, or you can call ahead and ask the operating agency. Dogs are not allowed on some public swimming beaches.

In short, responsible pet owners are welcome, neglectful ones are not. If your pet is allowed to cause problems, the next pet owner may well be turned away.

OREGON'S CAMPGROUNDS

Whether you're looking for a quiet place to pitch your tent, or a deluxe RV park, you'll find an abundance of improved campgrounds to choose from throughout Oregon. The following map shows the four sections used in organizing the state's hundreds of "pay" campgrounds. Each section offers many unique camping experiences.

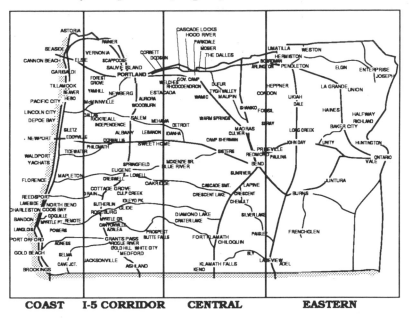

COAST   I-5 CORRIDOR   CENTRAL   EASTERN

The Oregon Coast experience

Most of Oregon's 360 miles of Pacific Ocean coastline is public land, providing an unparalleled opportunity for every visitor to find his or her own quiet spot at the beach.

Along the southern coast you'll encounter the state's "banana belt", the wild and scenic Rogue River and one of the world's largest coastal dune areas. The northern portion has historic lighthouses, wildlife refuges, protected estuaries, Indian shell mounds and spouting horns.

When fog blankets the coast you can generally escape its clutches with a short drive east, into the Coast Mountains. Rushing streams, cool forests, wildlife and rustic campgrounds are all found there.

15

Why to spend time in Oregon's I-5 Corridor

The I-5 corridor is extremely popular with travelers in a hurry, yet just off its path a myriad of experiences beckon. Most of Oregon's four dozen covered bridges are within this area, the scenery is gorgeous, wildlife is abundant and historic sights are easy to view.

The land surrounding the southern I-5 corridor holds Crater Lake National Park, Oregon Caves National Monument, the Oregon Vortex, historic Jacksonville and lots of great fishing streams. In the northern portion you'll discover pristine wilderness areas, towering Mt. Hood, the scenic Columbia River Gorge and the state's largest cities.

Reasons to visit Central Oregon

The eastern side of the Cascade Mountain Range, and central Oregon, offer plenty of sunshine. The sheer height of these mountains snag most rain clouds, making it the perfect place to go when the western side of the state is too wet for camping.

The largest collection of volcanic remains in the continental United States can be found in the southern half of central Oregon. Ice caves, lava cast forests, obsidian flows, giant cracks in the ground and Newberry Crater are all fun to visit. The John Day Fossil Beds, Smith Rock, ghost towns and the Deschutes, Metolius, Crooked and Columbia Rivers are all found to the north.

Things to do in Eastern Oregon

Cross Oregon to its very eastern edge, and you'll find a variety of unusual landscapes. In the northeast corner you'll encounter what residents refer to as the Little Switzerland of America. Hell's Canyon, the world's deepest, guards its eastern border. National Forests protect much of this land, making it a great place for campers.

The southeast corner of the state shelters colorful Leslie Gulch, the Steens Mountains, and a 30 mile long, 4 mile wide, lava flow where obsidian, agate and petrified wood are easy to find.

No matter where you go, Oregon is a camper's haven.

OREGON COAST
CAMPGROUNDS

See Page

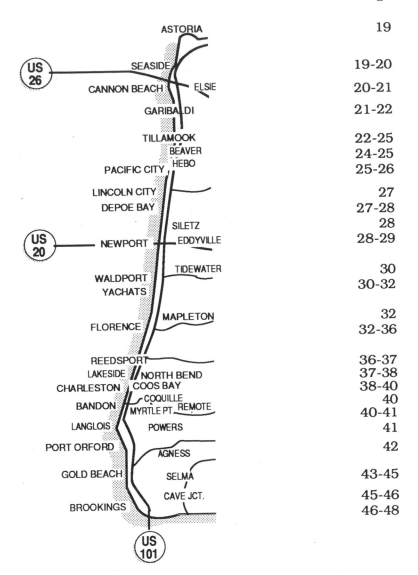

Location	See Page
ASTORIA	19
SEASIDE	19-20
CANNON BEACH — ELSIE	20-21
GARIBALDI	21-22
TILLAMOOK	22-25
BEAVER	24-25
PACIFIC CITY, HEBO	25-26
LINCOLN CITY	27
DEPOE BAY	27-28
SILETZ	28
NEWPORT — EDDYVILLE	28-29
TIDEWATER	30
WALDPORT / YACHATS	30-32
FLORENCE / MAPLETON	32
	32-36
REEDSPORT	36-37
LAKESIDE // NORTH BEND	37-38
CHARLESTON / COOS BAY	38-40
COQUILLE	40
BANDON / MYRTLE PT. REMOTE	40-41
LANGLOIS / POWERS	41
PORT ORFORD / AGNESS	42
GOLD BEACH / SELMA	43-45
CAVE JCT.	45-46
BROOKINGS	46-48

ASTORIA

(West of Astoria)

ASTORIA KOA (Private)
276 campsites - 142 w/full hookups, 87 w/water & elec., plus 47 tent sites, reservations - (503)861-2606, showers, laundry, groceries, swimming pool, spa, satellite tv, playground, pets okay, $$$$-$$$$$.
Located 10 miles west of Astoria, across from Fort Stevens.

FORT STEVENS (Oregon State Park)
604 campsites - 213 w/hookups for water/elec./sewer, 130 w/ elec., plus 261 tent units, mail reservations available, maximum site 69', group campsites, wheelchair access, picnic area, historical museum, self-guided walking tour, remains of Civil War era fort, showers, trailer waste disposal, boat launch, swimming, fishing, ocean beach access, beachcombing, bicycle trail, hiking trails, open year round, $$-$$$$.
Located 10 miles west of Astoria, near Warrenton - follow signs.

KAMPERS WEST KAMPGROUND RV PARK (Private)
243 campsites - 137 w/hookups for water/elec./cable tv, 50 w/water & elec., plus 56 tent units, reservation information - (503)861-1814, showers, laundry, ice, trailer waste disposal, river, fishing, pets okay, $$$-$$$$.
Located 10 miles west of Astoria. Follow Warrenton/Fort Stevens signs - located at 1140 NW Warrenton Dr.

(Southwest of Astoria)

SUNSET LAKE RV (Private)
50 units - 15 w/full hookups plus 35 w/water/elec./cable tv, tents okay, reservation information (503)861-1760, showers, laundry, trailer waste disposal, on Sunset Lake, fishing, hiking, open year round, $$$-$$$$.
Take US 101 south 9 miles, Sunset Beach Drive west .3 mile.

SEASIDE

PINE COVE MOTEL & TRAILER COURT (Private)
2 units w/full hookups plus 2 w/elec. only, no tents, reservations (503)738-5243, showers, laundry, trailer waste disposal, pets extra, open year round, $$$.
Located just beyond north end of town.

TRUCKE'S RV PARK (Private)
15 units w/hookups for water/elec./cable tv, tents okay, reservations (503)738-8863, trailers to 38', restrooms, store, tackle & bait, gas, diesel, near lake, fishing, pets okay, $$.
Located 1 block past first light - at 1921 S. Holladay Dr.

VENICE RV PARK (Private)
26 units w/full hookups, no tents, reservations - (503)738-8851, showers, laundry, picnic area, river, fishing, $$$$.
Near south end of Newana River bridge at 1032 24th Ave.

(South of Seaside)

CIRCLE CREEK CAMPGROUND (Private)
62 units - 30 w/full hookups, 14 w/water & elec., plus 18 tent sites, reservations (503)738-6070, showers, laundry, $$$-$$$$.
Take US 101 south 1 mile.

CANNON BEACH

RV RESORT AT CANNON BEACH (Private) [RV]
100 units w/full hookups, no tents, reservations - (503)436-2231, showers, laundry, wheelchair access, game room, playfield, playground, swimming & therapy pools, groceries, propane, gasoline, river, fishing, hiking, pets okay, $$$$$$$.
Is just off the Cannon Beach exit ramp, .6 mile past milepost 29.

SEA RANCH RESORT (Private) [A][RV]
71 units - 25 w/hookups for water/elec./sewer, 13 w/water & elec., plus 33 tent sites, information - (503)436-1268, showers, trailer waste disposal, nearby ocean access, swimming, fishing, hiking, summer horseback riding, pets okay, $$$-$$$$.
Located 6 blocks north of city center on old US 101.

WRIGHT'S FOR CAMPING (Private) [A]
18 campsites, information (503)436-2347, showers, laundry, wheelchair accessible, nearby beach & forest, pets okay, open Mem. Day thru Oct., $$$.
Take 2nd Cannon Beach exit - located just east of the viaduct.

(North of Cannon Beach)

BUD'S CAMPGROUND & RV PARK (Private)
32 units - 24 w/full hookups plus 8 tent sites, reservations - (503)738-6855, showers, laundry, wheelchair access, groceries, ocean fishing, crabbing, clamming, pets okay, $$$-$$$$.
Take US 101 north 11 miles - located just past Gearhart.

ECOLA (Oregon State Park) [A]
Hike-in camping, fire pits, creek, fishing, hiking, $-$$.
Leave US 101 at Cannon Beach's north exit, follow signs to park and hike Lewis & Clark Trail to Indian Creek and campground.

RIVERSIDE LAKE RESORT (Private) [A][RV]
80 units - 16 w/full hookups, 17 w/water/elec./cable tv, 19 w/water & elec., plus 28 tent sites, reservation information -

(503)738-6779, showers, laundry, river, swimming, fishing, pets okay, $$$-$$$$.
Follow US 101 north 7 miles.

(South of Cannon Beach)

NEHALEM BAY (Oregon State Park)
291 sites w/hookups for elec., maximum site 60', showers, wheelchair access, picnic area, trailer waste disposal, boat launch, fishing, ocean access, bicycle & horse trails, open year round, $$-$$$.
US 101 south 17 miles - is 3 miles beyond Manzanita junction.

NEHALEM BAY TRAILER PARK (Private)
40 units w/full hookups, no tents, reservation information - (503)368-5180, showers, laundry, groceries, ocean & river fishing, crabbing, clamming, small pets okay, $$$$.
Take US 101 south 14 miles.

NEHALEM SHORES RV PARK (Private)
25 trailer sites w/full hookups, no tents, reservations - (503)368-6670, showers, laundry, ice, river, fishing, small pets okay, $$$.
Take US 101 south 15 miles to Nehalem, then 7th St. north .2 mile, and North Fork Rd. .6 mile east to park.

OSWALD WEST (Oregon State Park)
36 hike-in campsites, picnic area, hiking, fishing, situated in a rain forest of massive spruce & cedar trees, $$.
Take US 101 south 10 miles and follow trail to campground.

(East of Cannon Beach)

SADDLE MOUNTAIN (Oregon State Park)
10 primitive campsites, picnic area, hiking, $$.
Take US 101 north 5 miles, US 26 east approximately 16 miles.

ELSIE

SPRUCE RUN (Clatsop County)
40 primitive sites, trailers to 25', flush toilets & drinking water only in summer, stream, swimming, fishing, rafting, bicycling, hiking, open year round, $$.
Located 5.2 miles south of Elsie on US 26.

GARIBALDI

BAR VIEW JETTY PARK (Tillamook County)
250 units - 40 w/hookups for water/elec./sewer, 20 w/elec. only, plus 190 tent sites, reservation information - (503)322-

3477, showers, handicap facilities, playground, trailer waste disposal, ocean access, fishing, hiking, pets okay, $$$.
US 101 north 2 miles, Cedar Ave. west to jetty and park.

BIAK BY THE SEA MOTOR HOME PARK (Private)
61 units w/full hookups, trailers to 35', reservation information - (503)322-0111, showers, laundry, ocean access, fishing, $$$.
Located west of city center 1 block on 7th St.

HARBOR VIEW INN (Private)
25 units - 2 w/hookups for elec. plus 23 w/out hookups, no tents, reservations (503)322-3251, wheelchair accessible, marina, on Tillamook Bay, pets okay, open year round, $$-$$$.
Located at marina - 302 S. 7th St.

HERON'S LANDING RV PARK (Private)
14 units w/full hookups, no tents, reservations (503)322-3773, trailers to 35', showers, on Tillamook Bay, pets okay, open year round, $$$$.
Take US 101 to Garibaldi Ave. - at 804 Garibaldi Ave.

MIAMI COVE RV PARK (Private)
14 units w/full hookups, no tents, reservations (503)322-3300, trailers to 56', pull thrus, showers, laundry, pets okay, open year round, $$$$.
Take US 101 to Garibaldi Ave. - at 503 E. Garibaldi Ave.

OLD MILL MARINA PARK (Private)
107 units - 55 w/hookups for water/elec./cable tv plus 63 w/out hookups, tents okay, reservations (503)322-0324, trailers to 40', showers, laundry, wheelchair access, playground, on Tillamook Bay, fishing, clamming, crabbing, pets okay, open year round, $$$-$$$$.
Take US 101 to 3rd St. - at 210 3rd St.

TILLAMOOK

BIG BARN MARINA & RV PARK (Private)
26 units w/hookups for water/elec./cable tv plus tent area, reservations (503)842-8596, trailers to 40', showers, laundry, wheelchair accessible, trailer waste disposal, on Tillamook River, boat ramp & dock, fishing, hiking, pets okay, open year round, $$-$$$$.
Follow Netarts Highway west 1 mile - located at 85 3rd St.

TRASK RIVER MOTOR HOME PARK (Private)
4 trailer sites w/hookups for water & elec., reservations - (503)842-6142, showers, laundry, river, fishing, $$.
Located at 3370 Geinger Rd.

BAY CITY RV PARK (Private)
18 pull thrus w/full hookups plus tent area, reservations (503)377-2124, trailers to 60', showers, laundry, wheelchair accessible, pets okay, open year round, $$$-$$$$.
Follow US 101 3 miles north of Tillamook Cheese Factory - located at 7930 Alderbrook Rd.

JETTY FISHERY (Private)
30 units - 15 w/hookups for water & elec. plus 15 tent sites, reservation information - (503)368-5746, groceries, ocean access, river, boat launch & rental, swimming, fishing, $$-$$$.
Take US 101 north 18 miles.

KILCHIS RIVER PARK (Tillamook County)
40 units, playfield, playground, trailer waste disposal, river, boat launch, swimming, fishing, hiking, open May to Oct., $$.
Follow US 101 .5 mile north of Tillamook Cheese Factory, then Kilchis River Rd. northeast 7 miles to park.

PACIFIC CAMPGROUND (Private)
67 units - 28 w/full hookups, 4 w/water & elec., 5 w/elec. only, plus 30 tent sites, reservations - (503)842-5201, showers, ice, $$-$$$.
Take US 101 north 2 miles.

SHOREWOOD TRAVEL TRAILER VILLAGE (Private)
6 units w/hookups for water/elec./sewer, no tents, reservation information - (503)355-2278, showers, laundry, ice, playground, trailer waste disposal, ocean access, fishing, $$$$.
Take US 101 north 12.7 miles, and go southwest 3 blocks at the Shorewood sign.

(Northeast of Tillamook)

BROWNS CAMP (Tillamook State Forest)
15 units, fire pits, picnic tables, off-road vehicle staging area, trails to Rogers Camp & University Falls, $$.
State 6 northeast 30 miles, Scoggins Creek Rd. south 1 mile.

ELK CREEK (Tillamook State Forest)
17 walk-in tent sites, at Elk Creek & Wilson River, trailheads to Kings Mtn./Elk Mtn./Old Wilson River Wagon Rd., $.
Follow State 6 northeast 27 miles.

GALES CREEK (Tillamook State Forest)
23 units - 19 standard plus 4 walk-in tent sites, picnic area, trailhead to Gales Creek trails, $-$$.
State 6 northeast 34 miles, Rigers Rd. north .7 mile.

JONES CREEK (Tillamook State Forest)
38 units - 28 tent/trailer units, 9 walk-in tent sites, plus group area, group reservations - (503)842-2545, maximum site 60', wheelchair access, nearby swimming/kayakking/fishing, $-$$. Follow State 6 northeast 21 miles.

(East of Tillamook)

TRASK PARK (Tillamook County)
60 units, trailers to 60', picnic area, trailer waste disposal, on Trask River, swimming, fishing, hiking, open May thru Sept., $$. Follow Trask River Rd. east 11.8 miles.

WILSON RIVER RV FISHERMAN PARK (Private)
85 units - 59 w/full hookups, 10 w/water & elec., plus 16 tent sites, reservations (503)842-2750, trailers to 40', showers, laundry, wheelchair accessible, playground, game room, trailer waste disposal, on Wilson River, fishing, hiking, pets okay, open year round, $$$-$$$$
Take State 6 east to milepost 5.

(West of Tillamook)

BAY SHORE TRAILER PARK (Private)
52 units w/hookups for water/elec./sewer plus 1 w/water & elec., no tents, trailers to 40', reservation information - (503)842-7774, showers, laundry, ice, ocean access, stream, boat launch & rental, fishing, crabbing, $$$-$$$$.
Take Netarts Highway west 6 miles, and Bilyeu Ave. .3 mile.

BIG SPRUCE TRAILER PARK (Private)
26 units - 23 w/hookups for water/elec./sewer plus 3 tent sites, trailers to 40', reservation information - (503)842-7443, showers, laundry, ocean access, stream, boat launch, swimming, fishing, $$$-$$$$.
Take Netarts Highway west 6.5 miles.

HAPPY CAMP (Private)
48 units - 27 w/full hookups plus 21 w/water/ elec./cable tv, no tents, reservations - (503)842-4012, showers, trailer waste disposal, ocean access, fishing, $$$.
Take Netarts Highway west 7 miles.

(South of Tillamook)

CAPE LOOKOUT (Oregon State Park)
250 units - 54 w/hookups for water/elec./sewer, 1 w/elec., 195 tent sites, plus group areas, maximum site 60', mail reservations available, showers, wheelchair access, picnic area, trailer waste disposal, ocean access, hiking, fishing, open year round, $$-$$$.
Follow Netarts Highway west to Cape Lookout Rd., and go south 8 miles to campground.

TILLAMOOK KOA (Private)
85 units - 21 w/full hookups, 8 w/water/elec./cable tv, 45 w/water & elec., plus 10 tent sites, reservations - (503)842-4779, showers, laundry, playground, groceries, propane, trailer waste disposal, river, fishing, hiking, pets okay, $$$-$$$$.
Take US 101 south 6 miles.

BEAVER

CAMPER COVE (Private)
24 campsites - 12 w/hookups for water/elec./sewer, 4 dry RV sites, plus 8 tent units, trailers to 40', reservation information - (503)398-5334, showers, laundry, trailer waste disposal, river, fishing, enclosed cooking area, hiking, pets okay, $$$-$$$$.
Located 2.5 miles north of town on US 101.

(East of Beaver)

ADLER GLEN (BLM)
10 units, handicap accessible, fishing, swimming, elev. 700', open year round, $.
Follow the Nestucca River Rd. east 18 miles.

DOVRE (BLM)
9 units, group shelter, fishing, swimming, elev. 1500', open year round, $.
Follow the Nestucca River Rd. east 21 miles.

FAN CREEK (BLM)
11 units, handicap accessible, fishing, swimming, elev. 1200', open year round, $.
Follow the Nestucca River Rd. east 24 miles.

HEBO

HEBO LAKE (Siuslaw NF)
16 units, trailers to 18', picnic shelter, lake - no motors, swimming, fishing, hiking, elev. 1600', $$.
Take US 101 north .1 mile, State 22 southeast .3 mile, and FSR 14 east 5 miles.

PACIFIC CITY

PACIFIC CITY TRAILER PARK (Private)
15 trailer sites w/full hookups, adults only, reservation information - (503)965-6820, showers, laundry, trailer waste disposal, river, fishing, $$$$.
Located on Pacific Ave., 1 block east of city center.

RAINES RESORT (Private)
14 units - 12 w/hookups for water/elec./sewer plus 2 tent sites, reservation information - (503)965-6371, showers, laundry, river, fishing, boat launch & rental, $$-$$$.
Follow Cape Dr. northwest 1 mile to just past the bridge, and take Ferry St. west .1 mile to resort.

RIVERVIEW LODGE CAMPGROUND (Private)
12 units w/hookups for water & elec., information - (503)965-6000, showers, laundry, river, swimming, fishing, boat rental, $$.
Take US 101 exit off US 101 and go west 1 mile.

(North of Pacific City)

CAPE KIWANDA RV PARK (Private)
159 units - 95 w/full hookups, 40 w/water & elec., plus 24 tent sites, reservations - (503)965-6230, showers, laundry, trailer waste disposal, groceries, ocean access, pets okay, $$$-$$$$.
Follow Cape Dr. northwest 1.2 miles.

ISLAND PARK (Tillamook County)
27 campsites, trailer waste disposal, ocean access, pond, boat launch, swimming, fishing, $$.
Follow Cape Dr. northwest to Sandlake Rd. - park is 4.4 miles north of Cape Kiwanda.

SAND BEACH (Siuslaw NF)
101 campsites plus two overflow trailer lots, trailers to 32', flush toilets, trailer waste disposal, ocean & sand dunes access, boating, fishing, ORV area, pets okay, $$.
Follow Cape Dr. and Sandlake Rd. northwest 9.6 miles and FSR S3001 southwest .5 mile.

WEBB PARK (Tillamook County)
30 sites, trailer waste disposal, sport fishing camp - noisy, ocean access, boat launch, $$.
Follow Cape Dr. northwest 2.2 miles.

WOODS PARK (Tillamook County)
7 units - 3 w/hookups for water/elec./sewer plus 4 tent sites, trailers to 40', Nehalem River, fishing, hiking, pets okay, $$-$$$.
Follow Cape Dr. northwest 1.2 miles.

(South of Pacific City)

NESKOWIN CREEK RV RESORT (Private)
100 units w/hookups for water/elec./sewer plus tent area, reservations (503)392-3082, trailers to 40', showers, laundry, wheelchair accessible, swimming pool, propane, rec room, trailer waste disposal, pets okay, open year round, $$$-$$$$.
Take US 101 south 8 miles to Newskowin - at 50500 US 101.

LINCOLN CITY

DEVIL'S LAKE (Oregon State Park)
100 units - 32 w/hookups for water/elec./sewer, 68 tent sites plus group area, mail reservations available, maximum site 62', showers, wheelchair access, on East Devil's Lake, boat launch, fishing, swimming, open year round, $$-$$$.
Located just off US 101 - well marked by signs.

(Northeast of Lincoln City)

EVERGREEN PARK (Private)
32 units - 25 w/hookups for water/elec./sewer plus 7 tent sites, reservation information - (503)994-3116, showers, laundry, groceries, trailer waste disposal, river, fishing, hiking, $$$-$$$$.
US 101 north 5 miles, State 18 east 6 miles.

H. B. VanDUZER FOREST (Oregon State Park)
Hiker/biker tent camping, no trailers, fishing, $.
US 101 north 5 miles, State 18 east 15 miles.

LINCOLN CITY KOA (Private)
85 units - 23 w/full hookups, 29 w/water & elec., plus 32 tent sites, reservations - (503)994-2961, showers, laundry, playground, gam & rec room w/kitchen, groceries, propane, trailer waste disposal, pets okay, $$$-$$$$.
US 101 north 4 miles, East Devils Lake Rd. southeast 1 mile.

(Southeast of Lincoln City)

COYOTE ROCK RV PARK (Private)
58 units - 38 w/full hookups plus 20 w/water/elec./cable tv, reservation information - (503)996-6824, showers, ice, river, boat launch & rental, fishing, bait/tackle & moorage, $$$-$$$$.
US 101 south 1.5 miles, State 229 east 1 mile.

SPORTSMAN'S LANDING (Private)
30 trailer sites w/full hookups, reservation information - (503)996-4225, showers, laundry, river, fishing, boat launch & rental, restaurant, $$$.
US 101 south 1.5 miles, State 229 east 3.9 miles.

DEPOE BAY

FOGARTY CREEK RV PARK (Private)
53 units w/full hookups, no tents, reservation information - (503)764-2228, showers, laundry, trailer waste disposal, propane, pets okay, $$$-$$$$.
Follow US 101 north 2 miles.

HOLIDAY RV PARK (Private) `RV`
110 sites w/full hookups - some w/ocean view, no tents, reservations - (503)765-2302, showers, laundry, indoor swimming & therapy pools, groceries, fishing, pets okay, $$$-$$$$$$.
Follow US 101 north 1 mile.

MARTIN'S TRAILER HARBOR (Private) `RV`
15 units w/hookups for water/elec./sewer, no tents, reservation information - (503)765-2601, showers, laundry, pets okay, $$$$.
US 101 just north of bridge to Collins St. - park is 2 blocks.

SEA & SAND RV PARK (Private) `RV`
95 units w/full hookups, no tents, reservations - (503)764-2313, trailers to 35', showers, laundry, wheelchair accessible, trailer waste disposal, ocean access, swimming, fishing, pets okay, $$$$.
Follow US 101 north 3.5 miles.

SILETZ

MOONSHINE PARK (Lincoln County) `A` `RV`
36 units, trailers okay, flush toilets, wheelchair accessible, picnic tables, playground, on Siletz River, boat launch, open May thru Oct., $$.
Take Upper Siletz Rd. east 6 miles to Logsden, and follow Upper Farm Rd. northeast 3.5 miles to campground.

NEWPORT

CITY CENTER TRAILER PARK (Private) `RV`
3 trailer sites w/full hookups, no tents, reservations (503)265-5731, trailers to 40', showers, laundry, 3 blocks from ocean, pets okay, open year round, $$$$.
Located at 721 N. US 101.

HARBOR VILLAGE TRAILER PARK (Private) `RV`
140 units w/full hookups, no tents, reservation information - (503)265-5088, showers, laundry, ocean access, pets okay, $$$.
Take US 20 east .5 mile, SW Moore Dr. south .5 mile, and SE Bay Blvd. east 1 block.

NEWPORT MARINA RV PARK (Port of Newport) `RV`
60 units w/full hookups, no tents, reservation information - (503)867-3321, showers, laundry, wheelchair access, groceries, trailer waste disposal, river, fishing, boat launch, $$$.
At the south end of the Yaquina Bay Bridge, take the Marine Science Center exit off US 101 - park is .5 mile east.

PACIFIC SHORES RV RESORT (Private) `RV`
287 paved units w/full hookups, no tents, reservations (800)666-6313, trailers to 55', showers, laundry, wheelchair access, playground, swimming pool, sauna, hot tub, game room, 2 mile path to beach, pets extra, open year round, $$$$-$$$$$$$.
Located at north end of town - 6225 US 101.

SPORTSMAN'S TRAILER PARK (Private) `RV`
60 trailer sites w/hookups for water/elec./sewer, no tents, reservation information - (503)867-3330, ocean access, river, fishing, boat launch & rental, $$$.
At the south end of the Yaquina Bay Bridge, take the Marine Science Center exit off US 101 - park is 1 block.

(North of Newport)

AGATE BEACH TRAILER & RV PARK (Private) `RV`
32 units - 27 w/full hookups plus 9 w/water/elec./cable tv, no tents, reservations - (503)265-7670, showers, laundry, lounge, trailer waste disposal, near ocean beaches, $$$$.
Follow US 101 north 3 miles.

BEVERLY BEACH (Oregon State Park)
279 units - 52 w/hookups for water/elec./sewer, 75 w/elec., 152 tent sites, plus group area, mail reservations available, maximum site 65', showers, wheelchair access, picnic area, trailer waste disposal, fishing, ocean access, hiking, open year round, $$-$$$.
Follow US 101 north 7 miles.

(South of Newport)

SOUTH BEACH (Oregon State Park)
254 units w/hookups for elec. plus group campsites, mail reservations available, maximum site 60', showers, handicap access, trailer waste disposal, at ocean, fishing, hiking, $$-$$$.
Follow US 101 south 2 miles.

WANDAMERE TRAILER PARK (Private) `A RV`
20 units - 3 w/hookups for water/elec./sewer, 6 w/water & elec., plus 11 tent sites, reservations (503)867-4825, showers, laundry, near ocean, pets okay, open year round - restrooms open March thru Oct., $$-$$$.
Follow US 101 south 2 miles, and turn left on 148th Dr.

EDDYVILLE

BIG ELK (Siuslaw NF) `A RV`
9 units plus 1 group site, trailers to 18', stream, swimming, fishing, $$.
Take US 20 east 10 miles, CR 547 south 7.5 miles, and CR 538 west 1.1 miles.

TIDEWATER

BLACKBERRY (Siuslaw NF)
32 units, trailers to 32', flush toilets, picnic area, on Alsea River, boat launch, swimming, fishing, $$.
Take State 34 southeast 6 miles.

RIVEREDGE (Siuslaw NF)
Group shelter, reservations required - (503)563-3211, wheelchair access inc. trail, stream, boat launch, swimming, fishing, hiking.
Take State 34 southeast 11 miles.

WALDPORT

ALSEA BAY TRAILER PARK (Private)
70 trailer sites w/hookups for water/elec./sewer, reservation information - (503)563-2250, showers, river, fishing, crabbing, clamming, hiking, sea lion watching, $$$-$$$$$.
On US 101 - at north end of bridge.

HANDY HAVEN RV PARK & CAR WASH (Private)
11 units w/full hookups, no tents, reservations - (503)563-4286, showers, laundry, groceries, trailer waste disposal, $$$$.
Located near city center - just east of US 101.

McKINLEY'S MARINA & RV PARK (Private)
15 units w/hookups for elec. & cable tv plus 20 dry sites, tents okay, reservations (503)563-4656, trailers to 70', on bay, crabbing, clamming, boat launch/gas & rentals, moorage, pets okay, open year round, $$-$$$.
Located about 1 mile east of the stop light - follow signs.

(North of Waldport)

SEAL ROCKS TRAILER COVE (Private)
44 units - 30 w/hookups for water/elec./sewer plus 14 w/elec. only, tents okay, trailers to 35', reservations - (503)563-3955, showers, trailer waste disposal, fishing, clamming, $$$$.
Take US 101 north 4.8 miles - located near Seal Rock.

(East of Waldport)

CANAL CREEK (Siuslaw NF)
9 units, trailers to 22', picnic area, narrow roads, $.
State 34 southeast 7 miles, FSR 3462 south 4.1 miles.

CHINOOK TRAILER PARK (Private)
42 units - 22 w/hookups for water/elec./sewer, 10 w/water & elec., plus 10 tent sites, reservation information - (503)563-3485, showers, laundry, river, fishing, $$-$$$$.
State 34 east 3.3 miles.

DRIFT CREEK LANDING (Private)
60 units - 52 w/hookups for water/elec./sewer plus 8 w/water & elec., no tents, reservations - (503)563-3610, showers, laundry, river, boat launch & rental, fishing, pets okay, $$$-$$$$. State 34 east 3.7 miles.

FISHIN' HOLE PARK & MARINA (Private)
21 units - 10 w/full hookups plus 11 w/water & elec., tents okay, reservation information - (503)563-3401, showers, laundry, river, boat launch & rental, fishing, crabbing, $$$-$$$$. State 34 east 3.8 miles.

HAPPY LANDING RV PARK & MARINA (Private)
29 units - 17 w/hookups for water/elec./sewer plus 12 w/water & elec., reservation information - (503)528-3300, showers, laundry, river, boat launch & rental, fishing, $$$-$$$$. State 34 east 7 miles.

KING SILVER RV PARK (Private)
33 units - 19 w/hookups for water/elec./sewer, 9 w/water & elec., plus 5 tent sites, reservations - (503)563-3502, trailers to 35', showers, laundry, ice, tackle/RV/marine supplies, river, fishing, covered moorage, boat launch & rental, $$$. State 34 east 3.6 miles.

KOZY KOVE MARINA & RV PARK (Private)
22 units w/full hookups, tents okay, reservation information - (503)528-3251, showers, laundry, groceries, restaurant, trailer waste disposal, river, boat launch & rental, fishing, $$$-$$$$. State 34 east 9.5 miles.

TAYLORS LANDING (Private)
27 units - 21 w/hookups for water/elec./sewer plus 6 w/water & elec., reservations (503)528-3388, showers, laundry, restaurant, tackle shop, river, boat moorage & rental, fishing, hiking, $$$. State 34 east 7.2 miles.

(South of Waldport)

BEACHSIDE (Oregon State Park)
81 units - 32 w/hookups for elec. plus 49 tent sites, mail reservations available, maximum site 30', showers, picnic area, ocean access, fishing, open year round, $$-$$$. Take US 101 south 4 miles.

TILLICUM BEACH (Siuslaw NF)
60 units - some w/ocean view, trailers to 32', flush toilets, fishing, pets okay, $$. Take US 101 south 4.7 miles.

YACHATS

CAPE PERPETUA (Siuslaw NF)
37 units plus group area, reservations required - (503)563-3211, trailers to 22', flush toilets, trailer waste disposal, stream, ocean access, fishing, hiking, pets okay, $$.
Follow US 101 south 2.7 miles.

ROCK CREEK (Siuslaw NF)
16 units, trailers to 22', flush toilets, ocean access, fishing, $$.
Follow US 101 south 10 miles.

SEA PERCH RV PARK & CAMPGROUND (Private)
52 units - 21 w/full hookups, 27 w/ water/elec./cable tv, plus 4 tents sites, reservations - (503)547-3505, showers, laundry, groceries, ocean access, swimming, fishing, $$$-$$$$$.
Follow US 101 south 6.5 miles.

MAPLETON

ARCHIE KNOWLES (Siuslaw NF)
9 units, trailers to 18', flush toilets, stream, $$.
Take State 126 east 3 miles.

CLAY CREEK (BLM)
21 units, trailers okay, wheelchair accessible, picnic shelter, on Siuslaw River, boating, swimming, fishing, $.
Take State 126 east 12.5 miles, and Siuslaw River Rd. south 16 miles to campground.

MAPLE-LANE TRAILER PARK & MARINA (Private)
46 units w/hookups for water/elec./sewer, reservations - (503)268-4822, showers, river, fishing, boat launch, $$$.
Located on State 126 at milepost #14.

WHITTAKER CREEK (BLM)
31 units, trailers okay, wheelchair accessible toilets, picnic area, non-motorized boating only, swimming, fishing, $$.
Take State 126 southeast 14 miles, and follow Whittaker Creek Rd. to campground.

FLORENCE

HAPPY PLACE RV PARK & STORAGE (Private)
52 units w/full hookups, tents okay, trailers to 52', reservations (503)997-1434, showers, laundry, wheelchair accessible, propane, fishing, hiking, pets okay, $$$-$$$$.
Located at 4044 US 101.

HARBOR VISTA CAMPGROUND (Private)
26 units - 20 w/hookups for water/elec. plus 6 tent sites, reservation information - (503)997-5987, showers, playground, trailer waste disposal, beach access, pets okay, $$-$$$.
Leave US 101 on Heceta Beach Rd. and follow to Harbor Vista Dr. - campground is at 87658 Harbor Vista Dr.

HECETA BEACH RV PARK (Private)
50 units - 19 w/hookups for water/elec./sewer, 28 w/water & elec., plus 3 tent sites, reservations - (503)997-7664, pull-thrus, showers, laundry, trailer waste disposal, pets okay, $$-$$$.
US 101 to Heceta Beach Rd. - located at 04636 Heceta Beach Rd.

LANE COUNTY HARBOR VISTA (Lane County)
26 units - 20 w/hookups for water/elec./sewer plus 6 tent sites, maximum site 60', showers, playground, picnic area, ocean view, trailer waste disposal, hiking trails, open year round, $$-$$$.
Leave US 101 on 35th St., go west 1 mile to Rhododendron Dr., follow to North Jetty Rd. and park.

PORT SIUSLAW RV PARK & MARINA (Port)
84 units - 60 w/full hookups plus 24 w/water & elec., tents okay, reservation information - (503)997-3040, showers, laundry, trailer waste disposal, river, boat launch, crabbing, fishing, $$$.
Leave US 101 3 blocks north of bridge on Maple, head 2 blocks southeast to 1st St, then 3 blocks east to park.

RV PARK AT SANDPINES (Private)
75 units w/full hookups, no tents, reservations (800)510-7388, showers, laundry, wheelchair access, trailer waste disposal, near beach, fishing, hiking, pets okay, open year round, $$$.
Leave US 101 on 35th St., go west 1 mile to Rhododendron Dr. - at 3850 Rhododendron Dr.

WAYSIDE RV & MOBILE PARK (Private)
22 units w/full hookups, no tents, reservation information - (503)997-6451, showers, laundry, lounge, trailer waste disposal, near ocean beaches, small dogs okay, no cats, $$$.
Take US 101 north 1.7 miles.

(North of Florence)

ALDER-DUNE LAKE (Siuslaw NF)
22 units, trailers to 32', flush toilets, lake - no motors, swimming, fishing, $$.
Follow US 101 north 7 miles.

BUCK LAKE MOBILE HOME & RV PARK (Private)
19 units - 12 w/hookups for water/elec./sewer plus 7 tent sites, reservations - (503)997-2840, showers, laundry, swimming, fishing, pets okay, $$$.
Follow US 101 north 7 miles.

CARL G. WASHBURNE (Oregon State Park)
66 units - 58 w/hookups for water/elec./sewer plus 8 tent sites, maximum site 45', showers, picnic area, ocean access, fishing, swimming, hiking, open year round, $$-$$$.
Follow US 101 north 14 miles.

LAKE VIEW MOBILE & RV PARK (Private) RV
4 RV sites w/full hookups, no tents, reservations - (503)997-6688, trailers to 40', showers, laundry, lake, swimming, fishing, no pets, $$$$.
Follow US 101 north 5.5 miles, and Mercer Lake Rd. east 1 mile.

RHODODENDRON TRAILER PARK (Private) RV
18 units w/full hookups, no tents, reservations - (503)997-2206, some pull-thrus, showers, laundry, pets okay, $$$$.
Take US 101 north 3 miles.

SUTTON CAMPGROUND (Siuslaw NF)
90 units plus 2 group sites, group reservations - (503)268-4473, trailers to 22', flush toilets, picnic area, trail to ocean, fishing, pets okay, group site $40 to $100/night - individuals $$.
Follow US 101 north 6 miles, and FSR 794 northwest 1.6 miles - bicycles can take access route off US 101.

(East of Florence)

CUSHMAN RV & BOAT DOCK (Private) RV
10 sites w/hookups for water/elec./sewer, reservations - (503)997-2169, showers, laundry, groceries, gas, on Siuslaw River, boat launch & marina, fishing, pets okay, $$$.
Take State 126 east 4 miles.

NIGHTINGALE'S FISHING CAMP (Private) RV
35 units w/hookups for water & elec. plus tent area, information (503)997-2892, trailers to 30', showers, laundry, wheelchair access, trailer waste disposal, on Siltcoos Lake, boat launch, moorage, gas, fishing, hiking, pets okay, open year round, $$$.
Take US 101 2 miles south of the bridge to Canary Rd., go east 9 miles and follow signs.

ADA FISHING RESORT (Private) RV
40 units w/full hookups, tents okay, reservations (503)997-2342, trailers to 38', showers, laundry, propane, on Lake Siltcoos, boat launch & rental, bait shop, gas, pets okay, open year round, $$$.
Take US 101 south 2 miles, and Canary Rd. east 13 miles.

(South of Florence)

CARTER LAKE (Siuslaw NF) RV
22 units, trailers to 22', information - (800)280-2267, flush toilets, lake, boat launch, swimming, fishing, hiking, $$.
Take US 101 south 8.5 miles, and FSR 1084 west .1 mile.

DARLINGS RESORT (Private) [RV]
15 units w/hookups for water/elec./cable tv, reservations - (503)997-2841, showers, laundry, groceries, lounge, lake, motor & paddle boat rentals, fishing, pets okay, $$$$.
Take US 101 south 5 miles and follow Darling Loop to resort.

DRIFTWOOD II (Siuslaw NF) [image][RV]
70 units, reservations required - (800)280-2267, trailers to 50', flush toilets, wheelchair access, ocean fishing, hiking, ORV, pets okay, $$.
Take US 101 south 7 miles, and FSR 1078 west 1.4 miles.

FISH MILL LODGES (Private) [RV]
11 units w/hookups for water/elec./sewer, no tents, reservations - (503)997-2511, showers, trailer waste disposal, lake, boat launch & rental, tackle shop, pets okay, $$$.
Take US 101 south 6 miles.

JESSIE M. HONEYMAN (Oregon State Park) [image][RV]
381 units - 68 w/hookups for water/elec./sewer, 75 w/elec., 238 tent sites, plus group areas, mail reservations available, maximum site 55', showers, wheelchair access, picnic area, trailer waste disposal, lakes, boat launch, fishing, swimming, trails, sand dunes, open year round, $$-$$$.
Take US 101 south 3 miles.

LAGOON (SILTCOOS) (Siuslaw NF) [image][RV]
40 units, reservations required - (800)280-2267, trailers to 22', flush toilets, river, swimming, fishing, hiking, ocean access, ORV, $$.
Take US 101 south 7 miles, and FSR 1076 west 1.3 miles.

LAKE'S EDGE RV PARK (Private) [RV]
13 units w/full hookups, no tents, trailers to 35', reservations - (503)997-6056, showers, laundry, fishing, boat launch & rental, hiking, pets okay, $$$.
Take US 101 south 6 miles, Pacific Ave. east .5 mile, and Laurel St. east 1 mile.

LAKESHORE TRAVEL PARK (Private) [RV]
20 units w/full hookups, no tents, reservations - (503)997-2741, showers, laundry, lake, swimming, fishing, pets okay, $$$$.
Take US 101 south 4.5 miles - located near milepost #195.

LODGEPOLE (Siuslaw NF) [RV]
3 RV sites - on blacktop, $$.
Take US 101 south 7 miles, and FSR 1078 west 1.8 miles.

SILTCOOS LAKE RESORT (Private) [RV]
16 RV sites w/hookups for water/elec./sewer, trailers to 32', reservation information - (503)997-3741, showers, playground,

lake, boat launch & rental, swimming, fishing, bait/tackle shop, hiking, pets okay, $$$$.
Take US 101 south 6 miles, Pacific Ave. 3 miles.

TYEE (Siuslaw NF)
14 units, trailers to 22', boat launch, swimming, fishing, $$.
Take US 101 south 6 miles, and FSR 1068 southeast .1 mile.

WAXMYRTLE (SILTCOOS) (Siuslaw NF)
56 units, trailers to 22', reservations (800)280-2267, flush toilets, ocean/dune access, river, fishing, hiking, ORV, $$.
Take US 101 south 7 miles, and FSR 1078 west 1.4 miles.

WOAHINK LAKE RV RESORT (Private)
40 units w/full hookups, no tents, reservations - (503)997-6454, showers, laundry, game room, on lake, atv dune access - no dune buggies, fishing, hiking, pets w/prior approval, $$$$.
Take US 101 south 4.5 miles.

REEDSPORT

COHO MARINA & RV PARK (Private)
49 units w/hookups for water/elec./sewers, no tents, trailers to 35', reservations - (503)271-5411, showers, trailer waste disposal, river, fishing, boat launch, $$$.
In Reedsport. Located on US 101 at 16th St.

SURFWOOD CAMPGROUND (Private)
163 units - 100 w/hookups for water/elec./sewer, 41 w/water & elec., plus 22 tent sites, reservation information - (503)271-4020, showers, laundry, swimming pool, playground, tennis, groceries, trailer waste disposal, stream, pets okay, $$.
Follow US 101 south 2 miles.

(North of Reedsport)

TAHKENITCH CAMPGROUND (Siuslaw NF)
7 campsites, trailers to 22', flush toilets, hiking, $$.
Take US 101 north 7 miles, and FSR 1090 west .1 mile.

TAHKENITCH LANDING (Siuslaw NF)
26 campsites, trailers okay, no drinking water, boat launch, fishing, elev. 100', $$.
Take US 101 north 8 miles.

(East of Reedsport)

LOON LAKE (BLM)
59 units, trailers okay, picnic area, boat launch, fishing, swimming, hiking, geology, nature study, elev. 700', $$-$$$.
Take State 38 east 12.5 miles, and Loon Lake Rd. south 7 miles.

LOON LAKE LODGE RESORT (Private)
100 units - 22 w/hookups for water & elec. plus 78 dry sites, tents okay, reservations - (503)599-2244, groceries, restaurant, lake, boat launch & rental, swimming, fishing, hiking, pets okay, $$-$$$.
Take State 38 east 12.5 miles, and Loon Lake Rd. south 8 miles.

(South of Reedsport)

EAST SHORE RECREATION SITE (BLM)
8 tent units, picnic facilities, boating, fishing, swimming, $$.
Follow US 101 south - located near Siskiyou Nat'l Forest.

NORTH EEL CREEK (Siuslaw NF)
16 campsites, trailers to 22', flush toilets, stream, hiking, $$.
Take US 101 south 12.1 miles.

UMPQUA BEACH RESORT (Private)
60 units - 50 w/hookups for water/elec./sewer plus 10 tent sites, reservations - (503)271-3443, showers, laundry, groceries, ocean access, stream, fishing, ATV dune access & rentals, $$-$$$$.
US 101 southwest 4 miles, Salmon Harbor Dr. west 1 mile.

UMPQUA LIGHTHOUSE (Oregon State Park)
64 units - 22 w/hookups for water/elec./sewer plus 42 tent sites, maximum site 45', showers, picnic area, boat launch, fishing, sand dunes, hiking trails, $$-$$$.
Take US 101 south 6 miles.

WILLIAM M. TUGMAN (Oregon State Park)
115 units w/hookups for elec., maximum site 50', showers, wheelchair access, picnic area, trailer waste disposal, boat launch, fishing, swimming, $$-$$$.
Take US 101 south 8 miles.

WINDY COVE COUNTY PARK (Douglas County)
96 units in 2 areas - 63 w/full hookups plus 33 tent sites, showers, wheelchair access, playground, lake, swimming, fishing, ocean access, $$-$$$.
US 101 southwest 4 miles, Salmon Harbor Dr. west .3 mile.

LAKESIDE

NORTH LAKE RESORT & MARINA (Private)
100 unit - 5 w/hookups for water/elec./sewer, 31 w/water & elec., plus 64 tent sites, reservation information - (503)759-3515, showers, groceries, playground, lake, boat launch & rental, swimming, fishing, $$$-$$$$.
Take North Lake Ave. 1 mile east to 2090 North Lake Ave.

SEADRIFT MOTEL & CAMPGROUND (Private)
42 trailers sites - 39 w/full hookups plus 3 w/water & elec., no tents, reservation information - (503)759-3102, showers, laundry, trailer waste disposal, $$$.
Located on US 101 .3 mile north of Lakeside exit.

NORTH BEND

BLUEBILL CAMPGROUND (Siuslaw NF)
19 units plus group area, reservations (800)280-2267, trailers to 22', flush toilets, lake, fishing, hiking, ocean/dune access, $$.
Take US 101 north 2.5 miles, CR 609 west .8 mile, and FSR 1099 northwest 2.3 miles.

FIRS TRAILER PARK (Private) [RV]
25 trailer sites w/full hookups, reservation information - (503)756-6274, showers, laundry, $$$.
Follow US 101 north 7 miles, and Wildwood Dr. east 1.1 miles.

HORSEFALL CAMPGROUND (Siuslaw NF) [A] [RV]
70 units plus additional 35 trailer sites in parking lot, reservations - (800)280-2267, flush toilets, showers, ORV access to sand dunes, $$.
Follow US 101 north 4 miles, and Horsefall Dunes Rd. to camp.

SPINREEL (Siuslaw NF) [A] [RV]
37 campsites, trailers okay, ORV access to sand dunes, trail, $$.
Take US 101 north 8 miles.

WILD MARE HORSE CAMP (Siuslaw NF) [A] [RV]
12 units, reservation information (800)280-2267, trailers okay, horse corrals, no ORV, $$.
Follow US 101 north 4 miles, and Horsefall Dunes Rd. to camp.

COOS BAY

(West of Coos Bay)

DRIFTWOOD RV PARK (Private)
30 trailer sites w/full hookups, reservation information - (503)888-6103, showers, laundry, ocean bay access, fishing, crabbing & clamming, small pets okay, $$$.
Take Cape Arago Highway west 7 miles.

KELLEY'S RV PARK (Private)
38 units w/full hookups, no tents, reservation information - (503)888-6531, showers, laundry, trailer waste disposal, $$$.
Take Cape Arago Highway west 4.5 miles.

PLAINVIEW TRAILER PARK (Private)
39 units - 33 w/full hookups, 1 w/water/elec./cable tv, plus 5 tent sites, reservation information - (503)888-5166, showers, laundry, ocean access, lake, fishing, pets okay, $$-$$$
Take Cape Arago Highway west 7.5 miles.

SAND BAR MOBILE & RV PARK (Private)
18 units w/full hookups - 7 pull-thrus, reservation information - (503)888-3179, laundry, bay fishing, crabbing, clamming, $$$$.
Take Cape Arago Highway west 5.5 miles.

SUNSET BAY (Oregon State Park)
139 units - 29 w/hookups for water/elec./sewer, 35 w/water & elec., 75 tent sites, plus group campsites, maximum site 47', mail reservations available, showers, wheelchair access, picnic area, swimming, fishing, hiking trail, $$-$$$.
Take Cape Arago Highway west to Sunset Bay.

(East of Coos Bay)

NESIKA PARK (Coos County)
20 campsites, picnic facilities, on Millicoma River, boating, fishing, swimming, hiking, $.
Follow Coos River Hwy. 21 miles east - is 5 miles past Allegheny.

ROOKE-HIGGINS PARK (Coos County)
18 campsites, on Millicoma River, boat ramp, boating, fishing, hiking, rockhounding, $.
Follow Coos River Hwy. 10 miles east.

CHARLESTON

BASTENDORFF BEACH PARK (Coos County)
81 units - 56 w/hookups for water & elec. plus 25 tent sites, trailers to 70', flush toilets, showers, picnic area, playground, trailer waste disposal, ocean access, fishing, hiking, pets okay, open year round, $$-$$$.
Take Cape Arago Highway south 2 miles.

CHARLESTON MARINA/TRAVEL PARK (Port)
119 units - 109 w/full hookups plus 20 tent sites, reservation information - (503)888-9512, showers, laundry, cooking facilities, playground, trailer waste disposal, propane, ocean access, river, boat launch, fishing, pets okay, $$-$$$.
Take Boat Basin Dr. north 2 blocks, Kingfisher Dr. east 1 block.

HUCKLEBERRY HILL MOBILE HOME PARK (Private)
10 trailer sites w/hookups for water/elec./sewer, reservation information - (503)888-3611, showers, laundry, trailer waste disposal, hiking, ocean fishing, crabbing & clamming in bay, $$.
Just west of the Charleston Bridge, on Cape Arago Highway.

SEA PORT RV PARK (Private) `RV`
26 RV sites w/full hookups, information - (503)888-3122, RVs to 40', laundry, near ocean, fishing, clamming, crabbing, $$$.
Cross the Charleston Bridge and take Boat Basin Dr. to park.

COQUILLE

HAM BUNCH CHERRY CREEK (Coos County)
15 units, community kitchen, stream, fishing, hiking, $.
Take State 42 southeast 9 miles, and Dora Rd. east 7 miles.

LAVERNE PARK (Coos County)
84 units - 20 w/hookups for water & elec. plus 64 w/out hookups, flush toilets, showers, community kitchen, playfield, playground, trailer waste disposal, fish ladder, swimming, hiking, rockhounding, open May thru Oct., $$.
Follow the Coquille/Fairview Rd. northeast 15 miles.

BANDON

BANDON RV PARK (Private) `RV`
40 trailer sites w/full hookups, no tents, reservation information - (503)347-4122, showers, laundry, pets okay, $$$.
Located 1 block west of US 101/State 42 junction at 935 E. 2nd.

BLUE JAY CAMPGROUND (Private)
40 campsites - 3 w/hookups for water/elec./sewer, 8 w/water & elec., 9 w/elec. only, plus 20 tent units, reservation information - (503)347-7904, showers, open year round, $$$-$$$$.
US 101 south 4 miles, Scenic Beach Loop Dr. west .5 mile.

BULLARDS BEACH (Oregon State Park)
192 units - 92 w/hookups for water/elec./sewer plus 100 w/elec., maximum site 64', showers, wheelchair access, trailer waste disposal, boat launch, fishing, horse camp/trails, ocean access, bike trails, 1896 lighthouse, open year round, $$-$$$.
Take US 101 north 1 mile to campground.

REMOTE

REMOTE CAMPGROUND & CABINS (Private)
25 units w/full hookups, trailers to 35', reservation information - (503)572-5105, showers, laundry, river, swimming, fishing, $$$.
Follow State 42 east 1 mile.

SLEEPY HOLLOW RV PARK (Private)
14 units - 11 w/hookups for water/elec./sewer plus 3 tent sites, reservation information - (503)572-2141, showers, laundry, playground, river, swimming, fishing, $$-$$$.

Take State 42 west 8.5 miles - park is located just east of the bridge.

MYRTLE POINT

BENNETT PARK (Coos County)
18 units, picnic area, fishing, hiking, rockhounding, $.
Take the Dora-Sitkum Hwy. northeast 8 miles - campground is near Gravel Ford.

FRONA PARK (Coos County)
17 units, picnic facilities, fishing, $.
Take the Dora-Sitkum Hwy. northeast 18 miles.

LANGLOIS

BANDON-PORT ORFORD KOA (Private)
74 units - 16 w/hookups for water/elec./sewer, 24 w/water & elec., plus 34 tent sites, reservations - (503)348-2358, showers, laundry, playground, groceries, propane, trailer waste disposal, pond, hiking, pets okay, $$$$.
Follow US 101 south 3 miles.

LANGLOIS TRAVEL PARK (Private)
20 units - 11 w/hookups for water/elec./sewer, 4 w/water & elec., plus 5 tent sites, reservation information - (503)348-2256, showers, laundry, nearby windsurfing, $$.
Located on US 101 - at the south end of town.

POWERS

DAPHNE GROVE (Siskiyou NF)
14 units, trailers to 18', picnic area, on Coquille River, swimming, fishing, hiking, petroglyphs, elev. 800', $-$$$.
Take the Powers South Rd. south 4.2 miles, and FSR 33 south 10.4 miles.

POWERS COUNTY PARK (Coos County)
60 units - 40 w/hookups for water & elec. plus 30 tent sites, flush toilets, showers, playground, trailer waste disposal, lake - no motors, fishing, swimming, hiking, open year round, $$.
Located 1 mile north of town on Gaylord Rd.

ROCK CREEK (Siskiyou NF)
7 units, trailers okay, swimming, fishing, trails, elev. 1200', $.
Take the Powers South Rd. south 4.2 miles, FSR 33 south 13 miles, and FSR 3347 southwest 1.3 miles.

PORT ORFORD

AGATE BEACH TRAILER PARK (Private)
14 units - 12 w/hookups for water/elec./sewer plus 2 tent sites, reservation information - (503)332-3031, shower, laundry, ocean access, lake, agate hunting, surf fishing, $$-$$$.
Follow US 101 to 12th St. and go west .7 mile.

EVERGREEN PARK (Private)
15 units - 13 w/hookups for water/elec./sewer plus 2 tent sites, reservation information - (503)332-5942, showers, laundry, trailer waste disposal, $$-$$$.
Follow US 101 to 9th St. and go west 2 blocks.

PORT ORFORD RV TRAILER VILLAGE (Private)
49 units - 36 w/full hookups, 9 w/water/elec./tv, plus 6 tent sites, reservation information - (503)332-1041, showers, laundry, public kitchen, rec room, trailer waste disposal, $$-$$$.
Leave US 101 at the north end of town on Madrona Ave., go east 1 block, and follow Port Orford Loop .5 mile north.

(North of Port Orford)

CAPE BLANCO (Oregon State Park)
58 campsites w/hookups for elec., maximum site 70', showers, picnic area, trailer waste disposal, ocean access, black sand beach, fishing, hiking, historic Hughes House, $$-$$$.
Take US 101 north 4 miles, and follow park road west 5 miles.

ELK RIVER RV CAMPGROUND (Private)
50 units w/full hookups, tents okay, information - (503)332-2255, pull thrus, showers, laundry, trailer waste disposal, on Elk River, fishing, $$-$$$.
US 101 north 3 miles, Elk River Rd. southeast 1.7 miles.

(South of Port Orford)

HUMBUG MOUNTAIN (Oregon State Park)
108 units - 30 w/hookups for water/elec./sewer plus 78 tent sites, maximum site 55', showers, wheelchair access, picnic area, trailer waste disposal, ocean fishing, Oregon Coast Trail, $$-$$$.
Follow US 101 south 6 miles.

AGNESS

ILLAHE (Siskiyou NF)
14 units, trailers to 22', flush toilets, picnic area, on Rogue River, fishing, $-$$$.
Take the Agness/Illahe Rd. north 4.9 miles.

GOLD BEACH

HUNTER CREEK MOBILE & RV PARK (Private)
40 units w/full hookups, tents okay, reservations - (503)247-2322, showers, laundry, rec room, fishing, $$-$$$.
Take US 101 south .8 mile, and Hunter Creek Loop west .8 mile.

OCEANSIDE RV CAMP (Private)
95 units - 35 w/full hookups plus 60 w/water/elec./cable tv, no tents, reservation information - (503)247-2301, showers, tackle shop, ocean access, river, boat launch, fishing, $$$$.
Leave US 101 at Port of Gold Beach exit and head west .5 mile to the South Jetty and campground.

(North of Gold Beach)

ARIZONA BEACH (Private)
127 units - 11 w/hookups for water/elec./sewer, 85 w/water & elec., plus 31 tent sites, reservations - (503)332-6491, showers, laundry, playfield, trailer waste disposal, groceries, ocean access, stream, swimming, fishing, pets okay, $$$-$$$$.
Take US 101 north 14 miles.

HONEY BEAR CAMPGROUND (Private)
150 units - 55 w/full hookups, 18 w/water & elec., plus 77 tent sites, reservations - (503)247-2765, showers, laundry, wheelchair access, playground, trailer waste disposal, groceries, ocean access, stream, swimming, fishing, hiking, pets okay, $$$-$$$$.
Take US 101 north 7 miles, and Ophir Rd. north 2 miles.

NESIKA BEACH RV PARK CAMPGROUND (Private)
37 units - 17 w/full hookups, 10 w/water & elec., plus 10 tent sites, trailers to 35', reservation information - (503)247-6077, some pull thrus, showers, laundry, groceries, $$$-$$$$.
Take US 101 north 7 miles, and Nesika Rd. southwest .7 mile.

(East of Gold Beach)

AGNESS RV PARK (Private)
84 units - 53 w/hookups for water/elec./sewer plus 31 w/elec. only, reservations - (503)247-2813, showers, laundry, trailer waste disposal, river, boat launch, fishing, hiking, $$$.
Follow Jerry's Flat Rd. east 28 miles.

ANGLERS TRAILER VILLAGE (Private)
49 units w/full hookups, no tents, reservation information - (503)247-7922, showers, laundry, rec room, $$$.
Follow Jerry's Flat Rd. east 3.5 miles east - on the south bank of the Rogue River.

FOUR SEASONS RV RESORT (Private)
45 units w/full hookups, reservation information - (503)247-7959, showers, laundry, playfield, trailer waste disposal, groceries, river, boat launch, fishing, hiking, $$$-$$$$$.
Take the North Bank Rogue River Rd. east 6.5 miles.

INDIAN CREEK RECREATION PARK (Private)
125 units - 100 w/full hookups plus 25 tent sites, reservations - (503)247-7704, showers, laundry, wheelchair access, playfield, playground, groceries, river, fishing, pets okay, $$$-$$$$.
Follow Jerry's Flat Rd. east .5 mile.

KIMBALL CREEK BEND RV RESORT (Private)
79 units - 66 w/full hookups plus 13 tent sites, reservations - (503)247-7580, showers, laundry, trailer waste disposal, river, boat launch, fishing, hiking, $$$$-$$$$.
Take the North Bank Rogue River Rd. east 8 miles.

LOBSTER CREEK (Siskiyou NF)
7 units plus open camping on gravel bar, trailers to 28', flush toilets, wheelchair accessible, picnic area, on Rogue River, boat ramp, fishing, hiking, pets okay, $-$$.
Follow Jerry's Flat Rd. east 8.5 miles.

LUCKY LODGE RV PARK (Private)
42 units - 32 w/hookups for water/elec./sewer, 4 w/water & elec., plus 6 tent sites, trailers to 35', reservation information - (503)247-7618, showers, laundry, trailer waste disposal, river, fishing, $$$.
Take the North Bank Rogue River Rd. east 8 miles.

QUOSATANA (Siskiyou NF)
43 units plus group area, trailers to 32', flush toilets, wheelchair access - includes trail, trailer waste disposal, on recreational section of Wild & Scenic Rogue River, boat launch, fishing, paved trail thru myrtlewood grove, $$-$$$.
Follow Jerry's Flat Rd. east 14.2 miles.

SELMA

GRANTS PASS/REDWOOD HWY KOA (Private)
41 units - 26 w/hookups for water & elec. plus 15 w/water only, tents okay, reservations - (503)476-6508, showers, laundry, playfield, playground, rec. room, groceries, propane, trailer waste disposal, stream, $$$-$$$$.
Take US 199 northeast 7 miles - is between mileposts 14 and 15.

LAKE SELMAC RV RESORT (Private)
44 units - 9 w/hookups for water/elec./sewer, 21 w/water & elec., plus 14 tent sites, reservations - (503)597-4989, trailers to 70', showers, laundry, playground, groceries, rec room, snack

bar, on lake, boat launch & rentals, year-round fishing, hiking, horse corrals/trails & rental, pets okay, open year round, $$$.
Take US 199 to the Lake Selmac Junction, and follow Lake Shore Dr. 2.5 miles east to resort.

SELMAC LAKE (Josephine County)
96 campsites, trailers to 40', information - (503)474-5285, showers, playfield, playground, trailer waste disposal, lake, boat launch, swimming, fishing, hiking, $$$-$$$$.
Take US 199 to the Lake Selmac Junction, and follow Lake Shore Dr. east to the campground.

CAVE JUNCTION

(North of Cave Junction)

KERBY TRAILER PARK (Private)
14 units - 5 w/hookups for water/elec./sewer plus 9 w/water & elec., reservations - (503)592-2897, showers, laundry, $$.
Follow US 199 north 2.8 miles to Kerby.

(East of Cave Junction)

CAVE CREEK (Siskiyou NF)
18 campsites, trailers okay, hiking, elev. 2900', $-$$$.
Take State 46 east 16 miles, and FSR 4032 south 1 mile.

CAVES HIGHWAY (Private)
20 sites w/hookups for water/elec./sewer, reservations - (503)592-6481, showers, trailer waste disposal, $$$.
Take State 46 east 1 mile.

CHINQUAPIN GROUP CAMP (Siskiyou NF)
Group area holds 100 people, reservations required - (503)592-2166, picnic tables, BBQ, fire rings, nearby trails, $25-40.
Take State 46 east 12 miles - just past Grayback Campground.

GRAYBACK (Siskiyou NF)
36 units plus 2 handicap sites, trailers to 45', picnic area, flush toilets, handicap access - includes trail, picnic shelter, stream, swimming, fishing, inter. trail, elev. 1800', $$-$$$.
Take State 46 east 12 miles.

WOODLAND ECHOES FAMILY RESORT (Private)
16 units - 2 w/hookups for water & elec. plus 14 dry sites, tents okay, reservations - (503)592-3406, pull-thrus, showers, historical theme park, swimming, $$-$$$.
Take State 46 east 8 miles.

(South of Cave Junction)

SHADY ACRES RV PARK (Private)
29 units - 25 w/hookups for water/elec./sewer plus 4 tent sites, reservation information - (503)592-3702, showers, $$-$$$.
Follow US 199 south 1 mile.

TOWN & COUNTRY RV PARK (Private)
51 units - 39 w/hookups for water/elec./sewer plus 12 w/water & elec., tents okay, trailers to 60', reservation information - (503)592-2656, showers, laundry, tv, rec room, trailer waste disposal, on Illinois River, pets okay, open year round, $$$-$$$$.
Follow US 199 south 2 miles.

TRAILS END CAMPGROUND (Private)
100 units - 40 w/hookups for water/elec./sewer, 40 w/water & elec., plus 20 tent sites, reservation information - (503)592-3354, showers, trailer waste disposal, river, swimming, $$-$$$.
Follow US 199 south 2.5 miles, and take Burch Dr. southwest .1 mile to campground.

BROOKINGS

BEACH FRONT RV PARK (Private)
154 units - 48 w/full hookups, 70 w/water & elec., 36 w/out hookups, plus tent area, reservations - (800)441-0856, trailers to 40', showers, wheelchair access, laundry, trailer waste disposal, river, boat launch/dock/marina, fishing, swimming, restaurant, open year round, small pets okay, $$-$$$.
Leave US 101 on Lower Harbor Rd. - located at intersection of Lower Harbor Rd. and Benham Ln.

CHETCO RV PARK (Private)
120 trailer sites w/full hookups - 80 are pull-thrus, adult park, no tents, reservation information - (503)469-3863, showers, laundry, ice, trailer waste disposal, small pets okay, $$$$.
Located 1 mile south of the Chetco River Bridge, on US 101 .

DRIFTWOOD RV PARK (Private)
108 campsites - 100 w/full hookups plus 8 w/water/elec./sewer, no tents, reservations - (503)469-3213, showers, laundry, ocean access, fishing, nearby boat launch, pets okay, $$$-$$$$.
Leave US 101 on Lower Harbor Rd. - located .7 mile west.

PORTSIDE RV PARK (Private)
90 units w/full hookups, no tents, reservations - (503)469-6616, showers, laundry, rec room, propane, pets okay, $$$$.
Located on Lower Harbor Rd.

SEA BIRD RV PARK (Private) RV

60 trailer sites w/hookups for water/elec./sewer, senior park, no tents, reservation information - (503)469-3512, showers, laundry, cable tv, wheelchair access, ocean fishing, trailer waste disposal, pets okay, $$$.
Located on US 101, just south of the Chetco River Bridge.

SNUG HARBOR (Private)

26 campsites - 4 w/hookups for water/elec./sewer, 15 w/water & elec., plus 7 tent sites, reservation information - (503)469-3452, boat basin, ocean access & fishing, pets okay, $$.
Located on North Bank Rd. - .7 mile east of US 101.

(North of Brookings)

WHALESHEAD RV PARK (Private)

109 units - 100 w/full hookups, 4 w/water & elec., plus 5 tent sites, reservation information - (503)469-7446, showers, laundry, beach access, hiking, pets okay, $$$-$$$$.
Take US 101 north 7 miles to Whaleshead Rd. - located at 19936 Whaleshead Rd.

HARRIS BEACH (Oregon State Park) RV

156 units - 34 w/hookups for water/elec./sewer, 53 w/elec. only, 69 tent sites, plus group campsites, mail reservations available, maximum site 50', showers, wheelchair access, picnic area, trailer waste disposal, ocean access, fishing, hiking trails, open year round, $$-$$$.
Take US 101 north 2 miles.

(East of Brookings)

ATRIVERS EDGE RV RESORT (Private) RV

90 units - 84 w/hookups for water/elec./sewer, 6 w/out hookups, plus tent area, trailers to 38', reservations (503)469-3356, showers, laundry, rec hall, propane, trailer waste disposal, on Chetco River, boat ramp, pets okay, $$$-$$$$.
Take Southbank Chetco River Rd. east 1.5 miles.

LITTLE REDWOOD (Siskiyou NF) RV

12 units, trailers to 18', picnic area, on Chetco River, boating, swimming, fishing, $-$$$.
Take Northbank Chetco River Rd. northeast 7.5 miles, and FSR 376 northeast 6 miles to campground.

LITTLE REDWOOD BAR (Siskiyou NF) RV

Open camping along rocky river bar, trailers okay, on Chetco River, swimming, fishing, $-$$$.
Take Northbank Chetco River Rd. northeast 7.5 miles, and FSR 376 northeast 6 miles - located next to Little Redwood.

LOEB (Oregon State Park)
53 units w/hookups for elec., maximum site 50', showers, wheelchair accessible, picnic area, fishing, swimming, hiking, open year round, $$-$$$.
Take Northbank Chetco River Rd. northeast 10 miles.

LUDLUM PLACE (Siskiyou NF)
Group area/shelter, reservations - (503)469-2196, trailers to 32', no water, on river, fishing, swimming, $$$$.
Follow US 101 southeast 5.7 miles, Winchuck River Rd. northeast 6.3 miles, FSR 3907 east 1 mile, and FSR 4029 north 1.5 miles.

RIVER BEND PARK (Private) [A] [RV]
96 units - 83 w/full hookups, 8 w/water/elec./cable tv, plus 5 tent sites, reservations - (503)469-3356, showers, laundry, rec room, river, fishing, small boat ramp, pets okay, $$$-$$$$.
Take Southbank Chetco River Rd. east 1.5 miles.

WINCHUCK (Siskiyou NF) [A] [RV]
13 units, trailers to 18', on river, swimming, fishing, $-$$$.
Follow US 101 southeast 5.7 miles, Winchuck River Rd. northeast 6.3 miles, and FSR 3907 east 1.1 miles.

OREGON I-5 CORRIDOR CAMPGROUNDS

See Page

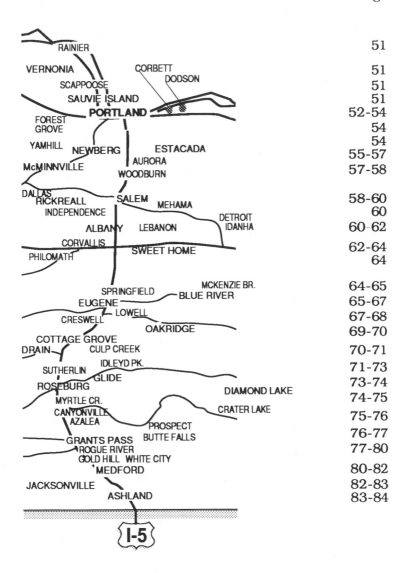

	See Page
RAINIER	51
VERNONIA / CORBETT / DODSON	51
SCAPPOOSE	51
SAUVIE ISLAND	51
PORTLAND	52-54
FOREST GROVE	54
YAMHILL	54
NEWBERG / ESTACADA / AURORA	55-57
McMINNVILLE / WOODBURN	57-58
DALLAS / RICKREALL / SALEM	58-60
INDEPENDENCE / MEHAMA	60
ALBANY / LEBANON / DETROIT / IDANHA	60-62
CORVALLIS / SWEET HOME	62-64
PHILOMATH	64
SPRINGFIELD / MCKENZIE BR. / BLUE RIVER	64-65
EUGENE	65-67
CRESWELL / LOWELL	67-68
OAKRIDGE	69-70
COTTAGE GROVE / DRAIN / CULP CREEK	70-71
SUTHERLIN / IDLEYD PK. / GLIDE	71-73
ROSEBURG	73-74
MYRTLE CR. / DIAMOND LAKE	74-75
CANYONVILLE / AZALEA / CRATER LAKE	75-76
GRANTS PASS / PROSPECT / BUTTE FALLS	76-77
ROGUE RIVER	77-80
GOLD HILL / WHITE CITY / MEDFORD	80-82
JACKSONVILLE	82-83
ASHLAND	83-84

I-5

49

RAINIER

HUDSON/PARCHER PARK (Columbia County)
66 units - 36 w/hookups for water & elec. plus tent area, reservations (503)556-9050, flush toilets, showers, playfield, playground, picnic tables, grills, trailer waste disposal, boating, fishing, windsurfing, open year round, $-$$$.
Take State 30 west to Larson Rd., and follow .4 mile.

SCIPIO'S GOBLE LANDING (Private)
60 units w/hookups for water & elec. plus tent area, reservations (503)556-6510, trailers to 40', showers, store, trailer waste disposal, on Columbia River, boat launch/rental/dock/moorage, gas & diesel, pets okay, open year round, $$.
Located on State 30 - between mileposts 40 & 41.

VERNONIA

BIG EDDY (Columbia County)
40 units - 10 w/hookups for water & elec. plus 30 tent sites, flush toilets, picnic tables, BBQ grills, playground, trailer waste disposal, on Nehalem River, boat launch, fishing, $$-$$$.
Follow State 47 north 7 miles.

CAMP WILKERSON (Columbia County)
7 units plus huge group camp, reservations required - (503)397-2353, flush toilets, picnic shelter, play areas, hiking trails, $$.
Take State 47 north 8 miles, turn onto Apiary Rd. and go 6 miles to park.

SCAPPOOSE

AIRPORT PARK (Columbia County)
17 units - 6 w/hookups for water/elec./sewer plus tent area, playground, adjacent to airport, $-$$$.
Leave State 30 just north of Scappoose, go east on West Lane Rd, and follow Honeyman Rd. to park.

SAUVIE ISLAND

REEDER BEACH RV PARK (Private)
47 units - 39 w/hookups for water/elec./sewer plus 9 w/water & elec., tents okay, reservations advised - (503)621-3970, showers, laundry, groceries, trailer waste disposal, on Columbia River, fishing, ice, $$$-$$$$.
Located on the Columbia River side of the island, at 26048 NW Reeder Beach Rd.

PORTLAND

FIR GROVE-EL RANCHO TRAILER PARK (Private)
6 units w/full hookups plus 2 tent sites, reservations (503)252-9993, trailers to 40', showers, laundry, wheelchair accessible, trailer waste disposal, pets okay, open year round, $$-$$$$.
Leave I-205 at exit #23B and take Columbia Blvd. west to 72nd St. - located at 5541 N.E. 72nd.

JANTZEN BEACH RV PARK (Private)
169 units w/hookups for water/elec./sewer, no tents, reservations (800)443-7248 or (503)289-7626, showers, laundry, swimming pool, playground, rec room, nearby shops, $$$$.
Take I-5 to exit #308, and follow North Hayden Island Dr. west .5 mile.

LEROSE RV PARK (Private)
20 units w/full hookups, no tents, reservations (503)639-1501, trailers to 40', pull thrus, showers, laundry, small pets okay, open year round, $$$.
Leave I-5 at exit #290 and go 5 blocks to 18040 SW Lower Boones Ferry Rd.

PORTLAND- FAIRVIEW RV PARK (Private)
407 units w/full hookups, reservations (503)661-1047, showers, laundry, pool, rec room, horseshoes, trailer waste disposal, lake fishing, pets okay, $$$$$.
Leave I-84 on the Parkrose exit and follow Sandy Blvd. east 2 miles to 21401 NE Sandy Blvd.

PORTLAND MEADOWS RV PARK (Private)
32 units w/hookups for water/elec./sewer, no tents, reservations (503)285-1617, trailers to 70', showers, laundry, wheelchair accessible, propane, trailer waste disposal, pets okay, open year round, $$$$.
Leave I-5 on the Columbia Blvd exit, go east 2 blocks to Martin Luther King Blvd, north 1 mile to Gertz Rd., and west to park.

ROLLING HILLS MOBILE TERRACE (Private)
108 units - 101 trailer sites w/full hookups plus 7 tent sites, reservation information - (503)666-7282, showers, laundry, wheelchair access, swimming pool, game room, trailer waste disposal, no pets in tent sites, $$$-$$$$$.
Leave I-84 westbound on Sandy Blvd. exit - park is west .7 mile at 20145 NE Sandy Blvd.

SOUTHGATE MOBILE HOME/RV PARK (Private)
25 units w/hookups for water/elec./sewer, no tents, reservation information (503)771-5262, showers, laundry, $$$$.
Leave I-205 on Foster Ave. exit, go west to 82nd Ave., and south to 7911 SE 82nd Ave.

TOWN & COUNTRY MOBILE ESTATES (Private)
21 units w/full hookups, no tents, information (503)771-1040, showers, laundry, rec room, $$$$.
Leave I-205 on Foster Ave. exit, go west to 82nd Ave., and south to 9911 SE 82nd Ave.

(South of Portland)

PHEASANT RIDGE RV PARK (Private) RV
130 units w/full hookups, no tents, reservations (800)532-7829, trailers to 42', pull thrus, showers, laundry, wheelchair accessible, pond, fishing, hiking, pets okay, open year round, $$$$$.
Leave I-5 on exit #286 and go east .5 mile to 8275 SW Elligsen Rd.

ROAMER'S REST RV PARK (Private) RV
93 units w/full hookups, no tents, reservations (503)692-6350, trailers to 70', pull thrus, showers, laundry, wheelchair accessible, Tualatin River, fishing, pets okay, open year round, $$$$$.
Leave I-5 at Tualatin exit #289, go right on State 212, then right on State 99 to 17585 S.W. Pacific Hwy.

TRAILER PARK OF PORTLAND (Private)
120 units - 100 w/full hookups plus 20 w/water & elec., tents okay, reservations (503)692-0225, showers, laundry, playground, groceries, trailer waste disposal, river, fishing, $$$-$$$$$.
Leave I-5 on exit #289, and take State 212 east .2 mile to park.

(East of Portland)

AINSWORTH (Oregon State Park) RV
45 campsites w/hookups for water/elec./sewer, maximum site 60'; showers, picnic area, trailer waste disposal, hiking, access to Columbia Gorge Trail, $$-$$$.
Take US 30 east 37 miles - is near I-84/US 30 junction.

BELLACRES MOBILE ESTATE (Private) RV
12 trailer sites w/hookups for water/elec./sewer, no tents, trailers to 35', reservation information - (503)665-4774, showers, laundry, game room, lounge, pets okay, $$$$.
Leave I-84 on the Wood Village exit and follow NE 238th Dr. south 2.6 miles (road becomes 242nd then Hogan Dr.), turn east on Division St. and go .6 mile to park.

COLUMBIA GORGE RV VILLAGE (Private) RV
105 units - 55 w/full hookups, no tents or tent trailers, reservations (503)665-6722, trailers to 54', showers, laundry, wheelchair accessible, on Sandy River, fishing, hiking, small pets okay, $$$$.

Leave I-84 on Troutdale exit - located in Troutdale, around the corner from city hall.

OXBOW (Multnomah County)
45 campsites, no hookups, trailers to 30', information - (503)663-4708, wheelchair access, fire pits, playfield, playground, river, boat launch, fishing, hiking, no pets, maximum stay 5 days, $$-$$$.
Follow Division St. east - located 8 miles east of Gresham.

CORBETT

CROWN POINT RV PARK (Private)
20 trailer sites w/hookups for water/elec./sewer plus a few tent sites, reservation information - (503)695-5207, showers, laundry, trailer waste disposal, store, pets okay, $$$-$$$$.
Take the Scenic Loop Highway .2 mile east of Corbett to milepost #9 and campground.

DODSON

FISHERY - COVERTS LANDING (Private)
15 sites w/hookups for elec., tents okay, reservations - (503)374-8577, showers, trailer waste disposal, ice, gas, boat launch & moorage, fishing, pets okay, $$.
Leave I-84 at exit #35 and follow signs.

FOREST GROVE

ROSE GROVE RV PARK (Private)
19 units w/hookups for water/elec./sewer, no tents, reservations (503)357-7817, trailers to 40', showers, laundry, pets okay, $$$.
Located at 3839 Pacific Ave.

SID'S FERNWOOD RV PARK (Private)
12 units w/hookups for elec. plus 2 tent sites, information (503)357-9491, showers, $$$$$.
Take State 8 northwest 9 miles, and State 6 northwest 1 mile - located at 57625 NW Wilson River Hwy.

YAMHILL

FLYING "M" RANCH (Private)
100 campsites, reservation information - (503)662-3222, showers, restaurant, lounge, pond, river, fishing, horse rental, $$.
Located at 23029 Flying "M" Rd.

NEWBERG

CHAMPOEG (Oregon State Park)
54 units - 48 w/hookups for elec., 6 walk-in tent sites, plus group area, maximum site 50', showers, wheelchair access, trailer waste disposal, boating, fishing, bicycle & hiking trails, interpretive center/OR's first gov., open year round, $$-$$$.
Follow State 99W to State 219 - park is about 7 miles southeast of town. (Also accessible via exit #278 off I-5.)

ESTACADA

METZLER (Clackamas County)
70 units - 46 w/hookups for water & elec. plus 24 tent sites, reservations (503)655-8521, flush toilets, showers, handicap facilities, picnic area, playground, basketball court, $$-$$$.
Follow State 211 south 4 miles, Tucker Rd. west .5 mile, and Metzler Park Rd. 1.6 miles to campground.

MILO McIVER (Oregon State Park)
45 sites w/hookups for elec. plus group area, maximum site 50', showers, wheelchair access, picnic area, trailer waste disposal, boat launch, fishing, horse/bicycle & hiking trails, $$-$$$.
Leave State 211 at Estacada and follow signs - is 5 miles west.

(Northwest of Estacada)

BARTON PARK (Clackamas County)
58 campsites - 55 w/hookups for water & elec. plus 3 w/water only, reservations - (503)650-3484, showers, handicap facilities, playground, trailer waste disposal, river, boat launch, swimming, fishing, open May thru Sept., $$-$$$.
Follow State 224 northwest 9 miles to park road.

(Southeast of Estacada)

ARMSTRONG (Mt. Hood NF)
12 units - some barrier-free sites by reservation (800)280-2267, trailers to 16', on Clackamas River, fishing, elev. 900', $$.
Take State 224 southeast 15.4 miles.

BIG SLIDE LAKE (Mt. Hood NF)
2 hike-in tent sites, swimming, fishing, elev. 4300', $.
Take State 224 southeast 26.7 miles, FSR 46 south 3.7 miles, FSR 63 south 5.4 miles, FSR 708 southwest 2.9 miles, FSR 708A 2 miles to Dickey Creek Trailhead, and hike 4 miles.

CARTER BRIDGE (Mt. Hood NF)
11 units, trailers to 22', wheelchair access, on Clackamas River, fishing, elev. 800', $$.
Take State 224 southeast 15 miles.

FISH CREEK (Mt. Hood NF)
24 units, trailers to 16', barrier free, on Clackamas River, fishing, hiking, elev. 900', $$.
Take State 224 southeast 15.6 miles.

INDIAN HENRY (Mt. Hood NF)
86 units - some barrier-free sites by reservation (800)280-2267, trailers to 22', flush toilets, trailer waste disposal, on Clackamas River, fishing, hiking, elev. 1200', $$.
Take State 224 southeast 23 miles, FSR 53 southeast .5 mile.

KINGFISHER (Mt. Hood NF)
23 units, trailers to 16', on Hot Springs Fork of Collawash River, fishing, elev. 1600', $$.
Take State 224 southeast 26.5 miles, FSR 46 south 3.5 miles, FSR 63 south 3 miles, and FSR 70 southwest 2 miles.

LAKE HARRIET (Mt. Hood NF)
13 units, trailers to 30', wheelchair access, lake - no motors, boat launch, fishing, elev. 2100', $$.
Take State 224 southeast 26.5 miles, and FSR 57 east 4 miles.

LAZY BEND (Mt. Hood NF)
21 units - some barrier-free sites by reservation (800)280-2267, trailers to 16', flush toilets, on Clackamas River, swimming, fishing, hiking, elev. 800', $$.
Take State 224 southeast 10.7 miles.

LOCKABY (Mt. Hood NF)
30 units - some barrier-free sites by reservation (800)280-2267, trailers to 16', on Clackamas River, fishing, elev. 900', $$.
Take State 224 southeast 15.3 miles.

PAUL DENNIS (Mt. Hood NF)
15 units, trailers to 16', lake - no motors, groceries, gas, ice, boat launch & rental, swimming, fishing, hiking trails, elev. 5000', $$.
Take State 224 southeast 27 miles, FSR 46 south 21.8 miles, FSR 4690 southeast 8.2 miles, and FSR 4220 south 6.3 miles.

PENINSULA (Mt. Hood NF)
35 units, trailers to 24', wheelchair access includes trails and fishing, lake - no motors, boat launch, swimming, fishing, hiking, elev. 4900', $$.
Take State 224 southeast 27 miles, FSR 46 south 21.8 miles, FSR 4690 southeast 8.2 miles, and FSR 4220 south 6.6 miles.

PROMONTORY (PGE)
58 sites, trailers to 20', reservation information - (503)630-5152, showers, playground, groceries, lake, fishing, boat launch & rental, hiking, $$$.
Take State 224 southeast 7 mile.

RAINBOW (Mt. Hood NF)
17 units - some barrier-free sites by reservation (800)280-2267, trailers to 16', river, swimming, fishing, hiking, elev. 1400', $$.
Take State 224 southeast 27 miles, and FSR 46 south .1 mile.

RIPPLEBROOK (Mt. Hood NF)
13 units - some barrier-free sites by reservation (800)280-2267, trailers to 16', stream, fishing, hiking, elev. 1500', $$.
Take State 224 southeast 26.5 miles.

RIVERSIDE (Mt. Hood NF)
16 units - some barrier-free sites by reservation (800)280-2267, trailers to 22', river, fishing, hiking, elev. 1400', $$.
Take State 224 southeast 27 miles, and FSR 46 south 2.7 miles.

ROARING RIVER (Mt. Hood NF)
19 units - some barrier-free sites by reservation (800)280-2267, trailers to 16', at junction of Roaring & Clackamas Rivers, fishing, hiking, elev. 1000', $$.
Take State 224 southeast 18.2 miles.

SKOOKUM LAKE (Mt. Hood NF)
2 tent sites, fishing, elev. 4500', $.
Take State 224 southeast 15.6 miles to Fish Creek, then follow FSR 54 and FSR 505 for 16.4 miles to lake and campground.

SUNSTRIP (Mt. Hood NF)
9 units - some barrier-free sites by reservation (800)280-2267, trailers to 18', trailer waste disposal, on Clackamas River, fishing, elev. 1000', $$.
Take State 224 southeast 18.6 miles.

AURORA

ISEBERG PARK RV (Private)
84 campsites w/hookups for water/elec./sewer, tents okay, reservations - (503)678-2646, showers, laundry, groceries, trailer waste disposal, rec room, miniature golf, hiking, pets okay, $$-$$$$.
Leave I-5 at exit #278 and follow signs east toward Aurora.

McMINNVILLE

FLAMINGO MOBILE & RV PARK (Private)
2 RV units - 1 w/hookups for water/elec./sewer plus 1 w/elec., no tents, no restrooms, pets okay, open year round, $$-$$$.
Located at 849 N. Hwy 99W.

MULKEY RV PARK (Private)

50 units - 8 w/hookups for water/elec./sewer, 16 w/water & elec., plus 26 tent sites, reservation information - (503)472-2475, showers, laundry, near landfill, river, fishing, $$$-$$$$.
Located on State 18, 4 miles southwest of town.

OLDE STONE VILLAGE MOBILE/RV PARK (Private) [RV]

28 units w/full hookups, no tents, reservations (503)472-4315, trailers to 60', pull thrus, showers, laundry, wheelchair accessible, swimming pool, rec room, small pets okay, $$$.
Located on State 18 - across from the airport.

WOODBURN

FEYRER PARK (Clackamas County) [A] [RV]

28 units - 20 w/hookups for water/elec. plus 8 tent sites, reservations (503)655-8521, showers, wheelchair access, picnic facilities, play area, volleyball, horseshoes, trailer waste disposal, on Molalla River, boat launch, fishing, $$-$$$.
Leave I-5 on exit #271, take State 211 east 16 miles, go thru Molalla to Feyrer Park Rd., and head southeast 1.9 miles to park.

RIVERPLACE RV PARK (Private) [RV]

108 units w/full hookups, no tents, reservations (503)266-1241, trailers to 42', showers, laundry, wheelchair accessible, small playground, hot tub, steam bath, propane, store, on Molalla River, fishing, pets extra, open year round, $$$$-$$$$$.
Leave I-5 on exit #271 and drive east 2 miles to 99E, then north 10 miles to Canby - located at 24310 Hwy. 99E.

WOODBURN I-5 RV PARK (Private) [RV]

148 units w/full hookups, reservations - (503)981-0002, paved pull thrus, showers, wheelchair access, laundry, heated pool in summer, playground, rec room, open year round, $$$$-$$$$$.
Take exit #271 off I-5 - located on west side of freeway.

DALLAS

HAWTHORNE ACRES MOBILE COURT (Private) [RV]

4 trailer sites w/full hookups, reservations - (503)623-6851, showers, laundry, nearby golf & fishing, $$$.
Take the Kings Valley Highway north of town - park is on left.

RICKREALL

POLK COUNTY FAIRGROUNDS (County)

242 units - 218 w/hookups for elec. plus 24 pull thrus w/water & elec., tents okay, information - (503)623-3048, showers, $$.
Follow State 99 west to the fairgrounds.

SALEM

SALEM CAMPGROUND & RV (Private)
204 units - 118 w/hookups for water/elec./sewer, 54 w/water & elec., plus 32 tent sites, reservations - (503)581-6736, showers, laundry, playground, game room, groceries, trailer waste disposal, $$$-$$$$.
Leave I-5 on exit #253, take State 22 southeast .2 mile, and Lancaster Dr., south .5 mile to park.

SALEM RV PARK (Private)
124 units w/full hookups, no tents, reservations (503)364-5490, trailers to 60', showers, laundry, wheelchair access, swimming pool, lounge, store, pets okay, open year round, $$$$.
Leave I-5 on the Market St. exit, go east .5 mile to 45th St. and north to Silverton Rd. - located at 4490 Silverton Rd. N.E.

TRAILER PARK VILLAGE (Private)
22 units w/hookups for water/elec./sewer, adults only, no tents, information - (503)393-7424, showers, laundry, ice, no pets, nearby groceries & restaurant, $$$.
Leave I-5 on exit #258 and take State 99E north .5 mile.

(East of Salem)

ELKHORN VALLEY (BLM)
22 units, trailers okay, fishing, swimming, hiking trails, open mid May thru Sept., elev. 1000', $.
Follow State 22 east 24 miles and Elkhorn Rd. north 10 miles to campground.

SILVER FALLS (Oregon State Park)
104 units - 53 w/hookups for elec., 51 tent sites, plus group areas, maximum site 60', showers, wheelchair access, picnic facilities, trailer waste disposal, bike trails, hiking trails, waterfalls, swimming, fishing, horse camp, $$-$$$.
Follow State 214 east 26 miles. The route is well marked by signs. This park is also accessible from Silverton.

(South of Salem)

FOREST GLEN (Private)
83 units w/hookups for water/elec./sewer, reservation information - (503)363-7616, showers, laundry, miniature golf, therapy pool, game room, ice, trailer waste disposal, hiking, $$$.
Leave I-5 5 miles south of Salem on exit #248, go east over freeway, and follow Enchanted Way south .5 mile to the campground.

MEHAMA

FISHERMEN'S BEND (BLM)
37 units - 21 w/hookups for water, 16 tent sites, plus group area, group reservations (503)375-5646, flush toilets, showers, basketball/volleyball/baseball facilities, trailer waste disposal, on North Santiam River, boat launch, fishing, elev. 750', $$.
Follow State 22 east of town 8.5 miles - located west of Mill City.

JOHN NEAL MEMORIAL PARK (Linn County)
40 units, trailers to 22', playground, playfield, river, boat launch, fishing, hiking, pets okay, $$.
Go south 1 mile to Lyons, east 1.5 miles to Memorial Park Rd., and north to the park.

SHADY COVE (Willamette NF)
9 units, no trailers, on Little North Santiam River, fishing, hiking, elev. 1400', $.
Take State 22 east .9 mile, CR 967 east 15.3 miles, FSR S80 east 1.1 miles, and FSR 581 east 2.1 miles.

INDEPENDENCE

ASH CREEK MOBILE PARK (Private)
77 units w/full hookups, no tents, trailers to 40', reservations (503)838-4552, showers, laundry, wheelchair accessible, nearby store, propane, trailer waste disposal, on Ash Creek, hiking, small pets okay, open year round, $$$$.
Located at 141 S. 17th St.

DETROIT

B & B RV COURT (Private)
12 RV sites w/full hookups, reservations - (503)854-3614, $$$.
Located at the junction of State 22 and Breitenbush Rd.

DETROIT LAKE (Oregon State Park)
311 units - 107 w/hookups for water/elec./sewer, 70 w/elec. only, 134 tent sites, plus group area, mail reservations available, maximum site 60', showers, picnic area, boat launch, fishing, swimming, $$-$$$.
Follow State 22 west 2 miles to park.

KANE'S HIDEAWAY MARINA (Private)
19 units w/hookups for water & elec., reservations - (503)854-3362, showers, lounge, trailer waste disposal, groceries, gas, on Detroit Lake, fishing, boating, $$$.
Leave State 22 on Clester Rd. and follow the signs.

MT. VIEW PARK RV & CAMPING (Private)
39 units - 26 w/full hookups plus 13 w/out hookups, tents okay, reservations - (503)854-3774, some pull-thrus, showers, wheelchair access, on North Santiam River, fishing, $$-$$$. Located at 577 Mountain Ave.

(North of Detroit)

BREITENBUSH (Willamette NF)
30 units plus group camp, trailers to 18', wheelchair access, groceries, gas, river, fishing, elev. 2200', $$. Take FSR 46 northeast 9.8 miles.

CLEATOR BEND (Willamette NF)
9 units, trailers to 18', river, fishing, elev. 2200', $$. Take FSR 46 northeast 9.6 miles.

HUMBUG (Willamette NF)
22 units, trailers to 22', on Breitenbush River, fishing, hiking, elev. 1800', $$. Take FSR 46 northeast 4.8 miles.

(South of Detroit)

HOOVER (Willamette NF)
37 units, trailers to 22', flush toilets, wheelchair access, on Detroit Lake, boat launch, swimming, fishing, water skiing, interpretive services, elev. 1600', $$. Take State 22 southeast 2.9 miles, and FSR 10 west .8 mile.

HOOVER GROUP CAMP (Willamette NF)
Group camp - 70 people max., reservations required - (503)854-3366, trailers to 18', picnic shelter, playfield, boating, swimming, fishing, water skiing, elev. 1600', $80/group. Take State 22 southeast 2.9 miles, and FSR 10 west .8 mile.

SOUTH SHORE (Willamette NF)
30 units, trailers to 22', picnic area, wheelchair access, on Detroit Lake, boat launch, swimming, fishing, water skiing, elev. 1600', $$. Take State 22 southeast 2.9 miles, and FSR 10 west 3.5 miles.

IDANHA

MOUNTAIN VIEW MOBILE PARK (Private)
28 units - 14 w/full hookups plus 14 tent sites, reservation information - (503)854-3774, showers, laundry, river, fishing, hiking, water sports, $$$. Leave State 22 on Church St., go 2 blocks south to Willow St., 2 blocks east to Mountain Ave., and 1 block to park.

BIG MEADOWS HORSE CAMP (Willamette NF)
9 campsites - each w/4 stall corral, trailers to 36', disabled mount/dismount ramp, fishing, hiking, $$-$$$.
Take State 22 east 20 miles, FSR 2267 west 1 mile, and FSR 2257 north .5 mile.

MARION FORKS (Willamette NF)
15 units, trailers to 22', stream, swimming, fishing, hiking, nearby salmon hatchery, elev. 2500', $$.
Take State 22 southeast 12 miles, and FSR 502 south .1 mile.

RIVERSIDE (Willamette NF)
37 units, trailers to 22', on North Santiam River, fishing, hiking, elev. 2400', $$.
Take State 22 southeast 9.6 miles.

WHISPERING FALLS (Willamette NF)
16 units, trailers to 22', flush toilets, on North Santiam River, waterfalls across river, fishing, elev. 1900', $$.
Take State 22 east 4.1 miles.

LEBANON

WATERLOO CAMPGROUND (Linn County)
60 units - 50 w/hookups for water & elec. plus 10 w/out hookups, tents okay, showers, handicap accessible, covered picnic area, trailer waste disposal, South Santiam River, boat dock, fishing, swimming, hiking, $$$.
Follow US 20 southeast of town 4 miles - located in Waterloo.

ALBANY

BABE THE BLUE OX RV PARK (Private)
100 trailer sites w/hookups for water/elec./sewer, reservations - (503)926-2886, showers, laundry, groceries, $$$$.
Leave I-5 on exit #233 and head east to Price Rd. - campground is located at 4000 Blue Ox Dr.

CORVALLIS-ALBANY KOA (Private)
105 campsites - 60 w/hookups for water/elec./sewer, 14 pull-thrus w/elec., plus 14 tent sites, reservations - (503)967-8521, showers, groceries, tv, laundry, playground, mini golf, heated pool, pets okay, $$$-$$$$.
Take exit #228 off I-5, drive 5 miles west on State 34 to Oakville Rd., and head south to campground.

CORVALLIS

BENTON COUNTY FAIRGROUNDS (County)
Paved RV sites w/hookups for water & elec. plus tent area, flush toilets, showers, wheelchair accessible, horse corrals, hiking, pets okay, closed in winter, $-$$.
Leave I-5 on State 34 and take a right on 53rd St. - fairgrounds are 2 miles.

SWEET HOME

(Northeast of Sweet Home)

SUNNYSIDE PARK (Linn County)
162 units - 103 w/hookups for water/elec. plus 59 tent sites, information - (503)967-3917, picnic shelter, showers, on Foster Res., boat launch, hiking, fishing, swimming, pets okay, $$$.
Take US 20 east 5 miles to Quartzville Dr. and go north 1 mile.

WHITCOMB CREEK (Linn County)
39 units, on Green Peter Lake, boat launch, swimming, fishing, hiking, $$.
Take US 20 east 5 miles to Quartzville Dr. and head northeast 9 miles to campground.

YELLOWBOTTOM (BLM)
21 units, trailers okay, picnic area, swimming, fishing, nature study, open mid May thru Sept., elev. 1500', $.
Take US 20 east 5 miles to Quartzville Dr. and head northeast 26 miles - camp is beyond reservoir.

(East of Sweet Home)

CASCADIA (Oregon State Park)
26 primitive units, maximum site 35', wheelchair access, picnic area, fishing, hiking trails, $$.
Follow US 20 east 14 miles.

FERNVIEW (Willamette NF)
11 units, trailers to 18', river, swimming, fishing, elev. 1400', $$.
Follow US 20 east 23.5 miles.

HOUSE ROCK (Willamette NF)
17 tent units in virgin old growth douglas fir, picnic area, river, swimming, fishing, hiking, elev. 1600', $$.
Follow US 20 east 26.5 miles, and FSR 2044 southeast .1 mile.

LOST PRAIRIE (Willamette NF)
4 units, trailers to 22', wheelchair access, stream, hiking, historic site, elev. 3300', $$.
Follow US 20 east 39.2 miles.

TROUT CREEK (Willamette NF)
24 units, trailers to 22', wheelchair access, swimming, fishing, near wilderness trailhead, elev. 1300', $$.
Follow US 20 east 18.7 miles.

YUKWAH (Willamette NF)
20 units, trailers to 32', wheelchair access, river, swimming, fishing, nature trail, elev. 1300', $$.
Follow US 20 east 19.3 miles.

PHILOMATH

ALSEA FALLS (BLM)
16 campsites, trailers okay, handicap accessible restrooms, picnic area, swimming, fishing, hiking, nature study, open mid May thru Sept., elev. 800', $.
Take State 34 southwest 19 miles. Just west of Alsea take the S. Fork Alsea Rd. southeast to waterfalls and campground.

MARYS PEAK (Siuslaw NF)
6 tent units, picnic area, hiking, elev. 3500', $$.
Take State 34 southwest 9.1 miles and follow Marys Peak Rd. northwest 9.2 miles to campground.

McKENZIE BRIDGE

BELKNAP WOODS RESORT (Private)
38 units - 25 w/hookups for water/elec./sewer plus 13 w/water & elec., reservations - (503)822-3512, showers, laundry, trailer waste disposal, natural hot springs, river, fishing, hiking, $$$$.
East 5 miles on State 126, north .3 mile on Belknap Springs Rd.

McKENZIE BRIDGE (Willamette NF)
20 units, trailers to 22', reservations - (800)280-2267, on McKenzie River, boating, fishing, hiking, open May to Oct., elev. 1400', $$.
Take State 126 west 1 mile.

PARADISE (Willamette NF)
64 units, trailers to 22', reservations - (800)280-2267, flush toilets, picnic area, on McKenzie River, fishing, hiking, open May to Oct., elev. 1600', $$.
Take State 126 east 3.5 miles.

(Northeast of McKenzie Bridge)

COLDWATER COVE (Willamette NF)
35 units plus 2 group sites, trailers to 22', reservations - (800)280-2267, wheelchair access includes trails, on Clear Lake -

no motors, boat launch & rental, fishing, hiking, snack bar, groceries, open May to Oct., elev. 3100', $$.
State 126 northeast 14.2 miles, FSR 1372 southeast .1 mile.

FISH LAKE (Willamette NF)
10 units, trailers to 22', lake - no motors - is low in summer, swimming, fishing, near lava beds, elev. 3200', $.
State 126 northeast 22.4 miles, FSR 1374 west .1 mile.

ICE CAP CREEK (Willamette NF)
22 units, trailers to 18', flush toilets, near Carmen Res./Koosah & Sahalie Falls, open May to Oct., elev. 3000', $$.
State 126 northeast 19.2 miles, FSR 14071 northeast .1 mile.

OLALLIE (Willamette NF)
17 units, trailers to 22', at confluence of McKenzie River & Olallie Creek, boating, fishing, elev. 2000', $.
State 126 northeast 11.1 miles.

TRAIL BRIDGE (Willamette NF)
28 units, trailers to 32', on res. - speed limits, boat ramp, fishing, hiking, open April to Nov., elev. 2000', $$.
State 126 northeast 13.2 miles, and FSR 1477 southwest .2 mile.

BLUE RIVER

LAZY DAZE MOTOR HOME PARK (Private) [RV]
16 trailer sites w/full hookups, reservations - (503)822-3889, showers, laundry, propane, McKenzie River, fishing, $$$.
Follow State 126 east 1.5 miles.

McKENZIE RIVER RV PARK (Private)
8 units w/full hookups plus riverfront tent area, reservations (503)822-6065, trailers to 40', pull thrus, showers, laundry, on McKenzie River, fishing, nearby hiking, pets okay, $$-$$$.
Follow State 126 east 1.5 miles.

MONA (Willamette NF)
23 units, trailers to 22', flush toilets, wheelchair access, on Blue River Res., boat launch, swimming, fishing, water skiing, elev. 1400', $$.
Take State 126 east 2 miles, FSR 15 northeast 3.9 miles, and FSR 15120 south .3 mile.

PATIO RV PARK (Private) [RV]
60 RV sites w/full hookups, no tents, reservations - (503)822-3596, showers, laundry, trailer waste disposal, playfield, on McKenzie River, fishing, hiking, $$$$.
State 126 east 6 miles, McKenzie River Dr. east 2.5 miles.

(Southeast of Blue River)

DELTA (Willamette NF)
39 units, trailers to 22', wheelchair access, picnic area, on McKenzie River, fishing, old growth nature trail, elev. 1200', $$.
Take State 126 east 3.5 miles, FSR 19 south .3 mile, and FSR 194 west .7 mile.

FRENCH PETE (Willamette NF)
17 units, trailers to 18', river, boating, swimming, fishing, water skiing, hiking, elev. 2000', $$.
Take State 126 east 3.5 miles, and FSR 19 south 11 miles.

FRISSELL CROSSING (Willamette NF)
12 units, trailers to 18', river, fishing, hiking, elev. 2600', $$.
Take State 126 east 3.5 miles, and FSR 19 south 23 miles.

HORSE CREEK GROUP CAMP (Willamette NF)
20 group units - reservations required (800)270-2267, trailers to 22', fishing, open May thru Oct. , elev. 1400', $30 for up to 50 people/$50 for 51 to 100.
Take State 126 east .2 mile, and CR 161 southeast 5.1 miles.

SLIDE CREEK (Willamette NF)
16 units, trailers okay, picnic area, lake, boating, swimming, fishing, water skiing, elev. 1700', $$.
Take State 126 east 3.5 miles, FSR 19 south 11.6 miles, and FSR 195 north 1.5 miles.

SPRINGFIELD

CHALET VILLAGE ANNEX (Private)
24 units w/hookups for water/elec./sewer, no tents, reservation information - (503)747-8311, showers, $$$.
Leave I-5 on exit #194 and follow Main St. to 54th St. and park.

(North of Springfield)

COBERG HILLS RV RESORT (Private)
215 campsites w/full hookups, reservations - (503)686-3152, pull-thrus, showers, laundry, fishing, restaurant, $$$-$$$$$.
Take I-5 north to exit #199 - park is in Coburg, at 33100 Van Duyn Rd.

EUGENE KAMPING WORLD (Private)
144 units - 56 w/full hookups, 44 w/water & elec., 14 w/out hookups, plus 30 tent sites, reservations - (503)343-4832, showers, laundry, playground, mini-golf, trailer waste disposal, groceries, $$$-$$$$.
Take I-5 north to exit #199 - campground is .3 mile west.

EUGENE

EUGENE MOBILE VILLAGE (Private) `RV`
30 units w/hookups for water/elec./sewer, no tents, reservations - (503)747-2257, showers, laundry, playground, trailer waste disposal, groceries, $$$.
Leave I-5 on exit #189, go east over highway, and take the Frontage Rd. 1 mile north.

SHAMROCK VILLAGE MOBILE/RV PARK (Private) `RV`
115 units - 30 pull thrus w/full hookups, 77 sites w/hookups for water/elec./sewer, plus 8 w/water & elec., no tents, reservations - (503)747-7473, showers, laundry, trailer waste disposal, river, fishing, $$$.
Leave I-5 on exit #191, take Glenwood Blvd. north .7 mile, and Franklin Blvd. southeast 1 mile.

(West of Eugene)

FERN RIDGE SHORES (Private) `RV`
61 units w/hookups for water/elec./sewer, no tents, information (503)935-2310, showers, laundry, shade trees, picnic facilities, ice, boat ramp & moorage, fishing, swimming, pets okay, $$$$.
Take State 126 west 7.3 miles to Ellmaker Rd., and go north to Jeans Rd. - campground is at 29652 Jeans Rd.

RICHARDSON PARK (Lane County) `A` `RV`
50 units w/hookups for water & elec. - 2 are barrier free, tents okay, trailers to 60', showers, laundry, picnic facilities, volleyball court, trailer dump station, on Fern Ridge Res., boat ramp/docks & moorage, swimming, open year round, $$$.
Take State 126 west 8.5 miles, and Territorial Rd. north 4 miles.

CRESWELL

SHERWOOD FOREST KOA (Private) `A` `RV`
140 units - 125 w/hookups for water/elec./sewer, 5 w/water only, plus 10 tent sites, reservations - (503)895-4110, showers, laundry, swimming pool, therapy pool, playground, trailer waste disposal, groceries, $$$-$$$$.
Leave I-5 at exit #182 and go .1 mile.

TAYLOR'S TRAVEL PARK (Private) `RV`
39 units - 17 w/hookups for water/elec./sewer, 7 w/water & elec., plus 15 w/water only, reservation information - (503)895-4715, showers, trailer waste disposal, $$$.
Leave I-5 at exit #182, head west to Highway 99S, go south 1.3 miles to Davisson Rd., then south .4 mile to park.

LOWELL

(Northeast of Lowell)

BEDROCK (Willamette NF)
19 campsites, trailers to 22', handicap accessible, picnic area, creek, swimming, fishing, hiking, elev. 1100', $$.
Take Unity Rd. north 1.8 miles, Place Rd. east .4 mile, Big Fall Creek Rd. east 9.5 miles, and FSR 18 east 4.8 miles.

BIG POOL (Willamette NF)
5 campsites, trailers to 24', handicap accessible, creek, fishing, hiking, elev. 1000', $.
Take Unity Rd. north 1.8 miles, Place Rd. east .4 mile, Big Fall Creek Rd. east 9.5 miles, and FSR 18 east 1.7 miles.

BROKEN BOWL (Willamette NF)
10 units, trailers to 24', flush toilets, wheelchair accessible, creek, fishing, swimming, hiking, elev. 1000', $$.
Take Unity Rd. north 1.8 miles, Place Rd. east .4 mile, Big Fall Creek Rd. east 9.5 miles, and FSR 18 east .9 mile.

CASCARA (Corps)
50 campsites, trailers okay, fire pits, on Fall Creek Res., boat ramp & dock, open mid May to mid Sept., $$.
Take Unity Rd. north 1.8 miles, Place Rd. east .4 mile, Winberry Creek Rd. southeast 4 miles, and Peninsula Rd. north 7 miles.

DOLLY VARDEN (Willamette NF)
6 tent units, stream, fishing, swimming, hiking, elev. 1000', $.
Take Unity Rd. north 1.8 miles, Place Rd. east .4 mile, and Big Fall Creek Rd. east 7 miles.

FISHERMAN'S POINT (Corps)
8 campsites, trailers okay, fire pits, on Fall Creek Res., open mid May to mid Sept., $$.
Take Unity Rd. north 1.8 miles, Place Rd. east .4 mile, Winberry Creek Rd. southeast 4 miles, and Peninsula Rd. north 7.1 miles.

PUMA (Willamette NF)
11 units, trailers to 24', handicap accessible, creek, swimming, fishing, hiking, elev. 1100', $$.
Take Unity Rd. north 1.8 miles, Place Rd. east .4 mile, Big Fall Creek Rd. east 9.5 miles, and FSR 18 east 6.5 miles.

(Southwest of Lowell)

DEXTER SHORES MOBILE/RV PARK (Private)
56 units w/full hookups plus tent area, reservations (503)937-3711, showers, laundry, wheelchair access, playground, trailer waste disposal, pets okay, open year round, $$$-$$$$.
Head southwest to the town of Dexter - at 39140 Dexter Rd.

OAKRIDGE

OAKRIDGE RV PARK (Private)
20 pull thrus w/full hookups plus tent area, reservations (503)782-2611, trailers to 70', showers, laundry, wheelchair accessible, trailer waste dispoosal, fishing, hiking, pets okay, open year round, $$-$$$.
Located at east end of town, on Hwy. 58.

(Northwest of Oakridge)

BLACK CANYON (Willamette NF)
72 units, trailers to 22', picnic area, wheelchair access includes trails & fishing, river, at head of Lookout Point Res. - speed limit, boat launch, fishing, swimming, hiking, elev. 1000', $$.
Take State 58 northwest 8.5 miles.

HAMPTON (Willamette NF)
4 units, trailers to 32', on Lookout Point Res., boat launch, swimming, fishing, water skiing, elev. 1100', $$.
Take State 58 northwest 10 miles.

SHADY DELL (Willamette NF)
9 units, trailers to 18', on N. Fork Willamette River, fishing, elev. 1000', $$.
Take State 58 northwest 7 miles.

(Northeast of Oakridge)

BLAIR LAKE (Willamette NF)
9 units - some hike-in sites, lake - no motors, fishing, swimming, hiking, elev. 4800', $.
Salmon Creek Rd. east 3 miles, FSR 24 northeast 8 miles, FSR 1934 northeast 7.4 miles, and FSR 733 east 1.5 miles.

SALMON CREEK FALLS (Willamette NF)
15 units, trailers to 18', picnic area, fishing, swimming, kayakking, elev. 1500', $$.
Salmon Creek Rd. east 3 miles, and FSR 24 northeast 3.7 miles.

(Southeast of Oakridge)

BLUE POOL (Willamette NF)
25 units, trailers to 18', flush toilets, picnic area, river, fishing, swimming, near McCredie Hot Springs, elev. 1900', $$.
Take State 58 southeast 8.8 miles.

CAMPERS FLAT (Willamette NF)
5 units, trailers to 24', reservations (800)283-2267, picnic area, fishing, hiking, elev. 2000', $$.
Take State 58 southeast 2.2 miles, Hills Creek Res. Rd. south .5 mile, and FSR 21 south 20 miles.

GOLD LAKE (Willamette NF)
25 units, trailers to 18', picnic area, lake - no motors, boat ramp, flyfishing, swimming, hiking, elev. 4800', $$.
Take State 58 southeast 25.6 miles, and FSR 500 northeast 2.2 miles.

PACKARD CREEK (Willamette NF)
33 units, trailers to 32', wheelchair access includes trails, picnic area, on Hills Creek Res., boat launch, swimming, water skiing, fishing, hiking, elev. 1600', $$.
Take State 58 southeast 2.2 miles, Hills Creek Res. Rd. south .5 mile, and FSR 21 south 5.2 miles.

SAND PRAIRIE (Willamette NF)
21 units, trailers to 32', flush toilets, wheelchair access includes trails, near head of Hills Creek Res., swimming, fishing, elev. 1600', $$.
Take State 58 southeast 2.2 miles, Hills Creek Res. Rd. south .5 mile, and FSR 21 south 11.6 miles.

TIMPANOGAS LAKE (Willamette NF)
10 units, trailers to 22', lake - no motors, swimming, fishing, trails, elev. 5200', $.
Take State 58 southeast 2.2 miles, Hills Creek Res. Rd. south .5 mile, FSR 21 southeast 38.4 miles, and FSR 2154 south 3 miles.

COTTAGE GROVE

VILLAGE GREEN RV PARK (Private)
42 trailer sites w/hookups for water/elec./sewer, information (503)942-2491 - reservation (800)343-ROOM, trailers to 63', pull thrus, wheelchair accessible, laundry, swimming pool, spa, game room, playground, trailer waste disposal, pets okay, $$$$.
Leave I-5 at exit #174 and follow Row River Rd. east .1 mile to 725 Row River Rd.

(East of Cottage Grove)

BAKER BAY (Lane County)
48 units plus 2 group sites, reservation information - (503)341-6940, trailers to 40', showers, picnic area, trailer waste disposal, on Dorena Res., boat dock & launch, fishing, $$-$$$$$.
Leave I-5 at exit #174, take Row River Rd. east 4 miles and Government Rd. southeast 3 miles.

SCHWARZ PARK/DORENA LAKE (Corps)
70 units plus 6 group sites, group information (503)942-1418, flush toilets, showers, wheelchair access, trailer waste disposal, lake, boat ramp, fishing, open April thru Sept., $$.
Leave I-5 at exit #174, take Row River Rd. east 4 miles and Government Rd. southeast 1 mile.

COTTAGE GROVE LAKE PRIMITIVE (Corps)
18 campsites, on lake, fishing, $$.
Leave I-5 at exit #170, take London Rd. south 3.5 miles, and
Reservoir Rd. east 1 mile.

PASS CREEK (Douglas County)
30 campsites w/hookups for water/elec./sewer, showers,
wheelchair access, picnic pavilion, playground, stream, $$-$$$.
Leave I-5 at exit #163 - campground is 10 miles south of Cottage
Grove, in the town of Curtin.

PINE MEADOWS (Corps)
92 campsites, flush toilets, showers, playground, trailer waste
disposal, on Cottage Grove Lake, swimming, fishing, open May
thru Sept., $$.
Leave I-5 at exit #170, take London Rd. south 3.5 miles, and
Reservoir Rd. east .5 mile.

CULP CREEK

RUJADA (Umpqua NF)
8 units plus 2 group sites, trailers to 22', flush toilets, picnic
area, play field, stream,fishing, swimming, hiking, elev. 1200', $.
Take Row River Rd. east 4 miles, and FSR 17 northeast 2 miles.

SHARPS CREEK (BLM)
10 units, trailers to 30', handicap accessible, play area, creek,
swimming, fishing, elev. 1200', open May to Nov., $.
Follow Row River Rd. east .5 mile and take Sharps Creek Rd.
south 4 miles to campground.

DRAIN

ELKTON RV PARK (Private)
46 units - 36 w/hookups for water/elec./sewer plus 10 tent
sites, reservation information - (503)584-2832, groceries, river,
fishing, $$-$$$$.
Take State 38 west of Drain 14 miles to Elkton, go 2 blocks west
of bridge and turn onto 2nd St. - park is 1 block.

IDLEYLD PARK

TIMBER RIVER RV PARK (Private)
16 units w/hookups for water/elec./sewer, tents okay,
information (503)496-0114, trailers to 70', showers, laundry,
nearby store, on Umpqua River, fishing, hiking, $$-$$$.
Located in town, at 22113 N. Umpqua Hwy.

MILLPOND (BLM)
12 units, trailers okay, picnic area w/shelter, playground, swimming, fishing, nature study. elev. 1100', $$.
Take State 138 east .5 mile, and Rock Creek Rd. north 5 miles.

ROCK CREEK (BLM)
18 units, trailers okay, picnic area, swimming, fishing, nature study, elev. 1200', $.
Take State 138 east .5 mile, and Rock Creek Rd. north 8 miles.

(East of Idleyld Park)

BOGUS CREEK (Umpqua NF)
15 campsites, trailers to 35', flush toilets, fire pits, whitewater boating, flyfishing, hiking, elev. 1100', $-$$.
Take State 138 east 14 miles.

CANTON CREEK (Umpqua NF)
5 units, trailers to 24', flush toilets, picnic shelter, on Steamboat Creek - no fishing, swimming, hiking, elev. 1200', $.
Follow State 138 east 18 miles to Steamboat, and take FSR 38 northeast .4 mile.

EAGLE ROCK (Umpqua NF)
25 units, trailers to 24', fire pits, access to North Umpqua River, white water boating, hiking, flyfishing, adjacent to Boulder Creek Wilderness, elev. 1676', $-$$.
Take State 138 east 30 miles.

HORSESHOE BEND (Umpqua NF)
24 units plus group area, group reservations - (503)496-3532, trailers to 24', flush toilets, wheelchair access, picnic facilities, on North Umpqua River, boat launch, flyfishing, hiking, elev. 1300', group site $40/night - individuals $$.
Follow State 138 east 25.6 miles, FSR 4750 south .1 mile, and FSR 4750-001 southwest .3 mile.

SUSAN CREEK (BLM)
33 units, trailers okay, showers, handicap accessible, swimming, hiking, $$.
Take State 138 east 2 miles.

SUTHERLIN

HI-WAY HAVEN RV PARK (Private)
99 units - 88 w/full hookups plus 11 w/water & elec., no tents, reservations - (503)459-4557, showers, laundry, wheelchair access, rec room, groceries, trailer waste disposal, fishing, $$$$.
Located at 609 Fort McKay Rd.

TREES OF OREGON RV PARK (Private)
34 units - 25 w/full hookups, 9 w/water/elec./cable tv, plus tent area, reservations (503)849-2181, trailers to 80', showers, laundry, wheelchair access, game room, trailer waste disposal, nearby fishing, hiking, pets okay, open year round, $$-$$$$.
Take State 99 north 2 miles.

TYEE (BLM)
15 units, on Umpqua River, swimming, fishing, elev. 200', $.
Follow State 138 northwest 12 miles, cross Bullock Bridge and turn right - campground is .5 mile.

GLIDE

CAVITT CREEK (BLM)
8 units, trailers okay, picnic area, swimming, fishing, nature study, elev. 1100', $.
Follow Little River Rd. south 6 miles and Cavitt Creek Rd. south 2 miles to campground.

LAKE IN THE WOODS (Umpqua NF)
11 units plus shelter, trailers to 35', flush toilets, fire pits, picnic area, lake - no motors, fishing, hiking trails to Hemlock & Yakso Waterfalls plus Hemlock Lake, elev. 3200', $.
Take Little River Rd. southeast 20 miles, and FSR 27 north 7 miles.

WOLF CREEK (Umpqua NF)
8 units plus 3 group sites, group reservations - (503)496-3532, trailers to 35', flush toilets, picnic facilities, swimming, fishing, hiking, elev. 1100', group site $45/night - individuals $.
Take Little River Rd. southeast 12.4 miles - campground is 1 mile past Job Corp Center.

ROSEBURG

ALAMEDA AVE. TRAILER COURT (Private)
35 units w/hookups for water/elec./sewer, no tents, reservations (503)672-2348, trailers to 40', showers, laundry, wheelchair accessible, store, trailer waste disposal, pets okay, open year round, $$$$.
Leave I-5 on exit #125, go east to N.E. Stevens and turn left, follow to Alameda Ave. - located at 581 N.E. Alameda Ave.

AMACHER PARK (Douglas County)
30 units - 20 w/hookups for water/elec./sewer plus 10 tent sites, showers, wheelchair access, playground, river, fishing, boat launch, $$-$$$.
Take I-5 north to exit #129, and follow old Highway 99 south .3 mile to the park.

NEBO TRAILER PARK (Private)
25 units w/hookups for water/elec./sewer, no tents, reservation information - (503)673-4108, showers, laundry, ice, trailer waste disposal, $$$.
Leave I-5 on exit #125 and take Garden Valley Rd. east .8 mile, and State 99 north .7 mile.

TWIN RIVERS VACATION PARK (Private)
93 units - 85 w/hookups for water/elec./sewer plus 8 tent sites, reservation information - (503)673-3811, showers, laundry, playground, groceries, swimming, fishing, $$$-$$$$.
Leave I-5 at exit #125 and, take Garden Valley Rd. west 5 miles, and Old Garden Valley Rd. west an additional 1.5 miles.

(Northeast of Roseburg)

WHISTLER'S BEND (Douglas County)
23 rustic sites plus group area, flush toilets, showers, playground, river, fishing, boat launch, $$.
Take State 138 northeast 12 miles, and Whistler's Bend Rd. west 2 miles.

(South of Roseburg)

UMPQUA SAFARI RV PARK (Private)
13 units - 10 w/full hookups, 3 w/water/elec./cable tv, plus tent area, reservations (503)679-6328, trailers to 40', showers, wheelchair accessible, trailer waste disposal, pets okay, open year round, $$-$$$$.
Leave I-5 south at exit #119 and take State 99 west 2.5 miles to the town of Winston - located at 511 NE Main.

MYRTLE CREEK

MILLSITE PARK & RV PARK (Private)
11 units - 8 w/hookups for water & elec., 3 w/elec., plus tent area, information - (503)863-3171, showers, wheelchair access, playground, trailer waste disposal, river, fishing, hiking, $-$$.
Located at 441 4th St.

DIAMOND LAKE

BROKEN ARROW (Umpqua NF)
148 units, trailers to 35', reservations - (800)283-2267, flush toilets, wheelchair access, picnic facilities, trailer waste disposal, on Diamond Lake - speed limits, boat ramp, fishing, hiking, $$.
Take State 138 north .2 mile, and FSR 4795 west and south 3.8 miles to campground.

DIAMOND LAKE (Umpqua NF)
238 units, trailers to 35', reservations - (800)280-2267, flush toilets, picnic facilities, trailer waste disposal, on Diamond Lake - speed limits, boat launch, swimming, fishing, hiking, bicycling, interpretive services, elev. 5200', $$-$$$.
Take State 138 north .2 mile, and FSR 4795, west 2.5 miles.

DIAMOND LAKE RV PARK (Private)
140 units w/hookups for water/elec./sewer, reservation information (503)793-3318, showers, laundry, wheelchair access, trailer waste disposal, groceries, on Diamond Lake - speed limits, boat launch, swimming, fishing, hiking, elev. 5300', $$$$.
Go south to Diamond Lake South Shore Rd., then north 1 mile.

THIELSEN VIEW (Umpqua NF)
60 units, trailers to 30', handicap access, picnic facilities, on Diamond Lake - speed limits, boat launch, swimming, fishing, hiking, elev. 5200', $$.
Take State 138 north .2 mile, and FSR 4795, west and south 3.1 miles to campground.

(North of Diamond Lake)

LEMOLO LAKE RESORT (Private)
34 units - 29 w/hookups for water/elec./sewer, 3 w/water & elec., plus 2 tent sites, reservations (503)793-3300, trailers to 45', showers, laundry, wheelchair access, groceries, restaurant, lounge, gas, mini golf, on lake, boat rentals & moorage, pets okay, open April thru Sept., $$-$$$$.
Go north 6 miles on State 138 and 5 miles on Lemolo Lake Rd.

POOLE CREEK (Umpqua NF)
59 units, trailers to 35', reservations - (800)283-2267, on Lemolo Lake, boat launch, swimming, fishing, water skiing, elev. 4200', $$.
Go north 6 miles on State 138 and 4.2 miles on Lemolo Lake Rd.

CRATER LAKE

LOST CREEK (Crater Lake Nat'l Park)
16 tent sites, information - (503)594-2211, open July thru August, elev. 6000', $$.
Located in southern portion of Crater Lake National Park - follow signs to Pinnacles Rd. and campground.

MAZAMA (Crater Lake Nat'l Park)
200 campsites, trailers okay, information - (503)594-2511, showers, wheelchair access, trailer waste disposal, groceries, lake, fishing, hiking, open June thru Sept., elev. 6000', $$$.
Located in southern portion of Crater Lake National Park, .5 mile east of the Annie Spring entrance.

CANYONVILLE

CHARLES V. STANTON PARK (Douglas County)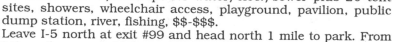
40 units - 20 w/hookups for water/elec./sewer plus 20 tent sites, showers, wheelchair access, playground, pavilion, public dump station, river, fishing, $$-$$$.
Leave I-5 north at exit #99 and head north 1 mile to park. From I-5 south you must take exit #101 and head east to park.

COW CREEK GAMING CENTER RV PARK (Tribal)
38 RV sites w/hookups for water/elec./sewer, no tents, pull thrus, information (503)839-1111, trailers to 70', restrooms are in casino, restaurant, pets okay, open year round, $$$-$$$$.
Leave I-5 at exit #99 and follow signs.

SURPRISE VALLEY MOBIL VILLAGE (Private)
25 units - 23 w/hookups for water/elec./sewer plus 2 tent sites, reservations - (503)839-8181, showers, laundry, $$-$$$.
Leave I-5 at exit #102 and follow Gazley Rd. 1 mile east.

AZALEA

MEADOW WOOD RESORT (Private)
63 trailer sites w/hookups for water & elec. - some w/sewer, reservation information - (503)832-2959, showers, laundry, trailer waste disposal, heated swimming pool, playground, $$$.
Take I-5 south to exit #86 and follow Frontage Rd. south 4 miles to 862 Autumn Ln.

PROSPECT

JOSEPH P. STEWART (Oregon State Park)
201 units - 151 w/hookups for elec., plus 50 tent sites, group area, maximum site 80', wheelchair access, trailer waste disposal, boat launch, fishing, swimming, hiking/bike trails, access to Upper Rogue River & Pacific Crest Trails,$$-$$$.
Take State 62 southwest 10 miles.

MT. HOME MOBILE VILLAGE (Private)
7 units w/full hookups, tents okay, reservation information - (503)560-3504, trailers to 36', showers, laundry, play area, nearby fishing, pets okay, open year round, $$.
Take 1st St. to Mill Creek Dr. - located at 51 Mill Creek Dr.

(North of Prospect)

ABBOTT CREEK (Rogue River NF)
23 units, trailers to 22', fishing, elev. 3100', $.
Take State 62 north 6.8 miles, and FSR 68 northwest 3.4 miles.

FAREWELL BEND (Rogue River NF)

61 units, trailers to 22', flush toilets, on Rogue River, fishing, elev. 3400', $$.
Take State 62 north 11.6 miles.

HAMAKER (Rogue River NF)
10 tent sites, river, fishing, hiking, elev. 4000', $$.
Follow State 62 north 12 miles, State 230 north 11 miles, FSR 6530 southeast .6 mile, and FSR 900 south .6 mile.

UNION CREEK (Rogue River NF)
78 units, trailers to 18', fishing, hiking, elev. 3200', $$.
Take State 62 north 10.8 miles, and FSR 3136 west .2 mile.

BUTTE FALLS

FOURBIT FORD (Rogue River NF)
7 tent units, stream, fishing, elev. 3200', $.
Take the Butte Falls-Fish Lake Rd. southeast 6 miles, FSR 30 east 2 miles, and FSR 37 northeast .8 mile.

PARKER MEADOWS (Rogue River NF)

8 tent units, picnic area, fishing, elev. 5000', $.
Take the Butte Falls-Fish Lake Rd. southeast 6 miles, FSR 30 east 2 miles, and FSR 37 northeast 11 miles.

SOUTH FORK (Rogue River NF)

6 units, trailers to 18', stream, fishing, remote, elev. 4000', $.
Take the Butte Falls-Prospect Rd. northeast 11.1 miles, and Lodgepole Rd. northeast 7.7 miles.

WHISKEY SPRINGS (Rogue River NF)
35 units, trailers to 18', picnic area, hiking, elev. 3200', $.
Take the Butte Falls-Fish Lake Rd. southeast 6 miles, FSR 30 east 2 miles, and FSR 37 east .3 mile.

WILLOW LAKE RESORT (Private)

73 units - 25 w/hookups for water/elec./sewer, 20 w/water & elec., plus 28 tent sites, reservations - (503)865-3229, showers, trailer waste disposal, groceries, restaurant/lounge, swimming, fishing, boat launch & rental, hiking, elev. 3000', $$$.
Take the Butte Falls-Fish Lake Rd. southeast 6 miles, and follow Willow Lake Rd. 2 miles southwest to resort.

GRANTS PASS

RIVERPARK RV RESORT (Private)

47 units w/full hookups plus tent sites, reservations - (800)677-8857, trailers to 70', showers, laundry, trailer waste disposal, on Rogue River, fishing, hiking, pets okay, open year round, $$$$.

Leave I-5 on exit #55, turn left on Parkdale, left on State 99, and go south 2 miles to 2956 Rogue River Hwy.

ROGUE VALLEY OVERNIGHTERS (Private) RV
110 trailer sites w/full hookups, reservations - (503)479-2208, showers, laundry, trailer waste disposal, $$$-$$$$.
Leave I-5 at exit #58 and go south 1 block to NW 6th St. - located at 1806 NW 6th St.

(North of Grants Pass)

GRANTS PASS OVER-NITERS (Private) RV
40 units - 29 w/hookups for water/elec./sewer plus 11 w/water & elec., reservation information - (503)479-7289, showers, laundry, swimming pool, propane, $$$-$$$$.
Leave I-5 at exit #61, turn east, take Frontage Rd. north .5 mile.

INDIAN MARY PARK (Josephine County) A RV
91 units - 42 w/hookups for water/elec./sewer plus 49 tent sites, trailers to 35', showers, playfield, playground, river, boat launch, swimming, fishing, hiking, $$$-$$$$.
Leave I-5 at exit #61, and take the Merlin-Galice Rd. 7.6 miles west.

SUNNY VALLEY KOA (Private) A RV
88 units - 11 w/hookups for water/elec./sewer, 61 w/water & elec., plus 16 tent sites, reservations - (503)479-0209, showers, laundry, swimming pool, playground, game room, groceries, trailer waste disposal, petting zoo, $$$-$$$$.
Take I-5 north to the Sunny Valley exit #71 and campground.

(West of Grants Pass)

BEND O' THE RIVER CAMPGROUND (Private) A RV
25 units - 10 w/hookups for water/elec./sewer, 10 w/water & elec., plus 5 tent sites, reservation information - (503)479-2547, showers, laundry, playground, river, swimming, fishing, $$-$$$.
Follow G St. 7.5 miles west - becomes Upper & Lower River Rds.

BIG PINE (Siskiyou NF) A RV
13 units, trailers to 22', wheelchair access - includes trails, picnic area, fishing, world's tallest Ponderosa pine, sightless interpretive trail, elev. 2400', $-$$$.
Leave I-5 north of town on exit #61, take the Merlin-Galice Rd. northwest 12.4 miles, and FSR 25 southwest 12.8 miles.

GRIFFIN PARK (Josephine County) A RV
18 units - 14 w/hookups for water/elec./sewer plus 4 tent sites, reservations - (503)474-5285, showers, playfield, playground, trailer waste disposal, river, boat launch, swimming, fishing, hiking, $$$-$$$$.
Take US 199 west 4 miles, Riverbanks Rd. 2.5 miles to park.

SAM BROWN (Siskiyou NF)

33 units, trailers okay, wheelchair access, picnic shelters, amphitheater, creek, fishing, swimming, hiking trails, $-$$.
Leave I-5 north of town on exit #61, take the Merlin-Galice Rd. northwest 12.4 miles, FSR 25 southwest 13.4 miles, and FSR 2512 west .6 mile.

SAM BROWN HORSE CAMP (Siskiyou NF)

7 campsites - each w/corral, trailers to 22', wheelchair access, fire rings, picnic tables, exercise corral, trails, $-$$$.
Leave I-5 north of town on exit #61, take the Merlin-Galice Rd. northwest 12.4 miles, FSR 25 southwest 13.4 miles, and FSR 2512 west .6 mile.

SCHROEDER (Josephine County)

30 campsites w/hookups for water/elec./sewer, tents okay, trailers to 35', showers, tennis, playfield, playground, river, boat launch, fishing, $$$-$$$$.
Follow G St. 4 miles west - becomes Upper River Rd.

SPAULDING POND (Siskiyou NF)

3 campsites, wheelchair accessible, picnic tables, 3 acre stocked lake, 2 fishing docks, historic mill site, $-$$$.
Take US 199 southwest 15 miles, FSR 25 northwest 6 miles, and FSR 2524 west 3.5 miles.

TIN CAN (Siskiyou NF)

5 campsites, wheelchair access, creek, fishing, hiking, $-$$$.
Leave I-5 north of town on exit #61, take the Merlin-Galice Rd. northwest 12.4 miles, and FSR 25 southwest 5.1 miles.

WHITE HORSE (Josephine County)

39 units - 8 w/hookups for water/elec./sewer, 2 w/elec., plus 29 tent sites, trailers to 35', information - (503)474-5285, showers, playground, river, boat launch, fishing, hiking, $$-$$$.
Follow G St. 6 miles west - becomes Upper River Rd.

ROGUE RIVER

CIRCLE W RV PARK (Private)

25 units - 15 w/full hookups plus 10 w/water/elec./cable tv, reservations - (503)582-1686, showers, laundry, playground, store, ice, propane, trailer waste disposal, river, swimming, fishing, paddle boat rentals, $$$$.
Leave I-5 at exit #48 and take State 99 west 1 mile.

CYPRESS GROVE RV PARK (Private)

45 units w/full hookups, no tents, reservations (800)758-0719, trailers to 70', pull thrus, showers, laundry, wheelchair access, propane, pets okay, open year round, $$$$.
Leave I-5 south of town on exit #45 and follow signs.

HAVE-A-NICE DAY CAMPGROUND (Private)

40 units - 18 w/full hookups, 15 w/water & elec., plus 7 tent sites, reservations (503)582-1421, showers, laundry, playground, trailer waste disposal, river, fishing, boat launch, $$$$.
Leave I-5 at exit #48 and take State 99 west 1.5 miles.

RIVERFRONT RV TRAILER PARK (Private)

27 units - 19 w/full hookups, 2 w/water/elec./cable tv, plus 6 tent sites, reservation information - (503)582-0985, showers, laundry, ice, trailer waste disposal, river, boat launch, swimming, fishing, $$$-$$$$.
Leave I-5 at exit #48 and take State 99 west 2 miles.

VALLEY OF THE ROGUE (Oregon State Park)

173 units - 97 w/hookups for water/elec./sewer, 55 w/elec. only, 21 tent sites, plus group area, maximum site 75', showers, wheelchair access, picnic facilities, trailer waste disposal, boat launch, fishing, hiking, open year round, $$-$$$.
Leave I-5 south of town on exit #45.

GOLD HILL

GOLD'N ROGUE KOA (Private)

90 units - 20 w/full hookups, 54 w/water & elec., plus 16 tent sites, reservations - (503)855-7710, showers, laundry, pool, playground, trailer waste disposal, groceries, propane, $$$-$$$$.
Leave I-5 at exit #40, north .3 mile, Blackwell Rd. east .2 mile.

LAZY ACRES MOTEL & RV PARK (Private)

75 units - 60 w/hookups for water/elec./sewer plus 15 w/out hookups, tents okay, reservations - (503)855-7000, showers, laundry, playfield, playground, river, swimming, fishing, $$$.
Leave I-5 at exit #40, north .3 mile, State 99 west 1.5 miles.

WHITE CITY

(Northeast of White City)

BEAR MOUNTAIN RV PARK (Private)

37 units - 30 w/hookups for water/elec./sewer plus 7 w/water & elec., tents okay, reservations - (503)878-2400, showers, laundry, wheelchair access, playfield, playground, river, fishing, hiking, pets okay, open year round, $$$-$$$$.
Take State 62 northeast 19 miles.

FLYCASTERS RV PARK (Private)

30 units w/hookups for water/elec./sewer, reservations - (503)878-2749, showers, laundry, restaurant, lounge, river, swimming, fishing, $$$$.
Take State 62 northeast 13 miles.

ROGUE ELK CAMPGROUND (Jackson County)
37 campsites, trailers okay, reservation information - (503)776-7001, showers, playground, trailer waste disposal, river, boat ramp, fishing, swimming, hiking, pets okay, $$$.
Take State 62 northeast 18 miles.

SHADY TRAILS RV PARK (Private)
50 units - 20 w/full hookups, 30 w/water/elec./cable tv, plus tent area, reservations - (503)878-2206, showers, playground, trailer waste disposal, river, boat launch, fishing, $$$-$$$$.
Take State 62 northeast 16 miles.

(East of White City)

DOE POINT (Rogue River NF)
25 units, trailers to 22', flush toilets, on Fish Lake - speed limits, swimming, fishing, hiking, bicycling, elev. 4600', $$.
Take State 140 east 28.2 miles.

FISH LAKE (Rogue River NF)
17 units, trailers to 22', flush toilets, on Fish Lake - speed limits, boat launch, swimming, fishing, hiking, elev. 4600', $$.
Take State 140 east 29.7 miles.

FISH LAKE RESORT (Private)
60 units - 45 w/hookups for water/elec./sewer, 5 w/elec., 5 w/out hookups, plus 5 pack-in tent sites, reservations - (503)949-8500, showers, laundry, game room, groceries, fishing supplies, cafe, trailer waste disposal, lake, boat launch & rental, swimming, fishing, hiking, open May to Nov., elev. 4600', $$-$$$.
Take State 140 east 30 miles.

MEDFORD OAKS CAMPARK (Private)
54 units - 19 w/hookups for water/elec./sewer, 33 w/water & elec., plus tent area, reservations - (503)826-5103, showers, laundry, pool, playground, rec room, picnic pavilion, dance floor, groceries, trailer waste disposal, pond, fishing, $$$-$$$$.
Take State 140 east 6.8 miles.

WILLOW PRAIRIE HORSE CAMP (Rogue River NF)
9 tent units - horse campers only, elev. 4400', $$.
Take State 140 east 28 miles, FSR 37 north 1.6 miles, and FSR 3738 west 1.5 miles.

MEDFORD

EXPO LAKE RV PARK (Private)
55 units w/hookups for water/elec./sewer, tents okay, reservations (503)664-6365, showers, laundry, wheelchair access, fishing, hiking, pets okay, open year round, $$-$$$$.
Take I-5 north to exit #32 - located at County Fairgrounds.

HOLIDAY RV PARK (Private)
110 units w/hookups for water/elec./sewer, no tents, reservation information - (503)535-2183, showers, wheelchair access, laundry, groceries, swimming pool, stream, $$$$.
Take I-5 south to exit #24 - located on west side.

PEAR TREE CENTER (Private) [RV]
31 units w/full hookups, no tents, reservation information - (503)535-4445, showers, laundry, wheelchair access, pool, spa, playground, mini mart, restaurant, gas & propane, $$$$$.
Take I-5 south to exit #24 - located on east side.

JACKSONVILLE

(Southwest of Jacksonville)

BEAVER SULPHER (Rogue River NF)
10 tent sites, picnic area, stream, elev. 2100', $.
Take State 238 southwest 8 miles, Applegate Rd. south 9 miles, and FSR 20 east 3 miles.

CANTRALL-BUCKLEY PARK (Jackson County) [A] [RV]
42 units - 30 RV sites w/out hookups, 12 tent sites, plus group area, group reservations (503)776-7001, trailers to 25', showers, playground, stream, swimming, fishing, hiking, pets okay, $$.
Take State 238 southwest 13 miles.

CARBERRY (Rogue River NF) [A]
10 walk-in tent sites, wheelchair accessible, on Applegate Lake - 10 mph, fishing, hiking, elev. 2000', $.
Take State 238 southwest 8 miles, and Applegate Rd. south 10 miles.

FLUMET FLAT (Rogue River NF) [A] [RV]
27 units, trailers to 22', flush toilets, showers, laundry, wheelchair access, groceries, gasoline, ice, snack bar, river, swimming, fishing, interpretive trail, elev. 1700', $$.
Take State 238 southwest 8 miles, Applegate Rd. south 9.9 miles, and FSR 1090 1.2 miles to camp.

FRENCH GULCH CAMP (Rogue River NF) [A] [RV]
9 units, trailers to 18', wheelchair access, lake, hiking, elev. 2000', $.
Take State 238 southwest 8 miles, Applegate Rd. southwest 14 miles, FSR 1075 east 1.5 miles.

HART-TISH PARK (Rogue River NF)
4 units, trailers okay, wheelchair accessible, lake - 10 mph, boat launch, swimming, fishing, hiking, elev. 2000, $$.
Take State 238 southwest 8 miles, and Applegate Rd. southwest 15 miles.

SQUAW LAKES (Rogue River NF)
16 tent units, remote, lake - no motors, swimming, fishing, hiking, elev. 3000', $.
Take State 238 southwest 8 miles, Applegate Rd. southwest 14 miles, and FSR 1075 southeast 8 miles.

STRINGTOWN (Rogue River NF)
7 walk-in tent sites, on Applegate Lake - 10 mph, fishing, hiking, elev. 2000, $.
Take State 238 southwest 8 miles, Applegate Rd. southwest 14 miles, and FSR 1075 southeast 3 miles.

WATKINS (Rogue River NF)
14 walk-in tent sites, on Applegate Lake - 10 mph, fishing, hiking, elev. 2000', $.
Take State 238 southwest 8 miles, and Applegate Rd. southwest 17 miles.

ASHLAND

JACKSON HOT SPRING (Private)
127 units - 14 w/hookups for water/elec./sewer, 13 w/water & elec., plus 100 tent sites, information - (503)482-3776, showers, laundry, ice, mineral pool & baths, pets okay, $$$-$$$$.
I-5 north to exit #19, South Valley View Rd. .5 mile southwest.

(East of Ashland)

CAMPERS COVE (Private)
25 trailer units w/hookups for water/elec./sewer, reservations - (503)482-1201, showers, ice, lake, fishing, boat launch, hiking, pets okay, elev. 5000', $$$.
Take State 66 east 18 miles, Hyatt Lake Rd. northeast 3 miles, and Hyatt Prairie Rd. north 1.5 miles.

EMIGRANT CAMPGROUND (Jackson County)
42 sites, reservation information - (503)776-7001, showers, trailer waste disposal, lake, fishing, boat launch, swimming, playground, hiking, pets okay, $$$.
Take State 66 east 5 miles.

GLENYAN KOA (Private)
68 campsites - 11 w/hookups for water/elec./sewer, 35 w/water & elec., plus 22 tent units, reservations - (503)482-4138, showers, laundry, groceries, trailer waste disposal, swimming pool, pond, fishing, playground, pets okay, $$$$-$$$$$.
Take State 66 east 3.5 miles.

GRIZZLY CAMPGROUND (Jackson County)
Group camp - 20 vehicles max., trailers to 25', lake, fishing, boat launch, hiking, pets okay, elev. 4500', $65.

Take State 66 south 1 mile, Dead Indian Rd. east 20 miles, and Hyatt Prairie Rd. south 2 miles.

HOWARD PRAIRIE LAKE RESORT (Private)
300 campsites - 60 w/hookups for water/elec./sewer, 90 w/water & elec., plus 150 tent units, information - (503)482-1979, showers, laundry, wheelchair access, groceries, trailer waste disposal, lake, swimming, fishing, boat launch & rental, hiking, pets okay, elev. 4500', $$-$$$$.
Take State 66 south 1 mile, Dead Indian Rd. east 20 miles, and Hyatt Prairie Rd. south 3.5 miles.

HYATT LAKE (BLM)
48 units plus 2 group tent areas, group reservations - (503)770-2200, trailers okay, picnic area w/shelter, showers, basketball, volleyball, horse area, boat launch, fishing, swimming, hiking, nature study, open mid-May thru Oct., elev. 5000', $$.
Take State 66 east 16 miles, E. Hyatt Lake Rd. north 4 miles.

HYATT LAKE RESORT (Private)
36 units - 25 w/full hookups plus 11 tent sites, reservations - (503)482-3331, showers, ice, trailer waste disposal, lake, fishing, boat launch & rental, restaurant, gas, hiking, pets okay, $$-$$$.
Take State 66 east 18 miles, Hyatt Lake Rd. northeast 3 miles, and Hyatt Prairie Rd. north 1 mile.

KLUM LANDING (Jackson County)
30 units, lake, boat ramp, fishing, swimming, water skiing, hiking, pets okay, open mid April thru Oct., $$-$$$.
Take State 66 south 1 mile, Dead Indian Rd. east 20 miles, Hyatt Prairie Rd. south to Dam Rd., turn left - campground is 3 miles.

LILY GLEN (Jackson County)
15 units plus large group area, reservation information (503)776-7001, horse barn & corral, lake, fishing, hiking, pets okay, group site $100/night - individuals $$.
Take State 66 south 1 mile, and Dead Indian Rd. east 21 miles.

SUGAR PINE (Jackson County)
1 group campsite, reservations - (503)776-7001, lake, swimming, fishing, boat launch, hiking, pets okay, elev. 4500', $75 1st night/$60 additional nights.
Take State 66 south 1 mile, Dead Indian Rd. east 20 miles, and Hyatt Prairie Rd. south 2 miles.

WILLOW POINT (Jackson County)
40 units, information - (503)776-7001, lake, swimming, fishing, boat launch, hiking, pets okay, elev. 5000', $$.
Take State 66 south 1 mile, Dead Indian Rd. east 20 miles, and Hyatt Prairie Rd. south 5 miles.

CENTRAL OREGON CAMPGROUNDS

See Page

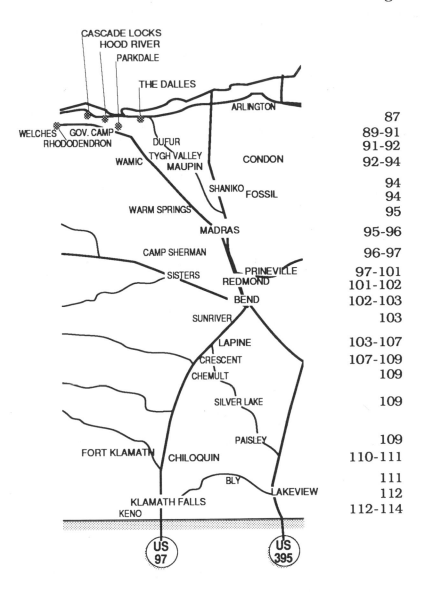

CASCADE LOCKS	
HOOD RIVER	
PARKDALE	
THE DALLES	
ARLINGTON	87
WELCHES GOV. CAMP	89-91
RHODODENDRON DUFUR	91-92
WAMIC TYGH VALLEY MAUPIN CONDON	92-94
SHANIKO FOSSIL	94
	94
WARM SPRINGS	95
MADRAS	95-96
CAMP SHERMAN	96-97
SISTERS PRINEVILLE	97-101
REDMOND	101-102
BEND	102-103
SUNRIVER	103
LAPINE	103-107
CRESCENT	107-109
CHEMULT	109
SILVER LAKE	109
PAISLEY	109
FORT KLAMATH CHILOQUIN	110-111
BLY	111
LAKEVIEW	112
KLAMATH FALLS	112-114
KENO	

US 97

US 395

CASCADE LOCKS

BRIDGE OF THE GODS RV PARK (Private)
15 sites w/full hookups, no tents, reservations (503)374-8628, showers, laundry, fishing, small pets okay, $$$.
Located right on US 30, just before you cross the bridge.

CASCADE LOCKS KOA (Private)
78 units - 40 w/hookups for water/elec./sewer plus 38 w/water & elec., reservations (503)374-8668, showers, laundry, groceries, swimming pool, trailer waste disposal, pets okay, $$$-$$$$.
At the east end of town take Forest Ln. 1 mile southeast.

CASCADE LOCKS MARINE PARK (Port)
38 sites - no hookups, showers, wheelchair access, playground, trailer waste disposal, river, boat launch, fishing, wind surfing, open year round - bathrooms close at 5 pm off-season, $$.
Located 3 blocks north of I-84's Cascade Locks exit.

(West of Cascade Locks)

EAGLE CREEK (Mt. Hood NF)
20 units, trailers to 22', flush toilets, wheelchair access, creek, swimming, fishing, hiking, elev. 200', pets okay, $$.
Take I-84 west 4.5 miles, then go east on I-84 for 2 miles, and take FSR 240 southeast .1 mile to campground.

OVERLOOK (Mt. Hood NF)
Tent & group campsites, flush toilets, picnic area, community kitchen, creek, $$.
Take I-84 west 4.5 miles, then I-84 east 2 miles, and take FSR 243 north .3 mile to campground.

(East of Cascade Locks)

HERMAN CREEK HORSE CAMP (Mt. Hood NF)
7 units, trailers to 24', wheelchair access, swimming, fishing, hiking, horse trails/corrals/hitch posts, bicycling, $$.
Take the County Road that parallels I-84 east 1.6 miles.

WYETH (Mt. Hood NF)
17 units, trailers to 32', flush toilets, stream, fishing, hiking, $$.
Follow I-84 east 7 miles to exit #51 and campground.

HOOD RIVER

AMERICAN ADVENTURE (Private)
250 units w/hookups for water & elec. plus 100 tent sites, (503)478-3750, showers, laundry, wheelchair access, trailer waste disposal, fishing, swimming, golf, pets okay, $$$-$$$$.
I-84 east 6 miles to exit #69 - in Mosier, at 2350 Carroll Rd.

VIENTO (Oregon State Park)
75 units - 58 w/hookups for elec. plus 17 tent sites, maximum site 30', showers, wheelchair accessible, stream, $$-$$$.
Take I-84 west 8 miles to exit #56 and campground.

(South of Hood River)

ROUTSON PARK (Hood River County)
20 tent sites, reservations (503)386-6323, flush toilets, stream, fishing, pets okay, $.
Follow State 35 south 7 miles.

TUCKER PARK (Hood River County)
69 units - 13 w/hookups for water & elec. plus 56 tent sites, reservations (503)386-6323, showers, pets okay, $$$.
Take Tucker Rd. out of Hood River and head south 6 miles.

PARKDALE

TOLL BRIDGE PARK (Hood River County)
85 units - 20 w/water/elec./sewer, 45 w/water & elec., plus 20 tent sites, reservations (503)386-6323, showers, handicap access, trailer waste disposal, fishing, hiking, pets okay, $$$.
Take Base Line Dr. 1 mile east - campground is west of State 35 .

(West of Parkdale)

LOST LAKE (Mt. Hood NF)
91 units plus group camp, reservations (800)280-2267, trailers to 24', showers, wheelchair access, lake - no motors, boat launch & rental, swimming, fishing, hiking, bicycling, elev. 3200', $$$.
Follow Hood River Highway north 6 miles, CR 501 southwest 5 miles, and FSR 13 southwest 9 miles.

WAHTUM LAKE (Mt. Hood NF)
8 hike-in tent units, lake, fishing, rough roads, elev. 3700', $.
Follow Hood River Highway north 6 miles, CR 501 southwest 5 miles, FSR 13 west 5 miles (bearing right at the Y), FSR 1310 northwest 8 miles to Wahtum Lake, and hike .3 mile to camp.

(South of Parkdale)

ROBINHOOD (Mt. Hood NF)
24 units, trailers to 18', picnic area, river, swimming, fishing, hiking, elev. 3600', $$.
Take State 35 south 12 miles.

SHERWOOD (Mt. Hood NF)
14 units, trailers to 16', river, fishing, hiking, elev. 3000', $$.
Take State 35 south 8 miles.

THE DALLES

LONE PINE RV PARK (Private)
22 RV sites w/full hookups, reservations - (503)296-9133, showers, laundry, playground, river, fishing, pets okay, $$$$. Leave I-84 on exit #87 - located near north end of overpass.

(West of The Dalles)

MEMALOOSE (Oregon State Park)
110 units - 43 w/water/elec./sewer plus 67 tent sites, trailers to 60', showers, wheelchair access, trailer waste disposal, $$-$$$. Take I-84 west 11 miles - this campground is not accessible from I-84 eastbound.

(East of The Dalles)

BOB'S BUDGET RV & TRAILER PARK (Private)
36 units - 26 w/hookups for water/elec./sewer plus 10 tent sites, reservations - (503)739-2829, pull thrus to 60', showers, laundry, wheelchair access, pets okay, $$-$$$. Take I-84 east 24 miles to Rufus exit #109, Old Highway 30 west .5 mile, and Wallace St. south .2 mile.

DESCHUTES RIVER (Oregon State Park)
34 primitive campsites, maximum site 30', fishing, boating, hiking trails, bicycle trails, wildlife viewing area, Oregon Trail display, $$. Take I-84 east 17 miles.

LEPAGE PARK (Corps)
Open camp area, reservation information - (503)296-1181, showers, trailer waste disposal, on John Day River, boat launch, fishing, swimming, pets okay, $. Take I-84 east 28 miles to exit #104, and follow the signs .2 mile to park.

ARLINGTON

TERRACE HEIGHTS MH PARK (Private)
10 trailer sites w/hookups for water/elec./sewer, reservations - (503)454-2757, showers, laundry, cable tv, pets okay, $$$$. Leave I-84 at exit #137 and take Main St. .5 mile south to park.

WELCHES

LOST CREEK (Mt. Hood NF)
9 units, trailers to 22', wheelchair accessible, fishing, hiking, $$. Take US 26 east 1 mile, LoLo Pass Rd. northeast 4.8 miles, and FSR 1825 east 4 miles.

MT. HOOD RV VILLAGE (Private)
420 units w/full hookups, tents okay, reservations - (503)622-4011, showers, wheelchair access, indoor pool & hot tub, weight room, laundry, groceries, propane, fishing, golf, $$$$-$$$$$.
Take US 26 west 2 miles.

RILEY HORSE CAMP (Mt. Hood NF)
14 sites, trailers to 16', reservations (800)280-2267, stream, horse loading/hitchracks & trails, fishing, hiking, elev. 2100', $$.
Take US 26 east 1 mile, LoLo Pass Rd. northeast 4.8 miles, FSR 1825 east 1.2 miles, and FSR 382 southeast .1 mile.

GOVERNMENT CAMP

ALPINE (Mt. Hood NF)
16 units, trailers to 18', no water, elev. 5400', $$.
Take US 26 east .8 mile, and Timberline Rd. northeast 4.6 miles.

STILL CREEK (Mt. Hood NF)
27 units, trailers to 18', reservation information - (800)280-2267, handicap access, fishing, elev. 3700', $$.
Take US 26 southeast 1.2 miles, and FSR 2650 south .5 mile.

TRILLIUM LAKE (Mt. Hood NF)
39 units, trailers to 22', reservation information - (800)280-2267, wheelchair access, lake - no motors, boat launch, swimming, fishing, bicycling, elev. 3600', $$-$$$.
Take US 26 southeast 2.2 miles, and FSR 2656 south 1.3 miles.

(South of Government Camp)

CLACKAMAS LAKE (Mt. Hood NF)
5 units, trailers to 32', reservation information - (800)280-2267, lake - speed limit, fishing, hiking, elev. 3400', $$.
Follow US 26 southeast 15 miles, FSR 42 south 8 miles, and FSR 4270 east .5 mile.

CLEAR LAKE (Mt. Hood NF)
3 units, trailers to 32', reservation information - (800)280-2267, handicap access, lake - 10 mph, swimming, fishing, hiking, elev. 3600', $$-$$$.
Follow US 26 southeast 9 miles, FSR 2630 south 1 mile, and FSR 220 south 1 mile.

FROG LAKE (Mt. Hood NF)
33 units, trailers to 22', reservation information - (800)280-2267, handicap access, lake - no motors, boat ramp, swimming, fishing, elev. 3800', $$-$$$.
Follow US 26 southeast 7 miles, FSR 2610 southeast 1 mile, and FSR 230 south .5 mile.

GONE CREEK (Mt. Hood NF)
50 units, trailers to 32', reservation information - (800)280-2267, handicap access, lake - 10 mph, boat ramp, swimming, fishing, hiking, elev. 3200', $$-$$$.
Follow US 26 southeast 15 miles, FSR 42 south 8 miles, and FSR 57 west 3.5 miles.

JOE GRAHAM HORSE CAMP (Mt. Hood NF)
14 units, trailers to 27', reservations advised - (800)280-2267, fishing, hiking, elev. 3400', $$.
Take US 26 southeast 15 miles, and FSR 42 south 8 miles.

HOOD VIEW (Mt. Hood NF)
43 units, trailers to 32', reservation information - (800)280-2267, handicap access, lake - 10 mph, boat ramp, swimming, fishing, hiking, elev. 3200', $$-$$$.
Follow US 26 southeast 15 miles, FSR 42 south 8 miles, and FSR 57 west 4 miles.

LITTLE CRATER LAKE (Mt. Hood NF)
16 units, trailers to 22', stream, hiking, elev. 3200', $$.
Follow US 26 southeast 15 miles, FSR 42 south 6 miles, FSR 58 west 2.7 miles, and FSR 230 west .3 mile.

OAK FORK (Mt. Hood NF)
47 units, trailers to 32', lake - speed limit, boat ramp, swimming, fishing, hiking, elev. 3200', $$-$$$.
Follow US 26 southeast 15 miles, FSR 42 south 8 miles, FSR 57 west 3 miles, and FSR 170 north .5 mile.

PINE POINT (Mt. Hood NF)
25 units, trailers to 32', reservation information - (800)280-2267, handicap access, lake - speed limit, boat launch, fishing, swimming, hiking trail, elev. 3200', $$-$$$.
Follow US 26 southeast 15 miles, FSR 42 south 8 miles, and FSR 57 west 5 miles.

RHODODENDRON

CAMP CREEK (Mt. Hood NF)
24 units, trailers to 22', flush toilets - barrier free, reservations (800)280-2267, fishing, hiking, elev. 2200', $$-$$$.
US 26 southeast 2.9 miles, Camp Creek Rd. south .1 mile.

TOLLGATE (Mt. Hood NF)
15 units, trailers to 16', reservations - (800)280-2267, stream, fishing, hiking, elev. 1700', $$-$$$.
Take US 26 southeast .5 mile.

DUFUR

DUFUR CITY PARK (Private)
15 sites w/water/elec./sewer, tents okay, reservations - (503) 467-2349, showers, swimming pool, trailer waste disposal, $-$$. Located in the town of Dufur - follow signs.

DUFUR RV PARK (Private)
26 units w/full hookups, no tents, trailers to 60', information (503)467-2449, showers, pets okay, open year round, $$$. Located at First & South Aikin Sts.

TYGH VALLEY

HUNT PARK/FAIRGROUNDS (Wasco County)
150 trailer sites w/hookups for water & elec., reservation information - (503)483-2288, showers, wheelchair access, playground, trailer waste disposal, stream, fishing, $-$$. Follow US 197 west 2 miles - located on Fairground Rd.

(Northeast of Tygh Valley)

BEAVERTAIL (BLM)
20 units, trailers okay, on Deschutes River, rough road, $. Take State 216 east 5 miles to Sherar's Bridge, and follow Deschutes River Rd. north 12 miles.

GET CANYON (BLM)
4 units, no drinking water, on Deschutes River, rough road, $. Take State 216 east 5 miles to Sherar's Bridge, and follow Deschutes River Rd. north 6.3 miles.

JONES CANYON (BLM)
7 units, no drinking water, on Deschutes River, rough road, $. Take State 216 east 5 miles to Sherar's Bridge, and follow Deschutes River Rd. north 6 miles.

MACKS CANYON (BLM)
18 units, boat launch, hiking, fishing, rough road, $. Take State 216 east 5 miles to Sherar's Bridge, and follow Deschutes River Rd. north 15 miles.

OAK BROOK (BLM)
4 units, no drinking water, on Deschutes River, rough road, $. Take State 216 east 5 miles to Sherar's Bridge, and Deschutes River Rd. north 5.5 miles.

RATTLESNAKE (BLM)
8 units, no drinking water, on Deschutes River, rough road, $. Take State 216 east 5 miles to Sherar's Bridge, and follow Deschutes River Rd. north 8 miles.

TWIN SPRINGS (BLM)
6 units, no drinking water, on Deschutes River, rough road, $.
Take State 216 east 5 miles to Sherar's Bridge, and follow
Deschutes River Rd. north 5 miles.

WAMIC

PINE HOLLOW LAKESIDE RESORT (Private)
82 units - 62 w/hookups for water & elec. plus 20 tent sites,
reservations - (503)544-2271, showers, laundry, restaurant,
lounge, groceries, trailer waste disposal, lake, boat launch &
rental, swimming, fishing, $$-$$$.
Take Pine Hollow Reservoir Rd. northwest 3.5 miles.

ROCK CREEK RESERVOIR (Mt. Hood NF)
33 units, trailers to 18', reservations (800)280-2267, wheelchair
access, lake - no motors, boat ramp, fishing, elev. 2200', $$-$$$.
Take Rock Creek Rd. west 6 miles, FSR 48 southwest 1.2 miles,
FSR 4820 west .2 mile, and FSR 120 north .2 mile.

CONDON

CONDON MOBILE HOME & RV PARK (Private)
17 trailer sites w/full hookups, reservation information -
(503)384-5666, showers, laundry, playground, $$$.
Park is on State 206, at west city limits.

MAUPIN

MAUPIN CITY PARK (City)
27 units w/hookups for water/elec./sewer, trailers to 24', tents
okay, trailer waste disposal, river, fishing, $$-$$$.
Located in downtown Maupin.

(North of Maupin)

BLUE HOLE (BLM)
5 units, no drinking water, wheelchair access - includes fishing,
reservations for accessible sites (503)395-2270, on Descutes
River, $.
Take Deschutes River Rd. north 3.5 miles.

OASIS FLAT (BLM)
12 units, no drinking water, on Deschutes River, narrow road, $.
Take Deschutes River Rd. north 1 mile.

WHITE RIVER (Tribal)
10 units, no drinking water, on Deschutes River, narrow road, $.
Take Deschutes River Rd. north 5 miles.

(West of Maupin)

BEAR SPRINGS (Mt. Hood NF)
21 units, trailers to 32', handicap accessible, reservations - (800)280-2267, fishing, elev. 3200', $$.
Follow State 216 west 25 miles.

(South of Maupin)

DEVIL'S CANYON (BLM)
5 units, no drinking water, on Deschutes River, narrow road, $.
US 197 southwest 1 mile, Deschutes River Rd. south 4.2 miles.

HARPHAM FLAT (Tribal)
20 units, no drinking water, on Deschutes River, narrow road, $.
US 197 southwest 1 mile, Deschutes River Rd. south 2.4 miles.

LONGBEND (BLM)
10 units, no drinking water, on Deschutes River, narrow road, $.
US 197 southwest 1 mile, Deschutes River Rd. south 4 miles.

NENA CREEK (BLM)
5 units, no drinking water, on Deschutes River, narrow road, $.
US 197 southwest 1 mile, Deschutes River Rd. south 6 miles.

OAK SPRINGS (BLM)
5 units, no drinking water, on Deschutes River, narrow road, $.
US 197 southwest 1 mile, Deschutes River Rd. south 4 miles.

WAPINITIA (BLM)
5 units, no drinking water, on Deschutes River, narrow road, $.
US 197 southwest 1 mile, Deschutes River Rd. south 2 miles.

SHANIKO

SHANIKO CORRAL & RV PARK (Private)
65 units - 10 w/water/elec./sewer plus 55 dry sites, tents okay, res. (503)489-3441, trailers to 40', showers, laundry, wheelchair access, trailer waste disposal, pets okay, year round, $$-$$$.
In Shaniko. Located at 2nd & E Sts.

FOSSIL

FOSSIL MOTEL & TRAILER PARK (Private)
12 trailer sites w/water/elec./sewer, res. (503)763-4075, $$-$$$.
Located on State 19 at Fossil Junction.

SHELTON (Oregon State Park)
36 primitive campsites, trailers to 30', picnic area, hiking, $$.
Take State 19 southeast 10 miles to park.

WARM SPRINGS

KAH-NEE-TA (Private)
92 units - 52 w/full hookups, 10 w/water/elec./sewer, 30 tent sites, plus group area, res. (800)554-4786, showers, laundry, ice, swimming & therapy pool, tennis, golf, mini golf, trailer waste disposal, fishing, boat & horse rental, hiking, $$$-$$$$$$$.
Take Kah-Nee-Ta Rd. north 11 miles.

MECCA FLAT (BLM)
10 units, boat-in or take rough road, no drinking water, on Lower Deschutes River, $.
Located 2 miles northeast of US 26.

MADRAS

COUNTY FAIRGROUNDS (Jefferson County)
65 units w/full hookups plus grassy tent area, reservations (503)475-4460, trailers to 60', pull thrus, showers, wheelchair accessible, trailer waste disposal, pets okay, $-$$$.
Take the Fairgrounds Rd. exit off US 97 and go 1 block.

TRAILS WEST RV PARK (Private)
30 units w/full hookups, tents okay, reservations (503)475-6062, pull thrus, showers, laundry, wheelchair accessible, nearby store, trailer waste disposal, pets extra, open year round, $$$$.
Located near south end of town - at 159 SW Bard Ln.

(North of Madras)

SOUTH JUNCTION (BLM)
18 units, no drinking water, on Lower Deschutes River, $.
Take US 97 northeast 25 miles to its junction with US 197, and follow South Junction Rd. southwest 11 miles.

TROUT CREEK (BLM)
18 units, no drinking water, on Lower Deschutes River, $.
Take US 97 northeast 3 miles, follow Clark Dr. north 9 miles to Gateway, and take Coleman Rd. 5 miles to campground.

(South of Madras)

BECKER'S HIGH CHAPARREL INN (Private)
15 units w/full hookups, no tents, trailers to 35', reservations (800)500-3021, groceries, propane, gas, no pets, $$-$$$.
Take the Culver Highway south 10 miles to the town of Culver - located at 5520 SW Peck Rd.

COVE PALISADES (Oregon State Park)
272 units - 87 w/water/elec./sewer, 91 w/elec., 94 tent sites, plus group area, mail reservations avail., trailers to 60', showers,

wheelchair access, picnic area, trailer waste disposal, on Crooked/Deschutes/Metolius Rivers, marina, boat launch, fishing, swimming, hiking, $$-$$$.
Leave US 97 just south of Madras and follow park signs - it's about 15 miles.

DESCHUTES RIVER RESORT (Private)
32 units - 26 w/full hookups plus 6 tent sites, information - (503)553-1011, pull thrus, trailers to 60', showers, laundry, playground, rec room, store, trailer waste disposal, on Deschutes River, fishing, rafting, pets okay, open year round, $$-$$$.
Take US 26 southwest 10 miles to 7228 NW Highway 26.

HAYSTACK RESERVOIR (Ochoco NF)
24 units, trailers to 32', flush toilets, lake, boat launch, swimming, fishing, water skiing, elev. 2900', $$.
Take US 97 south 9.3 miles, King Ln. southeast 3.3 miles, and FSR 58 north .6 mile.

PERRY SOUTH (Deschutes NF)
63 units, trailers to 22', wheelchair accessible, on Lake Billy Chinook, boat launch, swimming, fishing, water skiing, elev. 2000', $$.
Follow the signs to Cove Palisades State Park, cross Lake Billy Chinook bridge, and take FSR 63 and 64 northwest 12 miles - located on the Metoilus Arm of Lake Billy Chinook.

CAMP SHERMAN

BLACK BUTTE MOTEL & RV PARK (Private) [RV]
28 units - 19 w/hookups for water/elec./sewer plus 9 w/water & elec., reservations - (503)595-6514, showers, laundry, trailer waste disposal, river, fishing, playfield, playground, hiking, $$$$.
Located in town, on Camp Sherman Rd.

COLD SPRINGS RESORT & RV PARK (Private) [A] [RV]
45 units w/hookups for water/elec./sewer, tents okay, trailers to 45', reservations - (503)595-6271, showers, laundry, trailer waste disposal, river, flyfishing, hiking, pets okay, elev. 3000', $$$$.
Follow Camp Sherman Rd. north to Cold Springs Resort Ln.

(North of Camp Sherman)

ALLEN SPRINGS (Deschutes NF)
17 units, group site, trailers okay, fishing, hiking, elev. 2800', $$.
Take FSR 14 north 5 miles.

ALLINGHAM (Deschutes NF) [A] [RV]
10 units, group site, trailers okay, fishing, hiking, elev. 2900', $$.
Take FSR 14 north 1 mile.

CAMP SHERMAN (Deschutes NF)
15 units, 2 group sites, trailers to 22', picnic shelter, river, fishing, hiking, elev. 3000', $$.
Take FSR 14 north .2 mile.

GORGE (Deschutes NF)
18 units, 6 group sites, trailers to 22', river, fishing, hiking, elev. 2900', $$.
Take FSR 14 north 2 miles.

LOWER BRIDGE (Deschutes NF)
12 units, group site, trailers to 22', river, fishing, hiking, elev. 2800', $$.
Take FSR 14 north 7 miles.

PINE REST (Deschutes NF)
8 tent sites, picnic shelter, river, fishing, hiking, elev. 2900', $$.
Take FSR 14 north 1.5 miles.

PIONEER FORD (Deschutes NF)
18 units, trailers to 22', wheelchair access, river, fishing, hiking, elev. 2800', $$.
Take FSR 14 north 7 miles.

SHEEP SPRINGS HORSE CAMP (Deschutes NF)
11 units, trailers to 18', horse facilities, elev. 3200', $$$.
Take FSR 14 north 1 mile, FSR 1217 west 1 mile, FSR 1420 north 2 miles, FSR 400 and campground road north 3 miles.

SMILING RIVER (Deschutes NF)
38 units, trailers to 22', wheelchair accessible, river, fishing, hiking, elev. 2900', $$.
Take FSR 14 north 1.3 miles.

SISTERS

CIRCLE 5 TRAILER PARK (Private)
24 units - 21 w/hookups for water/elec./sewer plus 3 w/water & elec., tents okay, reservation information - (503)549-3861, showers, laundry, trailer waste disposal, elev. 3200', $$$-$$$$.
Take US 20 southeast .7 mile.

COLD SPRING (Deschutes NF)
23 units, trailers to 22', stream, birdwatching, elev. 3400', $$.
Follow State 242 west 5 miles.

MOUNTAIN SHADOW RV PARK (Private)
106 units w/full hookups, no tents, reservations (503)549-7275, trailers to 60', pull thrus, showers, laundry, wheelchair accessible, swimming pool, hot tub, pets okay, $$$$-$$$$$.
Located in Sisters, at 540 US 20.

SISTERS KOA (Private)
100 units - 60 w/full hookups plus 30 tent sites, reservations - (503)549-3021, showers, laundry, spa, mini golf, playground, restaurant, video rental, groceries, propane, gas, trailer waste disposal, pond, swimming, fishing, elev. 3200', $$$$-$$$$$.
Take US 20 southeast 4 miles.

(Northwest of Sisters)

BIG LAKE (Willamette NF)
49 units, trailers to 18', flush toilets, reservations (800)280-2267, lake, boat launch, swimming, fishing, water skiing, near wilderness trailheads, open June thru Sept., elev. 4600', $$.
Take US 20 west 21.7 miles, and FSR 2690 south 3.4 miles.

BIG LAKE WEST (Willamette NF)
11 tent units plus walk-in sites, reservations (800)280-2267, on Big Lake, boating, swimming, fishing, open June thru Oct., $$.
Take US 20 west 21.7 miles, and FSR 2690 south 4.3 miles.

BLUE BAY (Deschutes NF)
25 units plus 6 group sites, trailers to 22', on Suttle Lake - speed limits, boat launch, swimming, fishing, hiking, elev. 3400', $$.
Take US 20 west 13 miles, and FSR 2070 south 1 mile.

BLUE LAKE RESORT (Private)
38 units - 9 w/water/elec./sewer, 16 w/water & elec., plus 12 w/water, reservations - (503)595-6671, showers, trailer waste disposal, on Suttle Lake - speed limits, boat launch & rental, swimming, fishing, hiking, pets extra, elev. 3500', $$-$$$$.
Take US 20 west 13 miles, and FSR 2070 south 2.5 miles.

INDIAN FORD (Deschutes NF)
25 units plus 10 group sites, trailers to 22', stream, fishing, birdwatching, elev. 3200', $$.
Take US 20 northwest 5 miles, and FSR 11 east .1 mile.

LINK CREEK (Deschutes NF)
23 units plus 8 group sites, trailers to 22', on Suttle Lake - speed limits, swimming, fishing, water skiing, hiking, elev. 3400', $$.
Take US 20 northwest 13 miles, and FSR 2070 south 2 miles.

SCOUT LAKE (Deschutes NF)
13 units, trailers to 22', reservations - (503)549-2111, lake - no motors, swimming, hiking, elev. 4000', $$.
Take US 20 northwest 13 miles, FSR 2070 southwest 1 mile, and FSR 2066 south .5 mile.

SOUTH SHORE (Deschutes NF)
39 units plus group sites, trailers to 22', on Suttle Lake - speed limit, boat ramp, swimming, fishing, hiking trails, elev. 3400', $$.
Take US 20 northwest 13 miles, and FSR 2070 south 1.5 miles.

SUTTLE LAKE RESORT/MARINA/CAMP (Private)
21 campsites, tents okay, reservations (503)595-6662, trailers to 60', showers, playground, store, restaurant, on lake, boat launch, fishing, hiking, pets okay, open April thru Oct., $$-$$$. Take US 20 northwest 13 miles, and FSR 2070 south 1.8 miles.

PRINEVILLE

CROOK COUNTY RV PARK (Crook County)
81 units w/hookups for water/elec.,/sewer plus 9 tent sites, reservations suggested (503)447-2599, showers, wheelchair access, trailer waste disposal, pets okay, $$-$$$$. Located next to the fairgrounds.

GREEN ACRES MOBILE & RV PARK (Private)
3 units w/hookups for water/elec./sewer plus tent sites, reservations (503)447-6439, trailers to 35', showers, laundry, wheelchair access, no pets, open year round, $-$$$. Take US 26 northwest 1 mile to 525200 US 26.

(East of Prineville)

CRYSTAL CORRAL PARK (Private)
42 units - 16 w/hookups for water/elec./sewer, 7 w/ water & elec., plus 20 tent sites, reservation information - (503)447-5932, showers, laundry, groceries, lake, swimming, fishing, boat launch, elev. 3200', $$-$$$$. Take US 26 east 6.5 miles.

LAKESHORE RV PARK & STORE (Private)
64 units - 43 w/hookups for water/elec./sewer, 11 pull thrus, plus 10 tent sites, reservations (503)447-6059, showers, laundry, groceries, playground, trailer waste disposal, on Ochoco Lake, swimming, fishing, boat launch & rental, elev. 3100', $$-$$$. Take US 26 east 7 miles.

OCHOCO LAKE (Oregon State Park)
22 primitive units, maximum site 30', picnic area, boat launch, fishing, hiking trails, $$. Take US 26 east 7 miles.

(South of Prineville)

CASTLE ROCK (BLM)
5 units, no drinking water, on Crooked River, boating, $. Follow State 27 south 12 miles.

CHIMNEY ROCK RECREATION SITE (BLM)
20 units plus group area, trailers to 30', picnic facilities, on Crooked River, boating, fishing elev. 1500', $. Follow State 27 south 15.6 miles.

COBBLE ROCK (BLM)
15 units, no drinking water, on Crooked River, boating, $.
Follow State 27 south 16.4 miles.

LONE PINE (BLM)
8 units, no drinking water, on Crooked River, boating, $.
Follow State 27 south 14.4 miles.

LOWER PALISADES (BLM)
15 units plus group area, no drinking water, on Crooked River, boating, $.
Follow State 27 south 14.8 miles.

POISON BUTTE (BLM)
6 units plus group area, no drinking water, on Crooked River, boating, $.
Follow State 27 south 17.4 miles.

POST PILE (BLM)
10 units, no drinking water, on Crooked River, boating, $.
Follow State 27 south 16.9 miles.

STILLWATER (BLM)
10 units plus group area, no drinking water, on Crooked River, boating, $.
Follow State 27 south 12.8 miles.

(Southeast of Prineville)

ANTELOPE FLAT RESERVOIR (Ochoco NF)
24 units, trailers to 32', picnic area, lake, boat launch, swimming, fishing, hiking, elev. 4600', $.
Paulina Hwy. southeast 29 miles, FSR 17 south 11.3 miles.

PRINEVILLE RESERVOIR (Oregon State Park)
70 units - 22 w/hookups for water/elec./sewer plus 48 tent sites, mail reservations available, maximum site 40', showers, picnic area, boat launch & dock, fishing, swimming, $$-$$$.
Take Paulina Hwy. south 1.7 miles, and Juniper Canyon Rd. southeast 15 miles.

PRINEVILLE RESERVOIR RESORT (Private)
71 units w/hookups for water & elec., reservations - (503)447-7468, showers, groceries, trailer waste disposal, lake, swimming, fishing, boat launch & rental, elev. 3200', $$$.
Take Paulina Hwy. south 1.7 miles, and Juniper Canyon Rd. southeast 17 miles.

SUN ROCKS RV PARK & CAMPGROUND (Private)
60 units - 38 w/hookups for water/elec./sewer plus 22 w/out hookups, tents okay, reservations (800)771-0941, trailers to 70', pull thrus, showers, laundry, wheelchair access, swimming pool

& hot tub in summer, playground, volleyball, basketball, ice, propane, pets okay, open year round, $$$-$$$$.
Take Paulina Hwy. south 1.7 miles, and Juniper Canyon Rd. southeast 13 miles to 14900 S. Juniper Canyon Rd.

(Northeast of Prineville)

OCHOCO DIVIDE (Ochoco NF)
28 units, trailers to 32', at Ochoco Pass summit, elev. 4700', $$.
Follow US 26 east/northeast 30.8 miles to campground.

OCHOCO FOREST CAMP (Ochoco NF)
6 units, picnic area, creek, hiking trails, elev. 4000', $$.
Take US 26 east 17 miles, and Ochoco Creek Rd. northeast 8.5 miles - campground is adjacent to ranger station.

WALTON LAKE (Ochoco NF)
30 units, trailers to 32', picnic area, lake - no motors, boating, fishing, swimming, hiking, elev. 5000', $$.
Take US 26 east 17 miles, Ochoco Creek Rd. northeast 8.5 miles, FSR 22 northeast 6.2 miles, and FSR 2220 .3 mile.

WILDCAT (Ochoco NF)
17 units, trailers to 22', picnic area, stream, fishing, hiking, adjacent to Mill Creek Wilderness, elev. 3700', $$.
Take US 26 east 9.2 miles, and Mill Creek Rd. northeast 11.9 miles to campground.

REDMOND

CROOKED RIVER RANCH RV PARK (Private)
96 units - 367 w/hookups for water/elec./sewer, 63 w/water & elec., plus 17 tent sites, reservation information - (503)923-1441, showers, laundry, swimming pool, playground, restaurant, lounge, golf course, trailer waste disposal, river, fishing, hiking, elev. 2600', $$$-$$$$.
Take US 97 north 6 miles, and Lower Bridge Rd. northwest 7 miles.

DESERT TERRACE (Private)
25 units - 20 w/hookups for water/elec./sewer plus 5 tent sites, reservation information - (503)548-2546, showers, laundry, elev. 3000', $$-$$$$.
Follow US 97 south 3 miles.

GREEN ACRES (Private)
50 units - 45 w/full hookups, 5 w/water & elec./cable tv, plus tent area, reservations - (503)923-0868, trailers to 40', showers, laundry, wheelchair access, propane, trailer waste disposal, pets okay, open year round, $$-$$$$.
Follow US 97 south 2 miles.

SMITH ROCK (Oregon State Park)

Walk-in tent area, on river, fishing, hiking, rock climbing, $-$$.
Take US 97 north 5 miles, Smith Rock Rd. northeast 4 miles.

BEND

BEND KEYSTONE RV PARK (Private)

31 units w/full hookups, no tents, trailers to 36', showers, laundry, no dogs, $$$.
Located in town, at 305 NE Burnside Ave.

CROWN VILLA RV PARK (Private)

131 trailer sites - 105 w/hookups for water/elec./ sewer/cable tv, plus 26 w/elec. only, no tents, reservations - (503)388-1131, showers, laundry, ice, trailer waste disposal, pond, playground, wheelchair access, $$$$-$$$$$$.
Follow US 97 south, just past the city limits, and go 2 miles southeast on Brosterhaus Rd.

SCANDIA RV & MOBILE PARK (Private)

35 campsites w/full hookups, no tents, reservation information - (503)382-6206, showers, laundry, $$$$.
Take US 97 2.5 miles south of its junction with US 20 - park is located near city limits.

(North of Bend)

BEND CAMPGROUND (Private)

100 units - 50 w/full hookups plus 50 w/water & elec., tents okay, reservations - (503)382-7738, showers, laundry, swimming pool, playground, groceries, gas, propane, pond fishing, $$$$.
Take US 97 north 2 miles.

TUMALO (Oregon State Park)

88 units - 21 w/hookups for water/elec./sewer, 67 tent sites, plus group area, maximum site 44', showers, fishing, hiking trails, $$-$$$.
Follow US 20 northwest 5 miles.

(Southwest of Bend)

ELK LAKE (Deschutes NF)

23 units, trailers to 22', picnic area, lake - speed limits, boating, swimming, fishing, hiking, elev 4900', $$.
Leave US 97 in town heading southwest on Century Dr. Hwy. for 31.5 miles to Elk Lake and campground.

LITTLE FAWN (Deschutes NF)

20 units plus 10 group sites - group reservations - (503)388-5664, trailers to 22', Elk Lake - speed limit, boat launch, swimming, fishing, elev. 4900', groups $50/night - individuals $.

Leave US 97 in town heading southwest on Century Dr. Hwy. for 31.3 miles, and take FSR 4625 southeast 2.1 miles.

POINT (Deschutes NF)
9 units, trailers to 22', on Elk Lake - speed limits, boat ramp, swimming, fishing, elev. 4900', $$.
Leave US 97 in town heading southwest on Century Dr. Hwy. for 33 miles to campground.

QUINN MEADOW HORSE CAMP (Deschutes NF)
24 units, reservations required - (503)388-5664, trailers to 18', stream, fishing, hiking & horse trails, elev. 5100', $$.
Leave US 97 in town heading southwest on Century Dr. Hwy. for 30 miles, and take FRS 450 southeast .3 mile.

SUNRIVER

SNOWY RIVER RV PARK (Private)
6 units w/full hookups plus tent area, reservations (503)593-2597, trailers to 40', showers, laundry, wheelchair access, trailer waste disposal, pets okay, open year round, $$-$$$$.
Located just southwest of Sunriver, at 56148 Solar Dr.

LaPINE

HIGHLANDER MOTEL & RV PARK (Private)
28 pull thrus w/full hookups plus grassy tent area, reservations (503)536-2131, trailers to 35', showers, propane, gas, trailer waste disposal, open year round, $$$.
Located in LaPine, at 51511 Hwy. US 97.

LAMPLITER MOTEL & RV PARK (Private)
36 units w/full hookups, tents okay, reservations (503)536-2931, trailers to 44', showers, laundry, wheelchair accessible, trailer waste disposal, pets okay, open year round, $$$.
Located in LaPine, at 51526 N. Hwy. US 97.

ROUNDUP TRAVEL TRAILER PARK (Private)
27 units w/hookups for water/elec./sewer, reservations - (503)536-2378, showers, laundry, trailer waste disposal, $$$$.
Leave US 97 on Huntington Rd., go south 1 block, and take Finley Butte Rd. east 1 block to park.

(Northeast of LaPine)

CHIEF PAULINA HORSE CAMP (Deschutes NF)
13 horse camp units, reservations required - (503)388-5674, trailers to 32', near Paulina Lake, elev. 6300', $$.
US 97 north 5 miles, Paulina/East Lake Rd. 15 miles east.

CINDER HILL (Deschutes NF)
110 units, trailers to 32', flush toilets, on East Lake - speed limit, boat launch, fishing, hiking, elev. 6300', $$.
US 97 north 5 miles, Paulina/East Lake Rd. 18 miles east.

EAST LAKE (Deschutes NF)
29 units, trailers to 32', flush toilets, lake - speed limit, boat launch, fishing, hiking, elev. 6300', $$.
US 97 north 5 miles, Paulina/East Lake Rd. 17 miles east.

EAST LAKE RESORT & RV PARK (Private)
38 units w/ water & elec., tents okay, trailers to 35', reservations (503)536-2230, showers, laundry, trailer waste disposal, lake, boat launch/rental, swimming, fishing, hiking, elev. 6300', $$$.
US 97 north 5 miles, Paulina/East Lake Rd. 18 miles east.

HOT SPRINGS (Deschutes NF)
43 units, trailers to 32', on East Lake - speed limit, fishing, hiking, elev. 6300', $$.
US 97 north 5 miles, Paulina/East Lake Rd. 17.6 miles east.

LITTLE CRATER (Deschutes NF)
50 units, trailers to 32', on Paulina Lake - speed limit, boat launch, fishing, swimming, hiking, elev. 6300', $$.
US 97 north 5 miles, Paulina/East Lake Rd. 15 miles east.

NEWBERRY GROUP CAMP (Deschutes NF)
Group area, reservations (503)388-5674, picnic area, on Paulina Lake - speed limit, fishing, swimming, hiking trails, elev. 6400'.
US 97 north 5 miles, Paulina/East Lake Rd. 12.5 miles east.

OGDEN GROUP CAMP (Deschutes NF)
Groups only, reservations (503)388-5674, on Paulina Creek, hiking trails, elev. 4300'.
US 97 north 5 miles, Paulina/East Lake Rd. 2.5 miles east.

PAULINA LAKE (Deschutes NF)
71 units, trailers to 32', flush toilets, lake - speed limit, boat launch, fishing, swimming, hiking, elev. 6300', $$.
US 97 north 5 miles, Paulina/East Lake Rd. 13.1 miles east.

PRAIRIE (Deschutes NF)
16 units, trailers to 32', stream, fishing, hiking, elev. 4400', $$.
US 97 north 5 miles, Paulina/East Lake Rd. 3 miles east.

(Northwest of LaPine)

CRANE PRAIRIE (Deschutes NF)
147 units, trailers to 22', on Crane Prairie Reservoir - speed limit, fishing, elev. 4400', $$.
US 97 north 2.4 miles, Pringle Falls Loop west 9 miles, Century Dr. west 8 miles, Odell/Lava Lake Rd. north 4.5 miles.

CRANE PRAIRIE RESORT (Private)
38 units w/hookups for water/elec./sewer, tents okay, reservations - (503)382-2787, boat & motor rentals, boat ramp, store, boat gas, fishing, on Crane Prairie Reservoir, $$$-$$$$. US 97 north 2.4 miles, Pringle Falls Loop west 9 miles, Century Dr. west 8 miles, Odell/Lava Lake Rd. north 4.5 miles.

CULTUS LAKE (Deschutes NF)
55 units, trailers to 22', picnic area, lake, boating, swimming, fishing, waterskiing, windsurfing, elev. 4700', $$. US 97 north 2.4 miles, Pringle Falls Loop west 9 miles, Century Dr. west 8 miles, Odell/Lava Lake Rd. north 6.4 miles, FSR 463 west 1 mile.

DESCHUTES BRIDGE (Deschutes NF)
12 units, trailers to 22', picnic area, on Deschutes River, fishing, elev. 4600', $$. US 97 north 2.4 miles, Pringle Falls Loop west 9 miles, Century Dr. west 8 miles, Odell/Lava Lake Rd. north 10 miles.

GULL POINT (Deschutes NF)
8 units plus group sites, trailers to 32', flush toilets, picnic area, trailer dump station, on north end of Wickiup Reservoir, boat ramp, swimming, fishing, water skiing, elev. 4300', $$. US 97 north 2.4 miles, Pringle Falls Loop west 9 miles, Century Dr. west 5.4 miles, FSR 4260 south 3.5 miles.

HIDDEN PINES RV PARK (Private)
18 units w/full hookups, reservations - (503)536-2265, tents okay, showers, laundry, trailer waste disposal, ice, propane, RV supplies, elev. 4200', $$$-$$$$. US 97 north 2.4 miles, Pringle Falls Loop west 2.5 miles, Pine Forest Rd. south .7 mile, Wright Rd. 1 block to park.

LAPINE (Oregon State Park)
145 units - 95 w/hookups for water/elec./sewer plus 50 w/elec. only, maximum site 85', showers, wheelchair access, picnic area, trailer waste disposal, Deschutes River, boating, fishing, $$-$$$. US 97 north 6 miles, LaPine Recreation Area Rd. west 3.2 miles.

LAVA LAKE (Deschutes NF)
43 units, trailers to 22', trailer waste disposal, lake - speed limits, boat ramp & rental, fishing, hiking, elev. 4800', $$. US 97 north 2.4 miles, Pringle Falls Loop west 9 miles, Century Dr. west 8 miles, Odell/Lava Lake Rd. north 13.5 miles, FSR 500 northeast 1 mile.

LAVA LAKE RV CAMPGROUND (Private)
24 units w/water/elec./sewer, tents okay, reservation information - (503)382-9443, showers, laundry, groceries, propane, gas, trailer waste disposal, lake - speed limits, boat launch & rental, swimming, fishing, hiking, elev. 4700', $$$$.

US 97 north 2.4 miles, Pringle Falls Loop west 9 miles, Century Dr. west 8 miles, Odell/Lava Lake Rd. north 18 miles.

QUINN RIVER (Deschutes NF)
41 units, trailers to 32', picnic area, on Crane Prairie Reservoir - speed limits, boat ramp, Odell River, fishing, near Billy Quinn Historical Grave Site, elev. 4400', $$.
US 97 north 2.4 miles, Pringle Falls Loop west 9 miles, Century Dr. west 8 miles, Odell/Lava Lake Rd. north 4 miles.

RIVERVIEW TRAILER PARK (Private)
20 units w/full hookups plus tent area, reservation information - (503)536-2382, trailers to 60', showers, laundry, propane, Little Deschutes River, swimming, fishing, hiking, elev. 4300', small pets okay, open year round, $$-$$$.
US 97 north 2.4 miles, Pringle Falls Loop west 1 mile, Huntington Rd. north 1 mile to park.

ROCK CREEK (Deschutes NF)
31 units, trailers to 22', on Crane Prairie Reservoir - speed limits, boat ramp, fishing, elev. 4400', $$.
US 97 north 2.4 miles, Pringle Falls Loop west 9 miles, Century Dr. west 8 miles, Odell/Lava Lake Rd. north 2.4 miles.

ROSLAND (Deschutes NF)
11 units, trailers to 22', no drinking water, on Little Deschutes River, swimming, fishing, elev. 4200', $$.
US 97 north 2.4 miles, Pringle Falls Loop west 1.5 miles.

SOUTH TWIN LAKE (Deschutes NF)
24 units, trailers to 22', flush toilets, lake - no motors, boat ramp, swimming, fishing, hiking, elev. 4300', $$.
US 97 north 2.4 miles, Pringle Falls Loop west 9 miles, Century Dr. west 5.4 miles, FSR 4260 south 1.6 miles.

TWIN LAKES RESORT (Private)
23 units w/hookups for water/elec./sewer, no tents, reservation information (503)593-6526, flush toilets, showers, picnic tables, restaurant, groceries, tackle shop, on South Twin Lake - no gas motors allowed, row & paddle boat rental, walk to Wickiup Reservoir, fishing, hiking, open March thru Oct., $$$.
US 97 north 2.4 miles, Pringle Falls Loop west 9 miles, Century Dr. west 5.4 miles.

WEST CULTUS (Deschutes NF)
12 tent sites, boat-in or hike-in only, on Cultus Lake, fishing, swimming, water skiing, elev. 4700', $.
US 97 north 2.4 miles, Pringle Falls Loop west 9 miles, Century Dr. west 8 miles, Odell/Lava Lake Rd. north 6.4 miles, FSR 463 northwest 1.5 miles, boat across lake 2.7 miles or take Trail #16 for 3.2 miles to campground.

WEST SOUTH TWIN LAKE (Deschutes NF)

24 units plus 2 group areas, trailers to 22', flush toilets, snack bar, on Deschutes River channel - speed limits, boat launch & rental, swimming, fishing, elev. 4300', $$.
US 97 north 2.4 miles, Pringle Falls Loop west 9 miles, Century Dr. west 5.4 miles, FSR 4260 south 1.7 miles.

CRESCENT

BIG PINES RV PARK (Private)

14 units - most w/full hookups plus tent area, reservations (503)433-2785, pull thrus, showers, laundry, store, propane, pets okay, $$$.
Follow US 97 south .5 mile to park.

CRESCENT RV PARK (Private)

25 units w/full hookups plus grassy tent area, reservations (503)433-2950, trailers to 90', pull thrus, showers, wheelchair accessible, store, trailer waste disposal, near river, fishing, hiking, pets okay, open year round, $$-$$$$.
Located in Crescent, on US 97 at Potter St.

CY BINGHAM PARK (Klamath County)

10 units, trailers okay, picnic tables, near river, pets okay, $.
Located .3 mile west of US 97 on Crescent Cutoff Rd.

(Northwest of Crescent)

EAST DAVIS LAKE (Deschutes NF)

33 units, trailers to 22', picnic area, on Davis Lake - speed limit, boating, fishing, elev. 4000', $$.
Take Crescent Cutoff Rd. west 9 miles, FSR 46 north 6.5 miles, and FSR 855 west 1.5 miles to south end of Davis Lake.

ODELL CREEK (Deschutes NF)

22 units, trailers to 22', on Odell Lake, boating, fishing, windsurfing, hiking trails, elev. 4800', $$$.
Take Crescent Cutoff Rd. west 11.5 miles, and State 58 northwest 5 miles - on east end of lake, at the head of Odell Creek.

PEBBLE BAY (Deschutes NF)

Boat-in camping along Odell Lake, swimming, fishing, water skiing, elev. 4800', $.
Take Crescent Cutoff Rd. west 11.5 miles, State 58 northwest 5 miles to Odell Lake, and boat to Pebble Bay on southwest shore.

PRINCESS CREEK (Deschutes NF)

46 units, trailers to 22', picnic area, on Odell Lake, boat launch, fishing, water skiing, wind surfing, elev. 4800', $$$.
Take Crescent Cutoff Rd. west 11.5 miles, and State 58 northwest 9 miles.

SHELTER COVE RESORT (Private)　
69 units - 58 w/hookups for elec. plus 11 w/out hookups, trailers to 40', tents okay, reservations (503)433-2548, showers, propane, gas, trailer waste disposal, on Odell Lake, boat launch & rental, moorage, fishing, hiking, open May thru Oct., $$-$$$.
Take Crescent Cutoff Rd. west 11.5 miles, State 58 northwest 6.9 miles, and FSR 5810 southwest 2.2 miles.

SUNSET COVE (Deschutes NF)　
27 units, trailers to 22', picnic area, on Odell Lake, boat launch, fishing, wind surfing, elev. 4800', $$$.
Take Crescent Cutoff Rd. west 11.5 miles, and State 58 northwest 6 miles.

TRAPPER CREEK (Deschutes NF)　
32 units, trailers to 22', on Odell Lake, boat launch, fishing, hiking, near Diamond Peak Wilderness, elev. 4800', $$$.
Take Crescent Cutoff Rd. west 11.5 miles, State 58 northwest 6.9 miles, and FSR 5810 southwest 1.8 miles.

WEST DAVIS LAKE (Deschutes NF)
25 units, trailers to 22', on Davis Lake - speed limit, fishing, elev. 4400', $$.
Take Crescent Cutoff Rd. west 9 miles, FSR 46 north 3.3 miles, FSR 4660 northwest 3.8 miles, and FSR 4669 east 2 miles to the south end of Davis Lake and campground.

(West of Crescent)

CRESCENT CREEK (Deschutes NF)
10 units, trailers to 22', on creek, fishing, elev. 4500', $$.
Take Crescent Cutoff Rd. west 8.2 miles.

CRESCENT LAKE (Deschutes NF)
47 units, trailers to 22', on lake, boat launch, swimming, fishing, wind surfing, water skiing, hiking, elev. 4800', $$$.
Take Crescent Cutoff Rd. west 11.5 miles, State 58 northwest 3.5 miles, and FSR 60 southwest 2.7 miles to north end of Crescent Lake.

SIMAX GROUP CAMP (Deschutes NF)
Group sites - reservations req. (503)433-2234, on Crescent Lake, boating, fishing, swimming, wind surfing, elev. 4850'.
Take Crescent Cutoff Rd. west 11.5 miles, State 58 northwest 3.5 miles, FSR 60 southwest 2 miles, and FSR 6015 south 1.6 miles.

SPRING (Deschutes NF)　
68 units, trailers to 22', on Crescent Lake, boat launch, swimming, fishing, water skiing, wind surfing, hiking trails, elev. 4800', $$$.
Take Crescent Cutoff Rd. west 11.5 miles, State 58 northwest 3.5 miles, FSR 60 southwest 9 miles.

WHITEFISH HORSE CAMP (Deschutes NF)
19 horse camp units - reservations req. (503)433-2234, trailers okay, stream, trails, horse facilities, at Crescent Lake, elev. 4800', $$$.
Take Crescent Cutoff Rd. west 11.5 miles, State 58 northwest 3.5 miles, FSR 60 southwest 6.7 miles.

CHEMULT

CRATER LAKE MOTEL & RV PARK (Private)
10 units w/full hookups plus tent area, reservation information - (503)365-2241, showers, laundry, wheelchair accessible, trailer waste disposal, space for horses, pets okay, open year round, $$-$$$$.
Located right in the town of Chemult.

DIGIT POINT (Winema NF)
64 units, trailers to 32', flush toilets, trailer waste disposal, on Miller Lake - speed limit, boat launch, swimming, fishing, hiking, mosquitoes, elev. 5600', $$.
Take US 97 north 1 mile, and FSR 9772 west 12 miles.

SAND CREEK STATION (Private)
14 units - 10 w/hookups for water/elec./sewer plus 4 w/water & elec., tents okay, information (503)365-4416, showers, wheelchair accessible, store, propane, gas, restaurant, horse corral, pets okay, open year round, $$.
Follow US 97 south 23 miles.

SILVER LAKE

EAST BAY (Fremont NF)
18 units, trailers to 32', on Thompson Res. - 10 mph speed limit, boat ramp, swimming, fishing, elev. 5000', $$.
Take East Bay Rd. south 12.5 miles (becomes FSR 28), and FSR 280014 west 1.5 miles.

PAISLEY

SUMMER LAKE HOT SPRINGS (Private)
9 pull thrus w/hookups for water/elec./sewer plus tent area, reservations (503) 943-3931, trailers to 70', showers, laundry, hot spring swimming pool, trailer waste disposal, parasailing viewing, nearby fishing, hiking, pets okay, open year round, $$.
Located right in Paisley - on Hwy 31 at milepost 92.

FORT KLAMATH

CRATER LAKE RESORT (Private)
25 units - 13 w/hookups for water/elec./sewer, 12 w/water &
elec., plus large tent area, reservation information - (503)381-
2349, showers, laundry, rec room, playfield, playground, trout
pond, stream, fishing, elev. 4100', $$$.
Take State 62 south 1.5 miles.

FORT KLAMATH LODGE & RV PARK (Private)
16 units - 11 w/hookups for water/elec./sewer plus 5 tent sites,
reservation information - (503)381-2234, showers, laundry, river,
fishing, elev. 4100', $$-$$$.
Located on State 62, near city center.

JACKSON F. KIMBALL (Oregon State Park)
6 primitive campsites, maximum site 45', no drinking water,
picnic tables, wildlife viewing, hiking, fishing, $$.
Take State 62 east to Ft. Klamath Junction, and Sun Mountain
Rd. north 3 miles.

(Northwest of Fort Klamath)

CRATER LAKE RV PARK (Private)
63 units - 7 w/hookups for water/elec./sewer, 41 w/water &
elec., plus 15 tent sites, reservation information - (503)381-2275,
showers, laundry, wheelchair access, playground, groceries,
trout pond, stream, swimming, fishing, elev. 4300', $$$-$$$$.
Take State 62 northwest 5 miles.

WILSON'S COTTAGES & CAMP (Private)
15 campsites, reservation information - (503)381-2209, store,
creek, fishing, cross country & snowmobile trails, ski rental, $$.
Take State 62 northwest 5 miles.

CHILOQUIN

CAMP KLAMATH RIVER CABINS & RV PARK (Private) [RV]
4 RV sites w/full hookups, no tents, trailers to 30', information
(503)783-2697, showers, on Sprague River, dock, fishing, space
for horses, pets okay, open May thru Oct., $$.
Follow Sprague River Rd east 2 miles, and Chiloquin Ridge Rd.
south 1 mile.

NEPTUNE PARK RESORT (Private) [A] [RV]
25 units - 8 w/hookups for water/elec./sewer, 12 w/water &
elec., plus 5 tent sites, reservation information - (503)783-2489,
showers, groceries, gas & propane, on Agency Lake, boat launch
& rental, swimming, fishing, elev. 4200', $$-$$$$.
Just north of Chiloquin, leave US 97 on Chiloquin Hwy. and go
west 6 miles to Lakeside Rd., then head south 3 miles.

COLLIER (Oregon State Park)
68 campsites - 50 w/hookups for water/elec./sewer plus 18 tent sites, maximum site 60', showers, wheelchair access, picnic area, trailer waste disposal, horse facilities, hiking trails, fishing, historic logging museum & pioneer cabins, $$-$$$.
Take US 97 north about 5 miles to Collier State Park.

SPRING CREEK (Winema NF)
26 units, flush toilets, picnic tables, fishing, $$.
Take US 97 north 7 miles, FSR 9738 west .2 mile, and FSR 9732 northwest 3 miles.

WILLIAMSON RIVER (Winema NF)
10 units, trailers to 32', fishing, elev. 4200', $.
Take US 97 north 5 miles, and FSR 9730 northeast 1 mile.

(South of Chiloquin)

SPORTSMAN'S RIVER RETREAT (Private)
25 units w/hookups for water/elec./sewer plus tent area, reservations - (503)783-2675, trailers to 60', showers, laundry, wheelchair access, playground, picnic area, store, propane, gas, trailer waste disposal, on Williamson River, boat launch/dock & moorage, trout fishing, swimming, pets okay, elev. 4100', $$$.
Follow US 97 south 9 miles, and Modoc Point Rd. northwest 6 miles.

WALT'S COZY CAMP (Private)
34 units - 12 w/hookups for water/elec./sewer, 2 w/water & elec., plus 20 tent sites, reservation information - (503)783-2537, showers, elev. 4200', $$$.
Located on US 97, south of Chiloquin at milepost #248.

WATER WHEEL CAMPGROUND (Private)
48 units - 10 w/hookups for water/elec./sewer, 18 w/water & elec., plus 20 tent sites, reservations - (503)783-2738, showers, laundry, playground, trailer waste disposal, groceries, propane, river, boat launch, swimming, fishing, elev. 4200', $$$-$$$$.
Located on US 97, near its junction with State 62.

BLY

GERBER RESERVOIR (BLM)
50 units, trailers okay, handicap accessible, trailer dump station, boat launch, fishing platform, swimming, hiking, $.
Leave State 140 at Bly and follow the signs southwest - it's about 19 miles to the campground on the west side of the reservoir.

LAKEVIEW

JUNIPERS RESERVOIR RV RESORT (Private)
46 units - 25 w/hookups for water/elec./sewer, 15 w/water & elec., plus 6 tent sites, reservation information - (503)947-2050, showers, laundry, wheelchair access, trailer waste disposal, reservoir, stream, fishing, hiking, wildlife viewing, $$$-$$$$.
Follow State 140 west 10 miles - located in the middle of an 8,000 acre cattle ranch/wildlife viewing area.

MILE-HI TRAILER & RV PARK (Private)
20 units w/hookups for water/elec./sewer, no tents, reservations (503)947-2232, trailers to 50', showers, laundry, pets okay, open year round, $$$.
Located in Lakeview, at 764 NE H St.

PARKWAY MOTEL & RV PARK (Private)
19 units - 18 w/hookups for water/elec./sewer plus 1 tent site, flush toilets, showers, reservations - (503)947-2707, $$-$$$.
Located on State 140, 2 blocks west of US 395.

(North of Lakeview)

HUNTER'S RV (Private)
10 sites w/full hookups, 13 w/water & elec., plus tent area, reservations (503)947-4968, showers, laundry, groceries, hot tub, restaurant, trailer waste disposal, ponds, elev. 5000', $$-$$$$.
Take US 395 north 2 miles.

VALLEY FALLS STORE & CAMPGROUND (Private)
16 units - 6 w/hookups for water/elec./sewer, 2 w/water, plus 8 tent sites, reservations (503)947-2052, hiking, elev. 4200', $-$$.
Take US 395 north 23 miles.

(South of Lakeview)

GOOSE LAKE (Oregon State Park)
48 campsites w/elec., trailers to 50', showers, picnic area, trailer waste disposal, boat launch, fishing, wildlife viewing, $$-$$$.
Take US 395 south 15 miles.

KLAMATH FALLS

GREENSPRINGS RV/MH PARK (Private)
12 units w/full hookups plus tent area, reservations (503)882-0823, trailers to 70', showers, laundry, wheelchair accessible, pets okay, open year round, $$-$$$$.
Located east of US 97 - at 2055 Greensprings Dr.

KLAMATH FALLS KOA (Private)

73 units - 36 w/hookups for water/elec./sewer, 30 w/water & elec., plus 7 tent sites, reservations - (503)884-4644, showers, laundry, pool, playground, trailer waste disposal, groceries, propane, stream, elev. 4100', $$$-$$$$.
Take 5th St., go left on Washburn, and take Shasta Way to 3435.

MOUNTAIN VU RV PARK (Private)

23 units w/hookups for water/elec./sewer plus tent area, reservations - (503)884-0897, trailers to 40', showers, laundry, trailer waste disposal, pets okay, open year round, $$-$$$.
Located at 6660 S. 6th St.

WISEMAN'S MOBILE COURT (Private) [RV]

20 trailer sites w/hookups for water/elec./sewer, reservations - (503)884-4327, maximum site 40', showers, laundry, trailer waste disposal, pets extra, elev. 4200', $$$.
Located at 6800 S. 6th St.

(North of Klamath Falls)

HAGELSTEIN PARK (Klamath County) [A] [RV]

10 campsites, trailers okay, flush toilets, wheelchair accessible, on Klamath Lake, boat launch, fishing, pets okay, $.
Take US 97 north 10 miles.

OREGON MOTEL 8 RV PARK (Private) [A] [RV]

40 units - 22 w/hookups for water/elec./sewer, 3 w/water & elec., plus 15 tent sites, reservations - (503)882-0482, showers, laundry, swimming pool, game room, elev. 4100', $$$.
Take US 97 north 3 miles.

(Northwest of Klamath Falls)

ASPEN POINT (Winema NF) [A] [RV]

61 units, trailers to 22', flush toilets, trailer waste disposal, at Lake of the Woods, boat launch, fishing, hiking, elev. 5000', $$.
Follow State 140 northwest 33 miles, FSR 3704 south .6 mile.

FOURMILE LAKE (Winema NF) [A] [RV]

25 units, trailers to 20', horse facilities, trailhead access to Skylakes Wilderness, fishing, boating, swimming, elev. 5800', $.
Follow State 140 northwest 35 miles, FSR 3661 north 5.5 miles.

LAKE OF THE WOODS RV RESORT (Private)

42 units - 27 w/hookups for water/elec./sewer, 5 w/elec. only, plus 10 tent sites, reservations - (503)949-8300, trailers to 35', showers, laundry, trailer waste disposal, propane, restaurant, groceries, on lake, boat launch/gas & rental, swimming, fishing, hiking, pets okay, open April thru Oct., elev. 5000', $$-$$$$.
Follow State 140 northwest 33 miles, FSR 3704 south 1 mile, and resort road west .5 mile.

ROCKY POINT RESORT & MARINA (Private)
35 units - 19 w/hookups for water/elec./sewer, 10 w/water & elec., plus 6 tent sites, reservations - (503)356-2287, showers, laundry, store, trailer waste disposal, lake, paddleboat rental, boat launch, swimming, fishing, hiking, elev. 4200', $$-$$$.
Follow State 140 northwest 28 miles, and Rocky Point Rd. north 3 miles.

SUNSET (Winema NF)
67 units, trailers to 22', flush toilets, handicap access, at Lake of the Woods, boat ramp, swimming, fishing, hiking, elev. 5000', $$.
Follow State 140 northwest 32.6 miles, FSR 3704 south 1 mile.

(South of Klamath Falls)

TINGLEY LAKE ESTATES (Private)
14 units - 4 w/hookups for water/elec./sewer, 6 w/water & elec., plus 4 tent units, reservations - (503)882-8386, showers, pond, swimming, fishing, boat rental, elev. 4100', $$$-$$$$.
Follow US 97 south 7 miles to the town of Midland, take Old Midland Rd. east 2 miles, and Tingley Ln. south .5 mile.

KENO

KENO CAMP (Pacific Power)
26 campsites, information (503)464-5035, showers, handicap access, picnic area, trailer waste disposal, on Klamath River, boat launch, fishing, swimming, open May thru Oct., $$.
Take State 66 northwest 2 miles.

TOPSY (BLM)
12 primitive tent sites, handicap accessible, picnic facilities, boat launch, swimming, elev. 3500', $.
Follow State 66 northwest 6 mile, and Topsy County Rd. south 1 mile.

EASTERN OREGON
CAMPGROUNDS

See Page

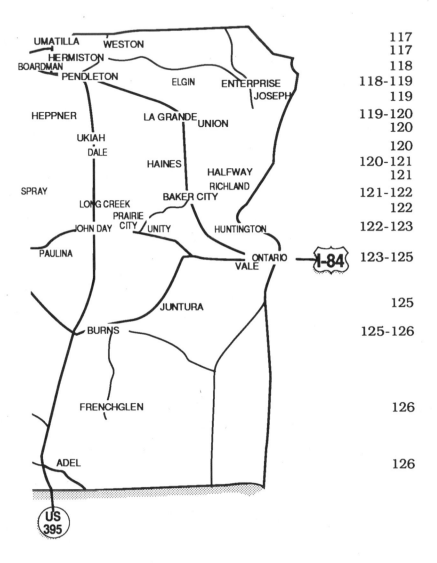

	See Page
	117
	117
	118
	118-119
	119
	119-120
	120
	120
	120-121
	121
	121-122
	122
	122-123
	123-125
	125
	125-126
	126
	126

UMATILLA

UMATILLA MARINA & RV PARK (Private)
35 units - 26 w/hookups for water/elec./sewer plus 9 w/out hookups, tents okay, reservations (503)922-3989, trailers to 65', pull thrus, showers, wheelchair access, trailer waste disposal, pets okay, open year round, $$-$$$.
From I-84/State 730 junction, go north .3 mile on Brownell Rd, then west .3 mile on 3rd St. - located at 1710 Quincy.

SHADY REST RV PARK (Private)
24 units - 18 w/hookups for water/elec./sewer plus 6 w/water & elec., reservations - (503)922-5041, showers, laundry, pool, $$$.
Take US 730 west .4 mile.

WESTON

WOODWARD (Umatilla NF) 🅰️ RV
18 units, trailers to 22', hiking & bike trails, elev. 4950', $.
Take State 204 east 17.5 miles.

JUBILEE LAKE (Umatilla NF) 🅰️ RV
51 units, trailers to 22', flush toilets, handicap access, lake - no motors, fishing, swimming, hiking, elev. 4800', $-$$.
Take State 204 east 15 miles, and FSR 64 northeast 12 miles.

TARGET MEADOWS (Umatilla NF) 🅰️ RV
20 units, trailers to 22', picnic area, hiking, elev. 4800', $.
Take State 204 east 15 miles, and FSR 6401 north 2.2 miles.

HERMISTON

BUTTERCREEK RECREATIONAL COMPLEX (Private) RV
24 trailer sites w/hookups for water/elec./sewer, reservation information - (503)564-9272, showers, laundry, trailer waste disposal, groceries, restaurant/lounge, $$$.
Located at junction of I-84 and State 207.

FORT HENRIETTA RV PARK (City) 🅰️ RV
7 units w/hookups for water/elec./sewer plus tent area, information (503)376-8411, showers, wheelchair access, fishing, trailer waste disposal, pets okay, open year round, $$-$$$.
Leave I-84 on exit #188 and go .5 mile south to Echo and park.

HAT ROCK CAMPGROUND (Private)
70 units - 27 w/hookups for water/elec./sewer, 33 w/water & elec., plus 10 tent sites, reservations - (503)567-4188, showers, pool, trailer waste disposal, river, boat launch, fishing, $$$.
Take US 395 north 5 miles, US 730 east 8 miles, and Hat Rock State Park Rd. north 1 mile.

BOARDMAN

BOARDMAN MARINA PARK (Private)
63 units w/full hookups, tents okay, trailers to 40', pull thrus, reservations (503)481-7217, showers, laundry, wheelchair access, trailer waste disposal, on Columbia River, boat launch, fishing, hiking, pets okay, open mid March thru mid Dec., $$$. Located just off I-84, at exit #164.

FRONTIER COURT (Private) [RV]
7 units w/full hookups, no tents, trailers to 60', res. (503)481-2356, showers, laundry, wheelchair access, pets okay, $$$. Located just south of I-84, at exit #164.

PENDLETON

BROOKE TRAILER COURT (Private) [RV]
22 sites w/hookups for water/elec./sewer plus 6 w/water & elec., reservations - (503)276-5353, showers, laundry, $$$$. Leave I-84 on exit #210, take State 11 northeast .8 mile, SE Court Ave. west 2.5 miles, and SE 8th St. north 2 blocks.

LUCKY SEVEN TRAILER PARK (Tribal)
26 units w/full hookups, tents okay, reservations (503)276-5564, trailers to 70', playground, pets extra, open year round. Follow Old Mission Hwy. east 5 miles.

RV PARK (Private) [RV]
32 RV sites w/full hookups, trailers to 40', information - (503)276-5408, laundry, playground, no dogs, $$$. I-84 to exit #210, take State 11 to Byers Ave. - 1500 SE Byers.

(South of Pendleton)

EMIGRANT SPRINGS (Oregon State Park) [A] [RV]
51 units - 18 w/water/elec./sewer, 33 tent sites, plus group area, trailers to 60', showers, Oregon Trail display, $$-$$$. Take I-84 southeast 26 miles.

INDIAN LAKE CAMPGROUND (Tribal) [A] [RV]
42 units w/hookups for water, tents okay, res. (503)443-3338, on Indian Lake - elec. motors only, boat rentals, fishing, hiking, horse trails, pets okay, year round - no water Oct. - March, $$. US 395 south to Pilot Rock, E. Birch Cr. Rd. southeast 19 miles.

ELGIN

MINAM (Oregon State Park) [A] [RV]
12 primitive sites, maximum site 71', picnic area, fishing, $$. Take State 82 northeast 15 miles.

ENTERPRISE

OUTPOST RV PARK (Private)
40 RV sites w/water/elec./sewer, reservation information - (503)426-4027, showers, elev. 3500', $$$$.
Take State 3 north .5 mile.

JOSEPH

BLACKHORSE (Hells Canyon Nat'l Rec. Area)
16 units, trailers to 32', river, fishing, hiking, elev. 4000', $.
Take State 350 east 7.7 miles, and FSR 39 southeast 28.7 miles.

HIDDEN (Hells Canyon Nat'l Rec. Area)
13 units, trailers to 32', river, fishing, hiking, elev. 4400', $.
Take State 350 east 7.7 miles, FSR 39 southeast 28.8 miles, and FSR 3960 southwest 7 miles.

INDIAN CROSSING (Hells Canyon Nat'l Rec. Area)
14 units, trailers to 32', river, fishing, horse ramp, elev. 4500', $.
Take State 350 east 7.7 miles, FSR 39 southeast 28.8 miles, and FSR 3960 southwest 8.8 miles.

OLLOKOT (Hells Canyon Nat'l Rec. Area)
12 units, trailers to 32', river, fishing, elev. 4000', $.
Take State 350 east 7.7 miles, and FSR 39 southeast 28.8 miles.

WALLOWA LAKE (Oregon State Park)
210 units - 121 w/hookups for water/elec./sewer, 89 tent sites, plus group area, mail reservations available, maximum site 90', showers, wheelchair access, picnic area, trailer waste disposal, boating, fishing, swimming, trails/Eagle Cap Wilderness, $$-$$$.
Follow Wallowa Lake Rd. south 6 miles.

HEPPNER

ANSON WRIGHT PARK (Morrow County)
30 units - 16 w/hookups for water/elec./sewer plus 14 tent sites, trailers to 30', showers, wheelchair access, picnic area, playground, stream, fishing - handicap accessible, hiking, rockhounding, open mid-May thru mid-Nov., elev. 2300', $$.
Follow State 207 southwest 26 miles.

CUTSFORTH PARK (Morrow County)
35 units - 20 w/hookups for water/elec./sewer plus 15 tent sites, trailers to 30', showers, wheelchair access, picnic area, playground, lake, fishing - handicap accessible, hiking, open mid-May thru mid-Nov., elev. 3400', $$.
Take State 207 southwest 2 miles, and Willow Creek Hwy. southeast 20 miles.

LA GRANDE

HILGARD JUNCTION (Oregon State Park)
18 campsites, maximum site 30', wheelchair access, trailer waste disposal, rafting, fishing, OR Trail display, open year round, $$.
Take I-84 northwest 8 miles.

HOT LAKE RV RESORT (Private)
100 pull thrus w/water/elec./sewer plus tent area, (503) 963-5253, trailers to 90', showers, laundry, wheelchair access, pool, trailer waste disposal, fishing, hiking, pets okay, $$$$.
I-84 to exit #265, State 203 southeast 5 miles, .3 mile to resort.

LA GRANDE RENDEZVOUS RV PARK (Private)
66 RV units w/water/elec./sewer, (503)962-0909, max. 70', showers, wheelchair access, pets okay, year round, $$$$-$$$$$.
Located at 2632 Bearco Loop.

SUNDOWNER MOBILE HOME PARK (Private)
24 trailer sites w/water/elec./sewer, reservations - (503)963-2648, showers, laundry, trailer waste disposal, elev. 2800', $$$.
Take State 82 east .3 mile, and Holmes St. south .2 mile.

UNION

CATHERINE CREEK (Oregon State Park)
18 units, maximum site 30', picnic area, fishing, $$.
Follow State 203 southeast 8 miles .

UKIAH

UKIAH-DALE FOREST (Oregon State Park)
25 units, trailers to 25', on N. Fork John Day River, fishing, $$.
Take US 395 southwest 3 miles.

DALE

MEADOWBROOK RV PARK (Private)
14 units w/elec., res. - (503)421-3104, showers, trailer waste disposal, groceries, propane, fishing, hiking, elev. 4000', $$$.
Follow US 395 south to milepost #71 and campground.

HAINES

ANTHONY LAKE (Wallowa-Whitman NF)
37 units, trailers to 22', ice, snack bar, small lake - no motors, boat launch & rental, swimming, fishing, hiking, wheelchair access includes trails & fishing, elev. 7100', $.

Follow the Elkhorn Scenic Byway northwest 17 miles, and FSR 73 west 7 miles.

GRANDE RONDE LAKE (Wallowa-Whitman NF)
8 units plus group area, trailers to 18', small lake - no motors, boat launch, swimming, fishing, elev. 7200', $.
Follow the Elkhorn Scenic Byway northwest 17 miles, FSR 73 west 8.5 miles, and FSR 43 northwest .5 mile.

MUD LAKE (Wallowa-Whitman NF)
8 units, trailers to 18', small lake, boating, swimming, fishing, periodic mosquito problems, elev. 7100', $.
Follow the Elkhorn Scenic Byway northwest 17 miles, and FSR 73 west 7.3 miles.

HALFWAY

LAKE FORK (Hells Canyon Nat'l Rec. Area)
10 sites, trailers to 22', stream, fishing, hiking, elev. 3200', $.
State Highway 86 east 9.2 miles, FSR 39 north 8.3 miles.

RICHLAND

EAGLE VALLEY RV/MH PARK (Private)
76 units - 25 w/full hookups, 16 w/water/elec./cable tv, plus 35 tent sites, reservations - (503)893-6161, showers, laundry, wheelchair access, playground, trailer waste disposal, $$-$$$.
Take State 86 east .2 mile - located near milepost #42.

HEWITT PARK (Baker County)
38 units - 17 w/hookups for water & elec., 16 w/out hookups, plus 5 tent sites, trailers to 32', flush toilets, wheelchair access - includes fishing dock, river, boat launch, fishing, hiking, open mid March thru mid Nov., pets okay, $$-$$$.
Follow signs at east end of town for 2.5 miles to park.

BAKER CITY

LARIAT MOTEL & RV PARK (Private)
6 RV sites w/full hookups, information - (503)523-6381, $$$.
Located at 880 Elm St.

MOUNTAIN VIEW TRAV-L-PARK (Private)
72 units - 60 w/full hookups plus 12 tent sites, reservations - (503)523-4824, showers, laundry, trailer waste disposal, swimming pool, playground, groceries, propane, $$$-$$$$.
Leave I-84 at exit #304, travel west .5 mile on Campbell, north 1 mile on Cedar, and west 1 mile on Hughes Ln.

OREGON TRAILS WEST RV (Private)
62 units - 51 w/hookups for water/elec./sewer, 7 w/water & elec., plus 4 tent sites, trailers to 40', pull thrus, reservations (503)523-3236, showers, laundry, horseshoe pits, groceries, propane, gas, pets okay, $$-$$$.
Campground is located just off I-84, at exit #302.

(Southwest of Baker City)

SUMPTER PINE RV PARK (Private)
10 units w/full hookups, tents okay, reservations (503)894-2328, trailers to 60', fishing, hiking, pets okay, open year round, $$$.
State 7 southwest 25 miles, Sumpter Rd. north 2 miles.

UNION CREEK (Wallowa-Whitman NF)
70 campsites - 24 w/hookups for water/elec./sewer, 34 standard units, 12 tent sites, plus group area, trailers to 22', flush toilets, wheelchair access, trailer waste disposal, on Phillips Reservoir, ice, firewood, bait, boat launch/rentals & gasoline, swimming, fishing, water skiing, hiking, bicycling, elev. 4100', $$-$$$.
Take State 7 southwest 20 miles.

SPRAY

ASHER'S RV PARK (Private)
20 campsites w/elec., tents okay, reservations - (503)934-2712, play area, hiking, fishing, fossil area, $$.
State 19 southeast to Kimberly - near the John Day Fossil Beds.

BULL PRAIRIE (Umatilla NF)
28 units, trailers to 32', picnic area, on Bull Prairie Lake, fishing, trail, elev. 4000', $.
State 207 northeast 14.5 miles, FSR 2039 northeast 3 miles.

LONG CREEK

HITCHING POST TRAILER COURT (Private)
19 units w/hookups for water/elec./sewer plus tent area, reservations (503)421-3043, trailers to 50', showers, laundry, propane, trailer waste disposal, pets okay, open year round, $$.
Located right in town - 2 blocks from the store.

JOHN DAY

CLYDE HOLLIDAY (Oregon State Park)
30 campsites w/elec., maximum site 60', showers, wheelchair access, picnic area, trailer waste disposal, fishing, $$-$$$.
Take US 26 west 7 miles.

DEPOT PARK (Prairie City)

16 units w/hookups for water/elec./sewer plus 9 tent sites, information (503)820-3605, showers, wheelchair access, trailer waste disposal, hiking, open May thru Oct., pets okay, $$-$$$.
Take US 26 west 13 miles to Prairie City and follow signs.

JOHN DAY TRAILER PARK (Private)

5 units w/hookups for water/elec./sewer, no tents, reservations (503)575-1557, trailers to 60', showers, laundry, near John Day River, small pets okay, restrooms closed in winter, $$$.
Located in John Day, at 660 W. Main.

UNITY

UNITY LAKE (Oregon State Park)

21 units w/hookups for elec., maximum site 60', wheelchair access, picnic area, trailer waste disposal, boat launch, swimming, fishing, elev. 4000', $$-$$$.
Take US 26 northwest 2.5 miles.

UNITY MOTEL & TRAILER PARK (Private)

10 trailer sites w/hookups for water/elec./sewer, reservations - (503)446-3431, showers, laundry, trailer waste disposal, $$.
Follow US 26 to the east end of town and park.

HUNTINGTON

FAREWELL BEND (Oregon State Park)

96 units - 53 w/hookups for elec, 43 primitive campsites, plus group sites, maximum site 56', showers, wheelchair accessible, picnic area, trailer waste disposal, river, boat launch, fishing, swimming, Oregon Trail display, open year round, $$-$$$.
Take I-84 southeast 5 miles.

SPRING (BLM)

14 sites, river, boat ramp, rough road, elev. 2500', $.
Take Snake River Rd. northeast 4 miles.

PAULINA

SUGAR CREEK (Ochoco NF)

11 units, trailers to 32', fishing, swimming, hiking, elev. 4000', $.
Take Paulina-Suplee Rd. east 3.5 miles, Beaver Creek Rd. north 6.5 miles, and FSR 58 east 1.8 miles.

WOLF CREEK (Ochoco NF)

11 units, trailers to 22', elev. 5700', $.
Take Paulina-Suplee Rd. east 3.5 miles, Beaver Creek Rd. north 6.6 miles, and FSR 42 north 1.6 miles to campground road.

ONTARIO

COUNTRY CAMPGROUNDS (Private)
15 units w/hookups for water/elec./sewer, tents okay, reservations - (503)889-6042, showers, laundry, trailer waste disposal, hiking, fishing, $$.
Located in town, at 660 Sugar Ave.

IDLE WHEELS VILLAGE (Private) [RV]
6 units w/hookups for water/elec./sewer, no tents, reservations - (503)889-8433, showers, laundry, trailer waste disposal, $$$.
Located in town, at 198 SE 5th St.

VALE

PROSPECTOR TRAVEL TRAILER PARK (Private)
34 units w/hookups for water/elec./sewer, reservations - (503) 473-3879, showers, laundry, trailer waste disposal, $$$-$$$$.
Take US 26 north .1 mile to Hope St. - park is 1 block east.

WESTERNER RV PARK (Private)
15 units w/hookups for water/elec./sewer - some have cable tv, tents okay, reservation information - (503)473-3947, showers, laundry, trailer waste disposal, river, fishing, $$.
Located at the junction of US 20 and US 26.

(West of Vale)

BULLY CREEK RESERVOIR (Malheur County)
66 units - 64 w/hookups for elec., information - (503)473-2969, showers, trailer waste disposal, lake, boat launch, fishing, $$.
Follow Graham Blvd. west 9 miles to reservoir and park.

(South of Vale)

LAKE OWYHEE (Oregon State Park) [A] [RV]
40 units - 10 w/elec. plus 30 tent sites, maximum site 55', showers, trailer waste disposal, boat launch, fishing, $$-$$$.
Follow Lake Owyhee State Park Rd south 41 miles.

LAKE OWYHEE RESORT (Private) [A] [RV]
61 units w/hookups for water & elec., trailers to 35', reservations - (503)339-2444, groceries, lake, boat launch & rental, tackle shop, swimming, fishing, open April thru Nov., $$.
Follow Lake Owyhee State Park Rd. south 38 miles.

SUCCOR CREEK (Oregon State Park)
19 units, no drinking water, picnic area, hiking, rockhounding, wildlife viewing area, colorful rock formations, $$.

Take Lake Owyhee State Park Rd. south 15 miles, go east 2 miles to State 201 and head south 13 miles south to Succor Creek State Recreation Area Rd. - park is southwest 16.5 miles.

JUNTURA

CHUKAR PARK (BLM)
16 units, swimming, hiking trails, elev. 3100', $.
Take US 20 west 4 miles, and Beulah Res. Rd. north 6 miles.

OASIS CAFE/MOTEL/RV PARK (Private)
22 trailer sites w/hookups for water/elec./sewer, reservation information - (503)277-3605, river, fishing, elev. 2900', $$$.
Located right on US 20, in Juntura.

BURNS

BROADWAY MOBILE HOME PARK (Private)
20 units w/hookups for water/elec./sewer, tents okay, information (503)573-6332, showers, laundry, store, trailer waste disposal, river, fishing, pets okay, open year round, $$$.
Located at 1318 N. Broadway.

R & L MOBILE HOME PARK (Private)
42 units w/full hookups plus tent area, trailers to 70', information (503)573-3955, pull thrus, showers, laundry, trailer waste disposal, pets okay, open year round, $$-$$$.
Take US 395/20 south 2 miles to Hines - at 12671 Hwy. 20.

SANDS OVERNIGHT TRAILER PARK (Private)
26 units - 10 w/hookups for water/elec./sewer plus 6 tent sites, reservations - (503)573-7010, showers, trailer waste disposal, pets okay, $$.
Take US 395/20 south 1 mile to park.

VILLAGE RV PARK (Private)
47 units - 43 w/hookups for water/elec./sewer plus 4 w/out hookups, no tents, reservation information - (503)573-7640, showers, laundry, playground, propane, river, fishing, pets okay, open year round, $$$-$$$$.
Take US 395/20 northeast to Seneca Dr. - at 1273 Seneca Dr.

(Northwest of Burns)

DELINTMENT LAKE (Ochoco NF)
24 units, trailers to 32', well water, wheelchair accessible toilets and fishing dock, boat launch, pets okay, elev. 5600', $$.
Go northwest on FSR 47 for 15 miles, and FSR 41 for approximately 30 miles to lake and campground.

EMIGRANT (Ochoco NF)
6 units, trailers to 22', well water, stream, fishing, pets okay, $.
Go northwest on FSR 47 for 15 miles, and FSR 41 for 20 miles.

FALLS (Ochoco NF)
5 units, trailers to 22', well water, stream, fishing, pets okay, $.
Go northwest on FSR 47 for 15 miles, and FSR 41 for 18 miles.

(East of Burns)

CRYSTAL CRANE HOT SPRINGS CAMP (Private)
6 units w/hookups for elec. plus large tent area, reservations
(503)493-2312, showers, laundry, wheelchair accessible, hot tub,
snack bar, pond, hiking, pets okay, $-$$$.
Take State 78 east 25 miles.

FRENCHGLEN

STEENS MT. RESORT/CAMPER CORRAL (Private)
75 sites - 32 w/hookups for water/elec./sewer, 37 w/water &
elec., plus large group tent area, some pull thrus, reservations -
(503)493-2415, showers, laundry, fire pits, trailer waste disposal,
groceries, propane, hiking, pets okay, elev. 4100', $$-$$$.
Located just south of the Frenchglen Hotel.

(Southeast of Frenchglen)

FISH LAKE (BLM)
20 units, trailers to 24', lake - stocked w/trout, boat dock,
swimming, fishing, hiking trails, elev. 7400', $.
Follow Steens Mountain Loop east 17 miles.

JACKMAN PARK (BLM)
4 units, water, hiking, bird watching, elev. 7700', $.
Follow Steens Mountain Loop east 20 miles.

PAGE SPRINGS (BLM)
30 units, trailers to 24', water, borders Malheur Wildlife Refuge,
river, fishing, hiking, open year round - water May thru Oct.,
elev. 4339', $.
Located 4 miles southeast of Frenchglen, on the Blitzen River.

ADEL

ADEL STORE & RV PARK (Private)
7 trailer sites w/hookups for water/elec./sewer, no tents,
reservations - (503)947-3850, groceries, nearby fishing, located
25 miles south of Hart National Antelope Refuge, $$.
This park is located in right Adel, next to grocery store.

WASHINGTON'S CAMPGROUNDS

Tenters will enjoy Washington's wealth of natural campsites; those traveling by RV will be thrilled with its luxurious resorts. Everyone will find plenty of places to choose from, no matter where their travels take them. For simplicity, the same four sections have been used in organizing both state's campgrounds.

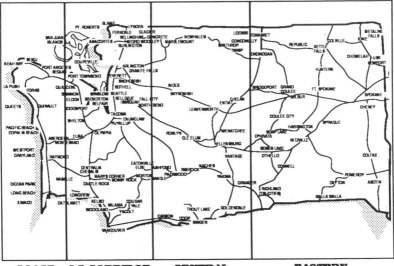

COAST   I-5 CORRIDOR   CENTRAL   EASTERN

The Washington Coast experience
The northern portion of Washington's Pacific Ocean coastline harbors America's last unspoiled wilderness beach. Together, the Olympic National Park and Olympic National Forest protect most of the north coast's best features. This area has lush rain forests, old growth forests, wildlife refuges, great whale watching, hiking trails and high-mountain lakes.

Along the southern Washington coast you'll encounter the world's longest driveable beach, a couple of wonderful old forts, aging lighthouses, colorful cranberry bogs, charter fishing boats and lots of great beachcombing areas.

Why to spend time in Washington's I-5 Corridor
A journey along I-5 provides access to several of the state's best-known attractions. These include Mt. St. Helens, where you can see an active volcano up close; Mt. Rainier

National Park, which protects the 14,410' Mt. Rainier; Puget Sound; the spectacular San Juan Islands; and the start of the luscious Cascade Loop.

History buffs will enjoy Port Townsend, Coupeville, Snohomish and Fort Lewis. The I-5 corridor is also where you'll find Olympia and Seattle. At 55-65 mph it all goes by in a quick blur, but anyone taking the time to leave the freeway will find lots to see and plenty of great camping areas.

Reasons to visit Central Washington
Heading east over the Cascade Mountains, toward central Washington, you'll find a slightly drier climate. These mountains do not run due north and south, so you'll find some of the cities in this section are actually on the western slopes.

The full glory of the Cascade Loop unfolds here. Most of the land it passes is protected by National Forests and Parks. Along the way, you'll have the chance to visit pristine wilderness areas, hike a multitude of trails, cruise a 55-mile long lake and watch bald eagles. A stop in the town of Winthrop is like a trip to the old west; Leavenworth resembles a Bavarian village.

Things to do in Eastern Washington
In eastern Washington you'll find a dry, desert climate. That's probably why some of this region's most popular campgrounds are those along the Snake, Columbia and Pend Oreille Rivers. Lake Conconully, Roosevelt Lake and Potholes Reservoir are also good places to cool off.

This section is the site of the state's largest limestone cave, the reconstructed 1880 Fort Spokane and the tragic Whitman Mission. Dry Falls and the Ginkgo Petrified Forest provide a unique opportunity to look back at prehistoric America. Spokane is this region's largest city and offers a wide range of recreational opportunities.

Camping in Washington is a great way to spend your vacation.

WASHINGTON COAST CAMPGROUNDS

See Page

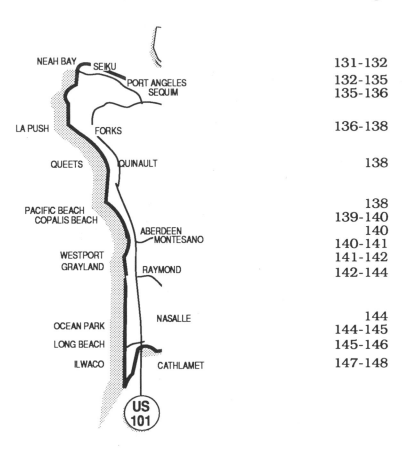

	See Page
NEAH BAY / SEIKU	131-132
PORT ANGELES	132-135
SEQUIM	135-136
LA PUSH / FORKS	136-138
QUEETS / QUINAULT	138
	138
PACIFIC BEACH	139-140
COPALIS BEACH	140
ABERDEEN / MONTESANO	140-141
WESTPORT	141-142
GRAYLAND / RAYMOND	142-144
	144
NASALLE / OCEAN PARK	144-145
LONG BEACH	145-146
ILWACO / CATHLAMET	147-148

NEAH BAY

CAPE FLATTERY RESORT (Tribal)
6 units w/hookups for water/elec./sewer plus tent area,
reservations (800)377-9439, trailers to 70', showers, laundry,
game room, play area, pets okay, open year round, $$-$$$.
Located right in Neah Bay - follow signs.

CAPE MOTEL & RV PARK (Private)
54 units w/hookups for water & elec. plus tent area, reservations
(360)645-2250, trailers to 70', showers, laundry, trailer waste
disposal, fishing, hiking, pets okay, open year round, $$$-$$$$.
Located in Neah Bay, just past the museum on Bayview Ave.

HOBUCK BEACH PARK (Private)
28 units, tents okay, reservations (360)645-2422, trailers to 30',
fishing, hiking, $$.
Located 3 miles southwest of town, on bay.

TYEE MOTEL & RV PARK (Private)
20 pull thrus w/hookups for water/elec./sewer, tents okay,
reservations (360)645-2223, trailers to 30', showers, trailer waste
disposal, fishing, pets okay, open year round, $$$.
Located right in Neah Bay.

SEIKU

BAYVIEW RV PARK (Private)
39 units w/full hookups plus tent area, reservations (360)963-
2750, trailers to 40', showers, laundry, wheelchair access,
fishing, pets okay, open year round, $$-$$$.
Located right in Sekiu, on Airport Rd.

COHO RESORT (Private)
150 units - 44 w/full hookups, 50 w/water & elec., plus 56 tent
sites, information (360)963-2333, trailers to 70', showers,
laundry, ice, trailer waste disposal, fishing, boat launch/rental &
gas, pets okay, open March thru Oct., $$-$$$.
Located at Sekiu's east end.

CURLEY'S RESORT (Private)
12 RV sites w/full hookups, reservations (360)963-2281, trailers
to 22', showers, fishing, pets okay, open April thru Oct., $$$.
Located right in Sekiu.

OLSON'S RESORT (Private)
190 units - 30 w/hookups for water/elec./sewer, 10 w/elec.,
plus 150 w/out hookups, tents okay, information (360)963-2311,
trailers to 40', showers, laundry, wheelchair access, groceries,
fishing, boat launch/rental & gas, open year round, $$-$$$.
Located right in Sekiu.

SURFSIDE CAMPLAND (Private)
20 units - 10 w/full hookups plus 10 tent sites, reservations (360)963-2723, trailers to 40', showers, laundry, trailer waste disposal, fishing, pets okay, open May thru Sept., $$-$$$.
Located right in Sekiu.

VAN RIPER'S RESORT & RV PARK (Private)
52 units - 42 w/hookups for water & elec. plus 10 tent sites, information (360)963-2334, showers, wheelchair access, snacks, ice, trailer waste disposal, fishing, boat launch & rental, salmon charters, pets okay, open March thru Sept., $$-$$$.
Located right in Sekiu.

(West of Seiku)

PILLAR POINT (County)
37 primitive sites, flush toilets, picnic shelter, small-boat launch & dock, fishing, open May thru Sept., $$.
Take State 112 west of Seiku 7 miles.

TRETTEVIKS TRAILER PARK (Private)
48 units - 28 w/hookups for water/elec./sewer plus 20 tent sites, information (360)963-2688, trailers to 70', laundry, swimming, fishing, pets okay, open mid April thru Sept., $$$.
Take State 112 west of Seiku 3 miles.

(East of Seiku)

MURALT'S MH/RV/CABINS (Private)
8 units w/full hookups plus 3 tent sites, reservations (360)963-2394, trailers to 40', showers, laundry, fishing, hiking, pets okay, open year round, $-$$$$.
Located 4 miles east of Seiku, in Clallam Bay.

SAM'S TRAILER & RV PARK (Private)
26 units - 20 w/hookups for water/elec./sewer plus 6 tent sites, reservation information - (360)963-2402, maximum site 40', 8 pull thrus, showers, laundry, ocean access, boat launch & moorage, fishing, pets okay, open year round, $$-$$$.
Located 4 miles east of Seiku, at the east end of Clallam Bay.

PORT ANGELES

AL'S RV PARK (Private)
35 units w/full hookups plus tent area, reservations (360)457-9844, trailers to 40', pull thrus, showers, laundry, wheelchair access, game room, playground, trailer waste disposal, nearby fishing & hiking, pets okay, open year round, $$$-$$$$.
US 101 east 1.5 miles, Lee's Creek Rd. north .3 mile.

ELMER'S TRAILER PARK (Private)
12 units w/hookups for water/elec./sewer, no tents, reservations (360)457-4392, trailers to 70', pets okay, open year round, $$$.
Follow US 101 east 1.5 miles.

HEART O' THE HILLS (Olympic Nat'l Park)
105 units, trailers to 21', wheelchair access, hiking, open year round, elev. 1807', $$.
Leave US 101 on Race St., and follow south 6 miles.

PEABODY CREEK RV PARK (Private)
36 units w/hookups for water/elec./sewer plus tent area, reservations (800)392-2361, trailers to 35', showers, laundry, propane, creek, pets okay, open year round, $$-$$$$.
Located in Port Angeles - at 127 South Lincoln.

WELCOME INN TRAILER & RV PARK (Private)
75 trailer sites w/full hookup, reservations (360)457-1553, trailers to 70', pull thrus, showers, laundry, wheelchair access, trailer waste disposal, pets okay, open year round, $$$$.
Located near the west end of Port Angeles, on US 101.

(West of Port Angeles)

ALTAIRE (Olympic Nat'l Park)
30 campsites, trailers to 21', handicap accessible restrooms, on Elwha River, elev. 450', open June thru Sept., $$.
US 101 west 7 miles, Olympic Hot Springs Rd. south 5 miles.

CAROL'S CRESCENT BEACH RV PARK (Private)
60 units w/hookups for water/elec./sewer, tents okay, reservations (360)928-3344, trailers to 35', showers, laundry, ocean beach, swimming, fishing, pets okay, seasonal, $$$$.
US 101 west 5 miles, State 112 west 6.5 miles to Joyce, Crescent Beach Rd. north 3 miles.

ELWHA (Olympic Nat'l Park)
41 campsites, trailers to 21', handicap accessible restrooms, on Elwha River, hiking, elev. 390', open year round, $$.
US 101 west 7 miles, Olympic Hot Springs Rd. south 3 miles.

FAIRHOLM CAMPGROUND (Olympic Nat'l Park)
87 units, trailers to 21', handicap access, trailer waste disposal, on Crescent Lake, swimming, fishing, boat launch & rental, hiking, open year round, elev. 580', $$.
Take US 101 west 26 miles.

HARRISON BEACH (Private)
10 tent/trailer units, information (360)928-3006, on water, fishing, hiking, no pets, open year round, $$$.
Take US 101 west 5 miles, State 112 west 15 miles, West Lyre River Rd. to Harrison Beach Rd. and camp.

INDIAN VALLEY MOTEL/RV/CAMP (Private)
8 units w/full hookups plus tent area, (360)928-3266, trailers to 30', shower, restaurant, pets okay, open year round, $$-$$$.
Take US 101 west 13 miles.

KLAHOWYA (Olympic NF)
55 units, trailers to 30', reservations (800)280-2267, flush toilets, handicap access, river, ramp, fishing, hiking, elev. 800', $-$$.
Take US 101 west 40 miles to milepost #212 and campground.

LINCOLN PARK (City)
35 units, trailers to 25', information (360)452-2928, flush toilets, showers, wheelchair access, pets okay, open summer only, $$.
Take US 101 west 5 miles, and State 112 just west of junction.

LYRE RIVER PARK (Private)
90 units - 55 w/hookups for water/elec./sewer, 18 w/water & elec., plus tent sites, reservations (360)928-3436, showers, laundry, wheelchair access, groceries, trailer waste disposal, on Lyre River - inner tubing, fishing, hiking, pets okay, $$$-$$$$.
Take US 101 west 5 miles, State 112 west 15 miles, and West Lyre River Rd. north .5 mile.

SALT CREEK RECREATION AREA (County)
90 units, information (360)928-3441, trailers to 70', flush toilets, showers, wheelchair access, trailer waste disposal, boat ramp, swimming, fishing, hiking, pets okay, open year round, $$.
Take US 101 west 5 miles, State 112 west 9 miles, and Camp Hayden Rd. north 3.5 miles.

SHADOW MOUNTAIN (Private)
60 units - 40 w/hookups for water/elec./sewer plus 20 tent sites, reservations (360)928-3043, trailers to 70', showers, laundry, wheelchair access, playground, store, propane, gas, trailer waste disposal, at Crescent Lake, boat launch, swimming, fishing, hiking, pets okay, open year round, $$$-$$$$.
Take US 101 west 15 miles.

SHADY TREE RV PARK (Private)
33 units w/hookups for water/elec./sewer plus grassy tent area, reservations (360)452-7054, trailers to 40', showers, wheelchair access, propane, pets okay, open year round, $$$-$$$$.
Take US 101 west 5 mile, and State 112 west .5 mile.

SILVER KING RESORT (Private)
70 units w/hookups for water & elec., tents okay, information (360)963-2800, trailers to 70', showers, laundry, wheelchair access, groceries, propane, gas, trailer waste disposal, fishing, boat launch & moorage, pets okay, open year round, $$-$$$.
Take US 101 west 5 miles, and State 112 west 30 miles to Jim Creek Recreation Area and resort.

SOL DUC HOT SPRINGS RESORT (Private)
20 units w/hookups for water & elec., no tents, reservations (360)327-3583, no restrooms, trailers to 28', hot springs extra, restaurant, groceries, pets extra, open mid May thru Sept., $$$$. US 101 west 28 miles, Soleduck River Rd. southeast 12 miles.

SOLEDUCK (Olympic Nat'l Park)
80 units, trailers to 21', handicap access, trailer waste disposal, on Soleduck River, swimming, fishing, hiking, elev. 1680', $$. US 101 west 28 miles, Soleduck River Rd. southeast 12 miles.

WHISKEY CREEK BEACH (Private)
50 units - 12 w/hookups for water & sewer plus 38 w/out hookups, tents okay, reservations (360)928-3489, trailers to 26', fishing, hiking, pets okay, open May thru Oct., $$-$$$. Take US 101 west 5 miles, State 112 west 9.5 miles, and Whiskey Creek Beach Rd. north to campground.

(East of Port Angeles)

CONESTOGA QUARTERS RV PARK (Private)
34 units w/hookups for water/elec./sewer, plus 11 w/out hookups, tents okay, reservations (800)808-4637, trailers to 40', showers, wheelchair access, playground, trailer waste disposal, charter fishing, pets okay, open year round, $$$-$$$$. Take US 101 east 7 miles, and Seibertt Creek Rd. 1 mile to park.

PORT ANGELES KOA (Private)
100 units - 20 w/full hookups, 50 w/water/elec./tv, plus 30 tent sites, (360)457-5916, trailers to 50', showers, laundry, wheelchair access, pool, playground, groceries, propane, trailer waste disposal, pets okay, open April thru Oct., $$$$-$$$$$. Take US 101 east 5 miles - located at O'Brien.

SEQUIM

RAINBOW'S END RV PARK (Private)
37 units w/full hookups plus tent area, (360)683-3863, trailers to 40', showers, laundry, wheelchair access, propane, trailer waste disposal, pets okay, open year round, $$$-$$$$. West of Sequim. US 101 west 1.5 miles.

SEQUIM BAY RESORT (Private)
43 units w/full hookups, (360)681-3853, trailers to 40', accessible showers, laundry, fishing, open year round, $$$$. Take West Sequim Bay Rd. northwest 2.5 miles.

SEQUIM WEST RV PARK & INN (Private)
29 units w/full hookups, no tents, reservations (800)528-4257, trailers to 65', showers, ice, pets okay, open year round, $$$$. Located at 740 West Washington (US 101).

(West of Sequim)

DUNGENESS RECREATION AREA (County)
65 units, information (360)683-5847, trailers to 40', showers, wheelchair access, playground, trailer waste disposal, pond, boat launch, swimming, fishing, hiking, open Feb. thru Oct., $$.
Take US 101 west 7 miles, and Kitchen Rd. north 4 miles.

SUNSHINE RV PARK (Private)
57 units w/hookups for water/elec./sewer plus tent area, reservations (360)683-4769, trailers to 40', pull thrus, showers, laundry, stream, pets okay, open year round, $$$-$$$$.
West of Sequim. US 101 west 4 miles.

(East of Sequim)

DUNGENESS FORKS (Olympic NF)
9 tent sites, stream, fishing, hiking elev. 1000', $.
US 101 east 4 miles, FSR 28 to FSR 2880, and south 7.5 miles.

EAST CROSSING (Olympic NF)
9 tent sites, stream, fishing, hiking, elev. 1200', $.
US 101 east 4 miles, FSR 28 to FSR 2860, and south 9 miles.

SEQUIM BAY (Washington State Park)
86 units - 26 w/hookups for water/elec./sewer plus 60 standard sites, trailers to 60', accessible showers, trailer waste disposal, boat launch, moorage buoys, fishing, scuba diving area, $-$$$.
Take US 101 east 4 miles.

SOUTH SEQUIM BAY RV PARK (Private)
30 units - 24 w/hookups for water/elec./sewer plus 6 w/water, tents okay, reservations (360)683-7194, trailers to 40', showers, trailer waste disposal, pets okay, open year round, $$-$$$.
US 101 east 5 miles, and Old Blyn Highway northeast .3 mile.

LA PUSH

LAPUSH OCEAN PARK (Tribal)
35 units - 15 w/hookups for water/elec./sewer plus 20 tent sites, reservations (800)487-1267, trailers to 50', showers, laundry, wheelchair access, propane, trailer waste disposal, ocean access, fishing, hiking, pets okay, open year round, $$$.
Located right in La Push.

MORA CAMPGROUND (Olympic Nat'l Park)
94 campsites, trailers to 21', handicap access, trailer waste disposal, ocean access, on Quinault River, swimming, fishing, hiking, open year round, $$.
Located right in La Push.

SHORELINE RESORT (Tribal)

55 units w/hookups for water & elec., no tents, reservations (800)487-1267, trailers to 50', showers, laundry, wheelchair access, surf fishing, hiking, pets okay, open year round, $$$$. Located right in La Push.

THREE RIVERS RESORT (Private)

24 units - 5 w/hookups for water/elec./sewer, 9 w/water & elec., plus 10 tent sites, reservations (360)374-5300, showers, laundry, playground, groceries, propane, restaurant, pets okay, $$-$$$. Take La Push Rd. east 6 miles.

FORKS

FORKS MOBILE HOME & RV PARK (Private)

7 trailer sites w/full hookups, reservations (360)374-5510, trailers to 32', laundry, pets okay, open year round, $$. Leave US 101 on Calawah Way and go east 3 blocks to park.

FORKS 101 RV PARK (Private)

56 units - 44 w/full hookups plus 12 tent sites, reservations (800)962-9964, trailers to 70', pull thrus, showers, laundry, no pets, open year round, $$$$. Located right in Forks, on US 101.

(North of Forks)

BEAR CREEK RV PARK & MOTEL (Private)

18 units w/hookups for water/elec./sewer, tents okay, reservations (360)327-3558, trailers to 40', showers, laundry, ice, restaurant, river, swimming, fishing, hiking, pets okay, $-$$$. Take US 101 north 15 miles - located near milepost #206.

OLD CHIEF'S MOBILE HOME PARK (Private)

27 units w/hookups for water/elec./sewer, tents okay, reservations (360)327-3247, trailers to 27', showers, laundry, wheelchair access, playfield, pets okay, open year round, $-$$. Take US 101 north 8 miles to Beaver and park.

(South of Forks)

BOGACHIEL (Washington State Park)

42 units - 6 w/hookups for water & elec. plus 36 standard sites, trailers to 35', flush toilets, showers, trailer waste disposal, on Bogachiel River, fishing, open year round, $-$$$. Take US 101 south 6 miles.

HOH RIVER (Olympic Nat'l Park)

89 units, trailers to 21', handicap access, trailer waste disposal, river, fishing, hiking, open year round, elev. 578', $$. Take US 101 south 14 miles, and Hoh River Rd. east 19 miles.

HOH RIVER RESORT & RV PARK (Private)
24 units - 20 w/full hookups plus 4 w/water & elec., tents okay, reservations (360)374-5566, showers, laundry, groceries, propane, on Hoh River, fishing, hiking, pets okay, $$-$$$.
Follow US 101 south 15 miles.

R & R SPORTS CENTER & RV PARK (Private)
7 units w/hookups for water/elec./sewer plus 4 w/water & elec., tents okay, reservations (360)374-9288, trailers to 35', showers, wheelchair access, pets okay, open year round, $$$.
Take US 101 south 13 miles, and Lower Hoh Rd. west 6 miles.

QUEETS

KALALOCH (Olympic Nat'l Park)
177 units, trailers to 21', handicap access, trailer waste disposal, ocean swimming, fishing, hiking, open year round, elev. 50', $$.
Take US 101 north of Queets 6 miles.

QUINAULT

FALLS CREEK (Olympic NF)
31 units, trailers to 16', flush toilets, wheelchair access, on Lake Quinault, boat ramp, swimming, fishing, hiking, $$-$$$.
Take South Shore Rd. northeast .2 mile.

GATTON CREEK (Olympic NF)
13 tent sites, on Lake Quinault, swimming, fishing, $$-$$$.
Take South Shore Rd. northeast .5 mile.

RAIN FOREST RESORT VILLAGE & RV PARK (Private)
31 units - some w/hookups for water/elec./sewer, no tents, information (360)288-2535, trailers to 38', showers, laundry, groceries, restaurant, on Lake Quinault, swimming, fishing, hiking, canoe rental, pets okay, open year round, $$$.
Take South Shore Rd. northeast 1.5 miles.

WILLABY (Olympic NF)
21 units, trailers to 16', flush toilets, on Lake Quinault, boat ramp, swimming, fishing, hiking, $$
Take South Shore Rd. northeast .5 mile.

PACIFIC BEACH

PACIFIC BEACH (Washington State Park)
138 units - 20 w/hookups for water & elec. plus 188 standard sites, trailers to 45', flush toilets, showers, trailer waste disposal, fishing, beachcombing, clamming, $$-$$$.
Located at Pacific Beach, just off State 109.

COPALIS BEACH

COPALIS BEACH RV PARK (Private)
43 units w/full hookups, 5 w/water & elec., plus tent area, reservations (800)867-2707, trailers to 40', showers, wheelchair access, playground, restaurant/lounge, trailer waste disposal, fishing, hiking, pets okay, open year round, $$-$$$$.
Located in Copalis Beach, on beach access road.

DRIFTWOOD ACRES OCEAN CAMP (Private)
25 units w/hookups for water/elec./sewer, 25 w/water & elec., plus large tent area, information (360)289-3484, trailers to 60', showers, fire pits, picnic tables, trailer waste disposal, river, fishing, pets okay, open Mem. Day thru Labor Day, $$$$-$$$$$.
Located on State 109, just north of the Copalis Beach bridge.

DUNES RV RESORT (Private)
29 units w/full hookups, 9 w/water & elec., plus 6 tent sites, (360)289-3873, trailers to 50', accessible showers, trailer waste disposal, fishing, hiking, pets okay, open year round, $$-$$$$.
Located on State 109, near milepost #20.5.

RIVERSIDE RV RESORT (Private)
67 units w/hookups for water/elec./sewer plus tent area, reservations (360)289-2111, showers, hot tub, trailer waste disposal, river, boat ramp, fishing, pets okay, open year round, $$$.
Located on State 109, just north of the Copalis Beach bridge.

ROD'S BEACH RESORT & RV PARK (Private)
80 units w/full hookups, no tents, reservations (360)289-2222, trailers to 40', showers, rec room, pool, playground, store, trailer waste disposal, fishing, pets okay, open March thru Oct., $$$.
On State 109, just south of Copalis Beach.

SHADE'S BY THE SEA (Private)
2 units w/full hookups, 33 w/water/elec./tv, plus 6 w/out hookups, (360)289-3358, showers, trailer waste disposal, $$$.
Located on State 109, just north of the Copalis Beach bridge.

TIDELANDS ON THE BEACH RV PARK (Private)
16 units w/hookups for water/elec./sewer, 39 w/water & elec., plus 50 tent sites, (360)289-8963, trailers to 40', showers, trailer waste disposal, pets okay, open year round, $$-$$$$.
Take State 109 south .6 mile.

(South of Copalis Beach)

BLUE PACIFIC MOTEL & RV PARK (Private)
19 units - 13 w/hookups for water/elec./sewer plus 6 w/water & elec., tents okay, reservations (360)289-2262, trailers to 38', showers, laundry, pets okay, open year round, $$$.
Take State 109 south of town 2.5 miles.

ILLAHEE RV PARK (Private)
35 units w/full hookups, 8 w/water & elec., plus 12 tent sites, (360)289-8795, trailers to 40', accessible showers, trailer waste disposal, fishing, pets okay, open year round, $$$-$$$$$.
Take State 109 south 5 miles, and State 115 south 3 miles to Ocean Shores' first beach access and park.

OCEAN CITY (Washington State Park)
29 units w/hookups for water/elec./sewer plus 149 campsites, group reservations (360)289-3553, trailers to 55', flush toilets, showers, disabled access, trailer waste disposal, fishing, $-$$$$.
Take State 109 south 5.5 miles.

SILVER MAPLE RV PARK (Private)
30 units w/full hookups plus 4 tent sites, reservations (360)289-0166, trailers to 40', showers, pets okay, open year round, $$$.
Take State 109 south 3.5 miles.

STURGEON TRAILER HARBOR (Private)
54 units w/hookups for water/elec./sewer plus 16 w/water & elec., no tents, reservations (360)289-2101, trailers to 35', showers, propane, horses & pets okay, open year round, $$-$$$.
Take State 109 south 3 miles to Ocean City and park.

ABERDEEN

ABERDEEN KOA (Private)
75 units w/full hookups plus 5 tent sites, reservations (800) 442-0101, trailers to 60', pull thrus, showers, wheelchair access, laundry, hot tub, game room, playground, groceries, propane, trailer waste disposal, fishing, hiking, pets okay, $$-$$$$.
Take State 105 southwest 1 mile.

ARTIC RV PARK (Private)
10 units w/full hookups plus 10 w/water/elec./tv, tents okay, reservations (360)533-4470, trailers to 70', showers, laundry, wheelchair access, trailer waste disposal, fishing, hiking, no big dogs, open year round, $$-$$$.
Take US 101 south to milepost #75 and park.

MONTESANO

COHO (Olympic NF)
58 campsites, trailers to 36', flush toilets, wheelchair access, on Wynoochee Lake, paved nature trail, elev. 900', $$.
Wynoochee Lake Rd. north 32 miles, FSR 23 north 1.5 miles.

LAKE SYLVIA (Washington State Park)
35 campsites plus group area, group reservations (360)249-3621, maximum site 30', flush toilets, showers, disabled access,

community kitchen, snack bar, groceries, trailer waste disposal, on lake, boat launch & rental, fishing, swimming, $-$$$.
Leave State 12 on the Lake Sylvia park road at Montesano.

SCHAFER (Washington State Park)　　　　　`A` `RV`
55 units - 6 w/hookups for water & elec. plus 47 standard sites, trailers to 40', flush toilets, showers, community kitchen, trailer waste disposal, on river, fishing, $-$$$.
Take State 12 east 5 miles, and Satsop River Rd. north 5 miles.

WESTPORT

COHO RV PARK (Private)　　　　　　　`RV`
76 units w/full hookups, reservations (800)572-0177, trailers to 60', pull thrus, showers, laundry, wheelchair access, ice, large meeting room w/kitchen, fishing & charter, crab pot & fish cleaning room, pets okay, open year round, $$$-$$$$.
Located in Westport, in the dock area.

CONNIE-LEE'S RV PARK (Private)　　　　`RV`
36 units w/hookups for water/elec./sewer, no tents, reservations (360)268-5555, trailers to 40', showers, laundry, wheelchair access, boat dock, fishing, hiking, pets okay, open year round.
Located at end of town, at 743 Neddie Rose Dr.

HAMMOND TRAILER PARK (Private)　　　`RV`
16 units w/hookups for water/elec./sewer, reservations (360)268-9645, trailers to 32', showers, laundry, nearby stores/restaurants/fishing, pets okay, open year round, $$.
From city center take Montesano St. south 1 mile - park is at 1845 Roberts Rd.

HARBOR RESORT (Private)　　　　　　`RV`
6 units w/full hookups, no tents, reservations (360)268-0169, showers, laundry, wheelchair access, store, trailer waste disposal, fishing, hiking, pets extra, open year round, $$$-$$$$.
Located at end of town, at 871 Neddie Rose Dr.

HOLAND CENTER RV PARK (Private)　　　`RV`
80 RV sites w/full hookups, reservations (360)268-9582, trailers to 38', showers, laundry, pets okay, open year round, $$$.
Located on State 105, 2 blocks off docks.

ISLANDER RV PARK (Private)　　　　　`RV`
55 units w/hookups for water/elec./sewer, no tents, reservations (360)268-9166, trailers to 40', pull thrus, showers, laundry, wheelchair access, ice, swimming pool, coffee shop, lounge, meeting room, waterfront sites, ocean access, fishing & charter, fish cleaning area, pets okay, open year round, $$$-$$$$.
On Revetment Dr., at northwest end of the boat basin.

JOLLY ROGERS (Private)
30 units w/full hookups, tents okay, reservations (360)268-0265, trailers to 40', showers, on jetty, harbor & surf fishing, pets okay, open year round, $$-$$$.
Located in the dock area, on the north side of the boat basin.

KILA HANA CAMPERLAND (Private)
70 units w/full hookups, 40 w/out hookups, plus 50 tent sites, reservations (360)268-9528, trailers to 60', pull thrus, showers, wheelchair access, rec hall, propane, trailer waste disposal, fishing, hiking, pets okay, open year round, $$-$$$.
Located 1 mile north of the State 105/105 spur intersection, at 931 S. Forrest Ave.

PACIFIC AIRE RV PARK (Private)
120 units w/full hookups plus large tent area, reservations (360) 268-0207, trailers to 40', showers, laundry, wheelchair access, pool, propane, pets okay, open year round, $$$-$$$$.
Located in dock area, at 1209 N. Montesano St.

PACIFIC MOTEL & RV PARK (Private)
80 units w/hookups for water/elec./sewer plus 20 tent sites, reservations (360)268-9325, trailers to 40', pull thrus, showers, heated pool, cable tv, rec room, open year round, $$$.
On State 105, just south of town.

TOTEM RV PARK (Private)
44 units w/full hookups, 24 w/water & elec., plus 7 w/out hookups, tents okay, reservations (360)268-0025, trailers to 40', showers, laundry, groceries, drive-in restaurant, trailer waste disposal, fishing, pets okay, open year round, $$-$$$.
Located in the dock area.

TWIN HARBORS (Washington State Park)
49 units w/hookups for water/elec./sewer plus 272 standard sites, mail reservations available, group area - reservations (360)268-9717, trailers to 35', flush toilets, showers, disabled access, trailer waste disposal, fishing, hiking, $-$$$$.
Located on State 105, 3 miles south of town.

GRAYLAND

GRAYLAND BEACH (Washington State Park)
60 units w/hookups for water/elec./sewer, mail reservations available, trailers to 40', flush toilets, showers, disabled access, self-guided trail, beachcombing, fishing, $-$$$$.
Located in Grayland, on State 105.

KENANNA RV PARK (Private)
90 pull thrus w/full hookups plus 20 tent sites, reservations (800)867-3515, showers, wheelchair access, laundry, rec room,

playfield, playground, groceries, ice, propane, trailer waste disposal, ocean access, sandy beach, fishing, pets okay, $$-$$$$.
Located on State 105, 2 miles south of town.

OCEAN GATE RESORT (Private)

48 units - 24 w/full hookups plus 24 tent sites, reservations (360)267-1956, trailers to 40', showers, playground, ocean access, surf fishing, pets okay, open year round, $$$.
Located in Grayland, on State 105.

TWIN SPRUCE RV PARK (Private)
49 units - 41 w/hookups for water/elec./sewer plus 8 w/water & elec., tents okay, reservations (800)438-1474, trailers to 70', showers, laundry, pets okay, open year round, $$$$.
Leave State 105 on Schmid Rd., park is east .1 mile.

WESTERN SHORES MOTEL /RV PARK (Private)

21 units w/hookups for water/elec./sewer, tents okay, reservations (360)267-6115, trailers to 40', showers, playground, nearby restaurant, pets okay, open year round, $-$$$.
Located in Grayland, on State 105.

(Southeast of Grayland)

BAYSHORE RV PARK (Private)
44 units w/full hookups plus 6 w/water & elec., reservations (360)267-2625, trailers to 40', showers, trailer waste disposal, ocean access, fishing, pets okay, open year round, $$$$.
Take State 105 south 8 miles, and Tokeland Rd. southeast 2 miles to Tokeland - located at 2941 Kindred.

WILLAPA RV PARK (Private)

14 units w/full hookups plus 2 tent sites, reservations (360)267-7710, trailers to 35', showers, laundry, wheelchair access, small store/deli, on bay, fishing, pets okay, open March thru Oct., $$$.
Take State 105 south 8 miles, and Tokeland Rd. southeast 2 miles to Tokeland and RV park.

RAYMOND

TIMBERLAND RV PARK (Private)
24 pull thrus w/hookups for water/elec./sewer plus tent area, reservations (360)942-3325, showers, pets okay, open year round, $$-$$$.
State 105 west .2 mile to Crescent St., park is 2 blocks south.

WILLAPA HARBOR GOLF & RV (Private)

20 units w/hookups for water & elec., no tents, reservations (360)942-2392, trailers to 70', showers, wheelchair access, golf, no pets, open year round, $$$.
Take Fowler St. off US 101 and follow 2 miles to golf course.

BAY CENTER KOA (Private)

10 units w/hookups for water/elec./sewer, 34 w/water & elec., 16 tent sites, plus bicycle camp w/shelter, reservations (360)875-6344, trailers to 40', showers, laundry, game room, small store, propane, playground, playfield, trailer waste disposal, on bay - sandy beach, fishing, hiking, pets & horses okay, open March thru Oct., $$$$-$$$$$.
Take US 101 southwest 15.5 miles, Bay Center Rd. west 3 miles.

BRUCEPORT PARK (City)

45 units - 9 w/hookups for water/elec./sewer, 6 w/water & elec., plus 30 tent sites, showers, laundry, picnic shelter, playground, groceries, beach access, open year round, $$.
Take US 101 south 11 miles.

SOUTH BEND MOBILE & RV PARK (Private)

10 units w/full hookups plus tent area, reservations (360)875-5165, trailers to 70', pull thrus, showers, laundry, trailer waste disposal, pets okay, open year round, $$-$$$.
Take US 101 south 5 miles to South Bend - park is located 4 blocks from downtown, at 524 Central.

NASALLE

CHRIS'S RV PARK & CAMPGROUND (Private)

100 units - 64 w/hookups for water & elec., 16 w/out hookups, plus 20 tent sites, reservations (360)777-8475, showers, laundry, picnic facilities, clubhouse w/tv, groceries & tackle, trailer waste disposal, on Columbia River, fishing, pets okay, $$-$$$.
Take State 401 south 9 miles.

NASALLE TRAILER COURT (Private)

24 trailer sites w/hookups for water/elec./sewer, no tents, reservations (360)484-3351, showers, laundry, $$$.
Located on State 4 just east of town.

SALMON CREEK ROADSIDE PARK (Private)

7 tent/trailer units, wheelchair access, creek, fishing, nature trail, nearby stores/restaurants, pets okay, open year round, $.
Located on State 4 at the east end of town.

OCEAN PARK

CLAM TIDE RV PARK (Private)

16 units w/hookups for water/elec./sewer plus 4 tent sites, reservations (360)665-3545, trailers to 36', showers, laundry, wheelchair access, near ocean, no dogs, open year round, $$$.
Located at 25210 Vernon Ave.

EVERGREEN COURT (Private)
30 units w/full hookups plus dry camp, tents okay, reservations (360)665-6351, showers, playground, trailer waste disposal, $$.
Take State 103 south 1 mile.

OCEAN AIRE TRAILER PARK (Private)
46 units w/full hookups, no tents, trailers to 35', reservations (360)665-4027, showers, laundry, well mannered pets okay, $$$.
Leave State 103 on 260th St., and go east .1 mile.

OCEAN PARK RESORT (Private)
94 units w/full hookups plus 6 w/water & elec., reservations (800)835-4634, showers, laundry, rec room, pool in summer, spa, playground, ice, propane, pets okay, open year round, $$$.
Leave State 103 on 259th St., and go east .1 mile.

WESTGATE RV PARK & MOTEL (Private)
36 units w/hookups for water/elec./sewer, no tents, reservations (360)665-4211, showers, ice, rec room, pets okay, $$$.
Take State 103 south 2 miles to Klipsan Beach.

LONG BEACH

ALOHA COURT (Private)
18 units w/full hookups plus 2 tent sites, reservations (360)642-2515, trailers to 40', showers, laundry, wheelchair access, trailer waste disposal, on Columbia River, fishing, hiking, pets okay, open year round, $$-$$$.
Located south of Long Beach, in Seaview, at 1701 30th St.

ANTHONY'S HOME COURT (Private)
25 units w/hookups for water/elec./sewer, reservations (360)642-2802, showers, laundry, pets okay, $$$.
Located at 1310 Pacific Highway North.

DRIFTWOOD RV PARK & MOTEL (Private)
44 units w/full hookups, 2 w/water & elec., plus 4 tent sites, reservations (360)642-2711, showers, handicap access, laundry, ice, near Columbia River & fishing, pets okay, $$$.
In Long Beach, on State 103.

OCEANIC CITY CENTER RV PARK (Private)
20 RV sites w/full hookups, reservations (360)642-3836, trailers to 40', showers, wheelchair access, open year round, $$$.
Located at the corner of Pacific and Fifth Sts.

PIONEER RV PARK (Private)
34 units w/full hookups, tents okay, reservations (360)642-3990, trailers to 35', showers, walk to ocean, hiking, near stores & restaurant, pets okay, open year round, $$$$.
On State 103, at north end of town.

SAND CASTLE RV PARK (Private) `RV`
38 units - 29 w/hookups for water/elec./sewer, no tents, reservations (360)642-2451, showers, laundry, $$$-$$$$.
On State 103, at north end of town.

SAND-LO MOTEL & TRAILER PARK (Private) `A` `RV`
15 units w/hookups for water/elec./sewer plus 4 tent sites - no fire pits, reservations (360)642-2600, showers, laundry, nearby groceries & restaurant, 4 blocks to beach, fish cleaning area, pets okay, $$$.
North of Long Beach. State 103 north 1 mile.

SOU'WESTER LODGE & TRAILER PARK (Private) `RV`
60 units w/hookups for water/elec./sewer/cable tv, reservation information - (360)642-2542, showers, laundry, ocean access, fishing, $$$.
Located south of Long Beach, in Seaview, on Seaview Beach Rd.

WILDWOOD SENIOR RV PARK (Private) `A` `RV`
50 units - 30 w/hookups for water/elec./sewer plus 20 tent sites, seniors only, reservations (360)642-2131, showers, trailer waste disposal, lake, fishing, pets okay, $$$$.
Take State 103 south to junction with US 101, US 101 east .5 mile, and Sandridge Rd. north .8 mile to park.

(North of Long Beach)

ANDERSEN'S RV PARK (Private) `A` `RV`
60 units w/full hookups plus 15 tent sites, reservations (800) 645-6795, trailers to 70', showers, laundry, playground, rec. hall, ice, propane, trailer waste disposal, nearby surf fishing, hiking, pets okay, open year round, $$$.
Take State 103 north 3.5 miles.

CRANBERRY RV & TRAILER PARK (Private) `RV`
20 units w/full hookups, no tents, adults only, reservations (360)642-2027, trailers to 40', pull thrus, showers, wheelchair access, rec room w/tv, ice, trailer waste disposal, walk to beach, fishing, hiking, pets okay, open March thru Oct., $$$.
Take State 103 north 3 miles, and Cranberry Rd. east .3 mile.

PACIFIC PARK TRAILER PARK (Private) `RV`
44 w/full hookups plus 6 w/water & elec., no tents, reservations (360)642-3253, showers, laundry, near ocean, pets okay, $$$.
Take State 103 north 2 miles.

PEGG'S RV PARK (Private)
30 units w/full hookups, no tents, reservations (360)642-2451, showers, laundry, rec room, ice, ocean access, pets okay, $$$.
Take State 103 north 4.5 miles.

ILWACO

BEACON CHARTERS & RV PARK (Private)
60 units - 40 w/full hookups plus 20 w/elec. only, no tents, reservations (360)642-2138, trailers to 40', showers, ice, on Columbia River, fishing & charters, hiking, nearby shops, pets okay, open year round, $$$.
Located in Ilwaco, at the east end of docks.

COVE RV PARK (Private)
40 units w/full hookups, no tents, reservations (360)642-3689, pull thrus, showers, laundry, trailer waste disposal, ocean access - by Baker Bay, fishing, pets okay, $$$.
Located in Ilwaco, at the west end of port area.

(South of Ilwaco)

CHINOOK COUNTY PARK (County)
100 campsites w/hookups, information (360)777-8442, showers, playground, on Columbia River, fishing, $-$$$.
Take US 101 southeast 5 miles to Chinook - park is located at east end of town.

FORT CANBY (Washington State Park)
250 campsites - 60 w/hookups for water/elec./sewer plus 190 standard units, mail reservations available, trailers to 45', flush toilets, showers, disabled access, trailer waste disposal, interpretive center, boat launch, fishing, ocean access, trails, pets okay, $-$$$$.
Follow signs southwest 2.5 miles.

ILWACO KOA (Private)
200 campsites - 36 w/hookups for water/elec./sewer, 90 w/elec. only, plus 74 tent units, reservations (360)642-3292, showers, laundry, playground, rec room, groceries, propane, trailer waste disposal, creek, pets okay, $$$$-$$$$$.
Located on US 101, about halfway between Ilwaco and Chinook.

MAUCH'S SUNDOWN RV PARK (Private)
49 units w/hookups for water/elec./sewer plus 10 w/water & elec., tents okay, reservations (360)777-8713, showers, laundry, ice, trailer waste disposal, on river, fishing, pets okay, $$-$$$.
Take US 101 southeast 8.5 miles - located just west of the Astoria Bridge.

RIVER'S END CAMPGROUND (Private)
100 units - 20 w/hookups for water/elec./sewer, 40 w/water & elec., plus 40 tent sites, reservations (360)777-8317, showers, laundry, ice, rec room, playground, trailer waste disposal, river, fishing, $$$$-$$$$$.
Take US 101 east 4.3 miles.

CATHLAMET

COUNTY LINE PARK (County)
12 tent/trailer sites, on Columbia River, fishing, handicap access - includes trail & fishing platform, $$.
Take State 4 east of Cathlamet 10 miles to county line and park.

NASSA POINT MOTEL & RV (Private) [RV]
2 trailer sites w/hookups for water & elec., no tents, no restrooms, reservations (360)795-3941, trailers to 40', on Columbia River, pets okay, open year round, $$$.
Take State 4 east of town 3 miles.

SKAMOKAWA VISTA PARK (Private) [A] [RV]
15 RV sites w/hookups for elec. plus space for 70 w/out hookups, tents okay, reservations (360)795-8605, trailers to 40', wheelchair accessible restrooms, showers, play area, ball courts & field, on Columbia River, fishing, swimming, pets okay, open year round, $$-$$$.
Take State 4 west 7 miles to Skamokawa and park.

WASHINGTON I-5 CORRIDOR CAMPGROUNDS

See Page

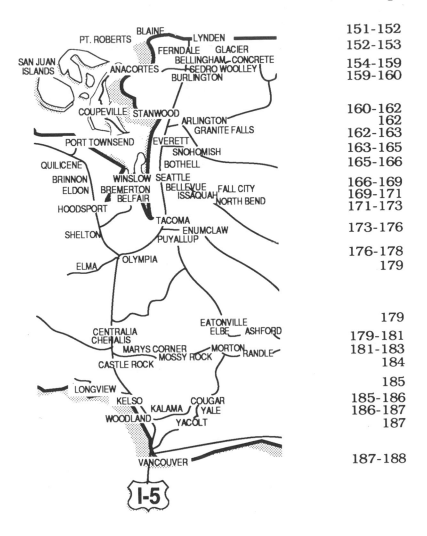

151-152
152-153

154-159
159-160

160-162
162
162-163
163-165
165-166

166-169
169-171
171-173

173-176

176-178
179

179
179-181
181-183
184

185
185-186
186-187
187

187-188

BLAINE

BELAIR TRAILER COURT (Private)
4 units w/hookups for water/elec./sewer, no tents, reservations (360)332-8633, trailers to 70', showers, laundry, trailer waste disposal, pets okay, open year round.
Take the first Blaine exit off I-5 and head toward town.

(South of Blaine)

BALL BAY VIEW RV PARK (Private)
42 units w/hookups for water/elec./sewer, 7 w/water & elec., plus 3 tent sites, reservations (360)371-0334, trailers to 38', showers, laundry, small pets okay, open year round, $$$-$$$$.
Take I-5 to exit #270, go west 4 miles, and take Birch Bay Dr. south 2 miles to Jackson Rd. - located at 7387 Jackson Rd.

BAY SHORE RESORT (Private)
7 units w/hookups for water/elec./sewer, no restrooms, no tents, reservations (360)371-7667, trailers to 40', laundry, on bay, fishing, hiking, no pets, open year round, $$$$$.
Take I-5 to exit #270, go west 4 miles, and take Birch Bay Dr. to 7930 Birch Bay Dr.

BEACHSIDE RV PARK (Private)
26 units w/hookups for water/elec./sewer plus 23 tent sites, reservations (360)371-5962, trailers to 40', showers, laundry, wheelchair access, trailer waste disposal, pets okay, open year round, $$$-$$$$.
Take I-5 to exit #270, go west 4 miles, and take Birch Bay Dr. south to 7630 Birch Bay Dr.

BIRCH BAY (Washington State Park)
167 units - 20 w/hookups for water & elec., 147 standard sites plus group area, mail reservations available, trailers to 70', flush toilets, showers, disabled access, trailer waste disposal, scuba diving area, fishing, hiking, $$-$$$.
Take I-5 to exit #270, go west 4 miles, and take Birch Bay Dr. south 3 miles to park.

BIRCH BAY TRAILER PARK (Private)
442 trailer sites - 337 w/full hookups plus 40 w/out hookups, reservations (360)371-7922, showers, laundry, rec room, propane, trailer waste disposal, swimming, fishing, $$$-$$$$.
Take I-5 to exit #270, go west about 4 miles, and then south to 8080 Harborview Rd.

EVERGREEN MANOR & RV PARK (Private)
16 units w/hookups for water/elec./sewer, no tents, reservations (360)384-1241, trailers to 35', showers, laundry, wheelchair access, pets okay, $$$.

Take I-5 to exit #266, Grandview Rd. east .5 mile, and Enterprise Rd. .01 mile to park.

PLAZA RV & MOBILE HOME PARK (Private)
18 units w/water & elec. plus 15 tent sites, reservations (360) 371-7822, trailers to 36', showers, laundry, wheelchair access, trailer waste disposal, small pets okay, open year round, $$-$$$. Take I-5 to exit #270 and Birch Bay-Lynden Rd. east 2 miles.

POINT ROBERTS

LIGHTHOUSE MARINE PARK (County)
30 tent/trailer sites, beach, lookout tower, on Strait, boat ramps, fishing, clamming, $$-$$$. Located at 811 Marine Dr.

WHALEN'S RV PARK (Private)
85 RV sites w/hookups for water & elec., reservations (360)945-2874, trailers to 70', accessible showers, trailer waste disposal, ocean access, fishing, pets okay, open May thru Sept., $$$$. Take Roosevelt Rd. east 1 mile to park.

LYNDEN

BERTHUSEN PARK (City)
25 units w/hookups for water & elec. plus dry sites, tents okay, trailers to 70', showers, wheelchair access, trailer waste disposal, old growth, stream, fishing, hiking, pets okay, $$-$$$. Follow signs from downtown - located on Berthusen Rd.

HIDDEN VILLAGE RV PARK (Private)
25 units w/hookups for water/elec./sewer, 38 w/water & elec., plus tent area, reservations (360)398-1041, showers, laundry, trailer waste disposal, pets okay, open year round, $$-$$$$. Take State 539 south 3 miles.

LYNDEN KOA (Private)
100 units - 45 w/hookups for water/elec./sewer, 25 w/water & elec., plus 30 tent sites, reservations (360)354-4772, pull thrus, showers, laundry, playground, swimming pool, groceries, restaurant, propane, trailer waste disposal, pond fishing, boat rental, miniature golf, pets okay, open year round, $$$$-$$$$$. Take State 546 east 3 miles and Line Rd. south 1.5 miles.

WINDMILL INN RV & TRAILER PARK (Private)
8 units w/hookups for water/elec./sewer, no tents, reservations (360)354-3424, trailers to 35', showers, pets okay, open year round, $$$. Located on Front St.

SILVER LAKE PARK (County)
50 units w/hookups for water & elec. plus 30 w/out hookups, tents okay, information (360)599-2776, trailers to 36', showers, wheelchair access, trailer waste disposal, on lake, swimming beach, boat launch/moorage & dock, fishing, canoe & paddleboat rentals, horse stalls, pets okay, open year round, $$$-$$$$.
Take State 546 east 5 miles, State 9 south 3 miles, South Pass Rd. east 17 miles and Silver Lake Rd. south 3 miles..

SUMAS RV PARK (Private)
19 units w/full hookups, 10 w/water & elec., 10 w/out hookups, plus tent area, reservations (360)988-8875, trailers to 35', accessible showers, laundry, trailer waste disposal, pets okay, $$-$$$.
Take State 546 east 5 miles, State 9 north to Sumas, and Cherry St. .01 mile to campground.

FERNDALE

FERNDALE CAMPGROUND (Private)
72 units w/full hookups, 33 w/water & elec., plus 60 w/out hookups, tents okay, reservations (360)384-2622, pull thrus, showers, laundry, game room, playfield, playground, groceries, trailer waste disposal, pond, pets okay, open year round, $$$.
Leave I-5 on exit #263 and take Portal Way north 1 mile.

MOUNTAIN VIEW RV PARK (Private)
25 RV sites w/hookups for water/elec./sewer, reservations (360)384-2860, trailers to 70', showers, pets okay w/approval, open year round, $$$$.
Leave I-5 on exit #263 and take Portal Way to 6006.

GLACIER

DOUGLAS FIR (Mt. Baker-Snoqualmie NF)
30 campsites, trailers to 32', picnic area, community kitchen, on Nooksack River, fishing, hiking, elev. 1000', $$.
Take State 542 east 2 miles.

EXCELSIOR CAMP (Mt. Baker-Snoqualmie NF)
1 group site, reservations (800)280-2267, not recommended for trailers, no water, on N. Fork Nooksack River, fishing, pets okay.
Take State 542 east 7 mile.

SILVER FIR (Mt. Baker-Snoqualmie NF)
21 campsites, trailers to 32', picnic area, community kitchen, along Nooksack River, fishing, elev. 2000', $$.
Take State 542 east 12.5 miles.

SAN JUAN ISLANDS

CLARK ISLAND (Washington State Park)
8 boat-in campsites, no water, mooring buoys, tide pools, hiking, fishing, scuba diving, open year round, $-$$.
Clark Island is 1.8 miles off the northeast tip of Orcas Island.

DOE ISLAND (Washington State Park)
5 boat-in campsites, no water, fishing, scuba diving, hiking, open year round, $.
Doe Island is just a short distance from Orcas Island's Doe Bay.

JONES ISLAND (Washington State Park)
21 boat-in campsites, mooring buoys, fishing, scuba diving, hiking, open year round, $-$$.
Jones Island is 1 mile west of Orcas Island's southwest tip.

MATIA ISLAND (Washington State Park)
6 boat-in campsites, no water, mooring buoys, fishing, scuba diving, tide pools, short trail, $-$$.
Matia Island is 2.5 miles north of Orcas Island.

PATOS ISLAND (Washington State Park)
4 boat-in campsites, no water, mooring buoys, fishing, scuba diving, tide pools, open year round, $-$$.
Patos Island is 5.5 miles north of Orcas Island.

POSEY ISLAND (Washington State Park)
Primitive boat-in camping, no water, fishing, scuba diving, tide pools, open year round, $.
Posey Island is just north of San Juan Island's Roche Harbor.

SHAW ISLAND'S SOUTH BEACH PARK (County)
11 units plus overflow area - 2 sites will take small trailers, small boat launch, beach, good biking, open year round, $$.
Shaw Island is accessible via Anacortes ferry. Take road to first left and turn onto paved road - park is .5 mile.

STUART ISLAND (Washington State Park)
19 primitive boat-in sites, mooring buoys & floats, no drinking water, fishing, $.
Stuart Island is northwest of San Juan Island.

SUCIA ISLAND (Washington State Park)
51 primitive boat-in sites, mooring buoys & floats, no drinking water, picnic shelter, scuba diving area, fishing, $.
Sucia Island is about 2.5 miles north of Orcas Island.

TURN ISLAND (Washington State Park)
10 primitive boat-in sites, mooring buoys, no drinking water, fishing, trails, $.
Turn Island is east of San Juan Island's Friday Harbor.

(On Lopez Island)

ODLIN PARK (County)
30 units, boat launch, fishing, hiking, open year round, $$$.
Lopez Island is accessible via the Anacortes ferry - park is 1.3
miles south of the ferry landing.

SPENCER SPIT (Washington State Park)
34 units, group area - reservations (360)468-2251, trailers to
20', disabled access, trailer waste disposal, fishing, $-$$$.
Park is located on the northeast side of Lopez Island.

(On Orcas Island)

DOE BAY VILLAGE RESORT (Private)
10 units w/hookups for water & elec. plus tent area, reservations
(360)376-2291, trailers to 32', showers, wheelchair access, hot
tub, mineral baths, sauna, game room, natural foods cafe/store,
fishing, hiking, pets extra, open year round, $$$-$$$$.
Orcas Island is accessible via the Anacortes ferry - follow the
main road and signs toward Olga.

MORAN (Washington State Park)
151 campsites, mail reservations available, trailers to 45', flush
toilets, showers, disabled access, trailer waste disposal, boat
launch & rental, fishing, located on Mt. Constitution, $-$$$.
On northeast side of Orcas Island, past Eastsound.

TOWN & COUNTRY (Private)
25 units w/hookups for water/elec./sewer, tents okay,
reservations (360)378-4717, showers, laundry, playground,
ocean access, lake, fishing, pets okay, open year round, $$-$$$.
Located northeast of harbor, on Orcas Island.

WEST BEACH RESORT (Private)
35 units w/hookups for water & elec. plus 35 tent sites, reservations (360)376-2240, trailers to 70', showers, laundry,
wheelchair access, hot tub, game room, playground, groceries,
marina, propane, scuba air, swimming, fishing, boat launch &
rental, hiking, pets extra, open year round, $$$$-$$$$$.
On Orcas Island, 3.5 miles west of Eastsound.

(On San Juan Island)

LAKEDALE CAMPGROUND (Private)
125 units - 18 w/hookups for water & elec., 82 tent sites, 15 site
bicycle camp, plus group sites, reservations (800)617-CAMP,
trailers to 70', showers, wheelchair access, store, trailer waste
disposal, 3 lakes, swimming, fishing, boat & bicycle rental, horse
corral & barn, pets okay, open April thru mid Oct., $$-$$$$$.
San Juan Island is accessible via Anacortes ferry - follow Roche
Harbor Rd. 4 miles north of Friday Harbor.

PEDAL INN CAMPGROUND (Private)
25 hike-in tent sites, no parking - bicyclers & hikers only, showers, laundry, small store, no ground fires, on pond, fishing, hiking, no pets, open April thru Oct., $.
On San Juan Island - take Cattle Point Rd. 4 miles, turn right on False Bay Dr. and follow signs.

SAN JUAN COUNTY PARK (County)
20 campsites, reservations (360)378-2992, trailers to 25', flush toilets, boat ramp, pets okay, $$-$$$.
On San Juan Island - take 2nd St. to West Valley Rd., go 6 miles to Mitchell Bay Rd. and follow 4 miles to park.

SNUG HARBOR MARINA (Private)
8 units w/hookups for water/elec./sewer plus 12 tent sites, reservations (360)378-4762, trailers to 30', showers, trailer waste disposal, groceries, propane, boat rental/launch & dock, fishing, swimming, hiking, pets extra, open year round, $$-$$$$$.
On San Juan Island - take Beaverton Valley Rd. 8 miles west of Friday Harbor to Mitchell Bay and marina.

ANACORTES

ANACORTES RV PARK (Private)
50 units, tents okay, reservations (360)293-3700, trailers to 35', showers, laundry, pets extra, open year round, $$$-$$$$.
Located at 1225 State Highway 20.

LIGHTHOUSE RV PARK (Private)
31 RV sites w/hookups for water/elec./sewer, reservations (360) 293-3344, trailers to 31', showers, no pets, open year round.
Follow signs toward ferry - located at 5809 Sands Way.

SADDLEBAG ISLAND (Washington State Park)
5 boat-in campsites, no water, fishing, scuba diving, trail, $.
Saddlebag Island is 2 miles northeast of Anacortes, at the north end of Padilla Bay.

WASHINGTON PARK (City of Anacortes)
46 units w/hookups for water & elec. plus 22 tent sites, trailers to 70', accessible showers, trailer waste disposal, swimming, fishing, boat launch, hiking, pets okay, open year round, $$$.
Take State 20 to 12th St., go west 2 miles and veer left to park.

BELLINGHAM

CRESTHAVEN MOBILE HOME PARK (Private)
3 units w/hookups for water, no tents, reservations (360)734-9223, trailers to 32', showers, pets okay, open year round, $$$.
Take I-5 north exit #250 (south #252) to 2500 Samish Way.

LARRABEE (Washington State Park)
26 units w/hookups for water/elec./sewer plus 61 standard sites, group area - reservations (360)676-2093, trailers to 60', flush toilets, showers, trailer waste disposal, on Puget Sound, tidal pools, boat launch, fishing, trails, $-$$$$.
Follow State 11 south 7 miles.

WILDWOOD RESORT (Private)
35 units - 3 w/hookups for water/elec./sewer, 2 w/water & elec., plus 30 w/out hookups, tents okay, reservations (360)595-2311, flush toilets, rec hall, groceries, on lake, boat launch/rental & moorage, fishing, swimming, water skiing, no pets, $$$-$$$$.
Take I-5 south to exit #240, Cain Lake Rd. east .5 mile, and head north at the Y for .2 mile to resort.

CONCRETE

(West of Concrete)

CREEKSIDE CAMPING (Private)
11 units w/hookups for water/elec./sewer, 13 w/water & elec., plus 3 w/out hookups, reservations (360)826-3566, showers, playground, trailer waste disposal, fishing, pets okay, $$$.
Take State 20 west 7 miles and Baker Lake Rd. north .2 mile.

TIMBERLINE RV PARK (Private)
39 units w/full hookups, tents okay, reservations (360)826-3131, showers, laundry, wheelchair access, groceries, propane, rec room, playfield, playground, pets okay, $$$.
Take State 20 west 5 miles, Russell Rd. north to Challenger Rd., and go east .3 mile to park - at 736 Wilde Rd.

(Northwest of Concrete)

BOULDER CREEK (Mt. Baker-Snoqualmie NF)
10 units plus group area, group reservations (800)280-2267, no water, trailers to 18', elev. 1100', group site $32.50/night - individuals $$.
Take State 20 west of town, Burpee Hill/Baker Lake Rd. north 9.6 miles, and FSR 11 north 5.4 miles.

HORSESHOE COVE (Mt. Baker-Snoqualmie NF)
34 units plus group area, group reservations (800)280-2267, trailers to 22', flush toilets, handicap access, on Baker Lake, boat launch, swimming, fishing, groups $43/night - individuals $$.
Take State 20 west of town, Burpee Hill/Baker Lake Rd. north 9.6 miles, FSR 11 north 2.4 miles, and FSR 1118 east 2 miles.

PANORAMA POINT (Mt. Baker-Snoqualmie NF)
16 campsites, trailers to 22', reservations (800)280-2267, on Baker Lake, boat launch, swimming, fishing, elev. 700', $$.

Take State 20 west of town, Burpee Hill/Baker Lake Rd. north 9.6 miles, and FSR 11 north 6.4 miles.

PARK CREEK (Mt. Baker-Snoqualmie NF)
12 units plus 2 group sites, group reservations (800)280-2267, no water, trailers to 18', elev. 800', group site $32.50/night - individuals $$.
Take State 20 west of town, Burpee Hill/Baker Lake Rd. north 9.6 miles, FSR 11 north 7.4 miles, and FSR 1144 west .1 mile.

SHANNON CREEK (Mt. Baker-Snoqualmie NF)
20 units, reservations (800)280-2267, trailers to 22', on Baker Lake, boating, swimming, fishing, elev. 800', $$.
Take State 20 west of town, Burpee Hill/Baker Lake Rd. north 9.6 miles, FSR 11 north 12.2 miles, and FSR 3830 east .5 mile.

(East of Concrete)

CLARK'S SKAGIT RIVER RV PARK (Private)
64 units - 50 w/full hookups, 6 w/out hookups, plus 8 tent sites, reservations (360)873-2250, showers, laundry, restaurant, museum, river, fishing, hiking, pets okay, $$-$$$.
Take State 20 east 14.5 miles - located 6 miles past Rockport.

HOWARD MILLER STEELHEAD PARK (County)
70 units - 60 w/hookups for water & elec. plus 10 tent sites, reservations (360)853-8808, showers, wheelchair access, playground, trailer waste disposal, river, boat launch, swimming, fishing, hiking, pets okay, $$-$$$.
Take State 20 east 10 miles and follow signs to park.

ROCKPORT (Washington State Park)
58 unites - 50 w/hookups for water/elec./sewer plus 8 standard sites, group area - reservations (360)853-4705, trailers to 45', flush toilets, showers, disabled access - includes trail, trailer waste disposal, old growth forest, fishing, hiking, pets okay, open April thru mid Nov., $-$$$.
Take State 20 east 8 miles.

WILDERNESS VILLAGE (Private)
38 units w/full hookups plus 6 tent sites, reservations (360)873-2571, showers, laundry, river, fishing, pets okay, $$-$$$.
Take State 20 east 14 miles.

SEDRO WOOLLEY

RIVER FRONT PARK RV (City)
40 RV sites w/hookups for water & elec., no tents, playground, picnic area, on Skagit River, boat launch, fishing, pets okay, open Mem. Day to Labor Day, $$.
Located in Sedro Woolley, just south of the highway.

RIVERVIEW PARK (Private)

6 units w/hookups for water & elec. plus 24 w/out hookups, no tents, reservations (360)595-2672, trailers to 70', wheelchair access, trailer waste disposal, river - no motors, fishing, swimming, innertube rental, no pets, open April thru Sept., $$$. Take State 9 north 16 miles to Acme and park.

BURLINGTON

BIG LAKE RESORT (Private)

22 units w/hookups for water/elec./sewer, 5 w/water & elec., plus tent area, reservations (360)422-5755, trailers to 40', showers, laundry, trailer waste disposal, swimming, fishing, boat moorage/dock & rentals, pets okay, open year round, $$$-$$$$. Take I-5 to exit #226, College Way east 2.5 miles, State 9 south 2 miles, and follow signs for Big Lake Blvd. and resort.

BLAKE'S RV PARK & MARINA (Private)

61 units - 29 w/hookups for water/elec./sewer plus 32 standard sites, tents okay, reservations (360)445-6533, trailers to 70', showers, laundry, wheelchair access, propane, on N. Fork Skagit River, boat launch/moorage & dock, fishing, hiking, pets & horses okay, open year round, $$$-$$$$. Leave I-5 on exit #221 and follow signs 6 miles to park.

BURLINGTON/CASCADE KOA (Private)

52 units w/full hookups, 10 w/water & elec., 18 w/elec., plus 40 tent sites, reservations (360)724-5511, showers, wheelchair access, laundry, propane, groceries, indoor pool, sauna, hot tub, playground, trailer waste disposal, fishing, $$$$-$$$$$. Take I-5 exit #232, Cook Rd. east .2 mile, and Old Highway 99 north 3.5 miles.

MOUNTAIN VIEW TRAILER PARK (Private)

15 trailer sites w/full hookups, adults only, reservations (360)424-3775, showers, laundry, pets okay, $$$. Take I-5 exit #225, go west to State 99S, and north .01 mile.

RIVERBEND PARK (Private)

75 units w/hookups for water/elec./sewer plus 30 tent sites, reservations (360)428-4044, showers, wheelchair access, rec room, trailer waste disposal, river, fishing, pets okay, $$$-$$$$. Take I-5 exit #227, College Way west to Freeway Dr., and go north .5 mile.

SKAGIT COUNTY FAIRGROUNDS (County)

35 units w/hookups for water & elec., tents okay, information (360)336-2332, showers, wheelchair access, playfield, pets okay, open year round, $$-$$$. South of Burlington. Take I-5 south 5 miles to Mt. Vernon - located at the south end of downtown Mt. Vernon.

(West of Burlington)

BAY VIEW (Washington State Park)
78 units - 9 w/hookups for water/elec./sewer plus 67 standard tent sites, group area - (360)757-0227, trailers to 40', flush toilets, showers, on Padilla Bay, open year round, $-$$$$.
Take State 20 west 6 miles; and follow signs 1.3 miles north.

COUPEVILLE

FORT CASEY (Washington State Park)
38 units, trailers to 40', flush toilets, showers, wheelchair access, historic defense post, boat launch, fishing, scuba diving, $-$$$.
Take Engle Rd. 3 miles south to west side of island.

FORT EBEY (Washington State Park)
50 units, trailers to 70', flush toilets, showers, disabled access, historic defense bunker, fishing, $-$$$.
Located on the west side of island, 6 miles from Coupeville.

(North of Coupeville)

DECEPTION PASS (Washington State Park)
246 campsites, trailers to 30', group area - information (360)675-2417, flush toilets, showers, wheelchair access, community kitchen, trailer waste disposal, boat launch/buoys/floats, fishing, scuba diving, pets okay, $-$$$.
Located 16 miles north of Coupeville, at bridge.

FERN HILL CAMPGROUND/RV PARK (Private)
25 units w/hookups for water/elec./sewer, 35 w/water & elec., plus 45 tent sites, reservations (360)384-2622, showers, laundry, playground, trailer waste disposal, ice, propane, $$$-$$$$$.
Take State 20 10 miles north to Oak Harbor and go west 1 mile to Miller Rd. and park.

JAMES ISLAND (Washington State Park)
13 boat-in campsites, no water, mooring buoys, fishing, scuba diving, short trail, $-$$.
From Deception Pass State Park, boat north - James Island is near northeast tip of Decatur Island.

NORTH WHIDBEY RV PARK (Private)
100 units w/full hookups plus 10 tent sites, reservations (360)675-9597, trailers to 70', showers, laundry, wheelchair access, play area, pets okay, open year round, $$$$.
Located 16 miles north of Coupeville, on the north end of island.

OAK HARBOR CITY BEACH (City)
56 units w/hookups for water & elec. plus overflow area, tents okay, information (360)679-5551, showers, tennis, playground,

160

trailer waste disposal, ocean access, swimming, fishing, boat launch, pets okay, open year round, $$-$$$.
Take State 20 north toward Oak Harbor - campground is just south of Oak Harbor, at Pioneer Rd.

(South of Coupeville)

BUSH POINT RESORT (Private)
18 RV sites w/out hookups plus grassy tent area, reservations (360)331-7368, trailers to 70', wheelchair access, on sound, boat launch & rental, fishing, pets okay, open May thru Oct., $$
Located south of Coupeville, in Freeland - at 326 Main St.

ISLAND COUNTRY FAIRGROUND (Private)
50 units w/hookups for water & elec., tents okay, reservations (360)221-4677, trailers to 70', showers, wheelchair access, near town, box stalls for horses, pets okay, open year round, $$-$$$.
Take State 20 south 5 miles, State 525 south 18 miles, and head north 4 miles to Langley - located at 819 Camano Ave.

MUTINY BAY RESORT (Private) [RV]
25 units w/hookups for water/elec./sewer, no tents, reservations (360)331-4500, trailers to 30', showers, ice, trailer waste disposal, ocean access, swimming, fishing, pets okay, $$$$.
Located south of Coupeville, in Freeland - take Fish Rd. south 1 mile, and follow Mutiny Bay Rd. to resort.

SOUTH WHIDBEY (Washington State Park) [A] [RV]
56 campsites, trailers to 45', flush toilets, showers, disabled access, group sites - reservations (360)321-4559, trailer waste disposal, scuba diving, fishing, beachcombing, clamming, $-$$.
Take State 20 south 5 miles, State 525 south 6 miles, and take the road leading southwest toward the water and campground.

STANWOOD

CAMANO ISLAND (Washington State Park) [A] [RV]
87 units, group area - reservations (360)387-3031, trailers to 45', flush toilets, showers, trailer waste disposal, boat launch, fishing, scuba diving area, nature trail, open year round, $-$$.
Take State 532 west 5 miles to Camano Island, and head south 7 miles to this state park campground.

(South of Stanwood)

CEDAR GROVE SHORES RV PARK (Private)
48 units w/full hookups plus 20 w/water & elec., no tents, reservations (360)652-7083, showers, laundry, rec room, lake, swimming, fishing, boat launch, pets okay, $$$$-$$$$$.
Take I-5 south to exit #206, Lakewood Rd. west 5 miles, and 52nd Ave. NW south .5 mile.

KAYAK POINT COUNTY PARK (County)

32 sites w/hookups for elec. & gray water, 2 w/handicap access - reservations (360)652-7992, flush toilets, boat launch, fishing, pets okay, open year round - no hookups Nov. to Feb., $$$.
Take Marine Dr. south 9 miles.

LAKE GOODWIN RESORT (Private)
68 units w/hookups for water/elec./sewer, 17 w/water & elec., plus 18 tent sites, reservations (360)652-8169, propane, playground, groceries, trailer waste disposal, swimming, fishing, water skiing, boat launch & rental, small pets okay, $$$-$$$$$.
Take I-5 south to exit #206, Lakewood Rd. west 5 miles, and follow signs.

WENBERG (Washington State Park)
10 units w/hookups for water & elec. plus 65 standard sites, trailers to 50', flush toilets, showers, groceries, trailer waste disposal, on east shore of Lake Goodwin, boat launch, fishing, swimming, open year round, $$-$$$$.
Take I-5 south to exit #206, Lakewood Rd. west 5 miles, and follow signs south 2 miles to campground.

ARLINGTON

RIVER MEADOWS PARK (County)

80 tent/trailer sites, no hookups, trailers to 70', wheelchair accessible restrooms, on river, fishing, swimming, canoeing, nature & mountain bike trails, pets okay, open year round, $$$.
Take Arlington Heights Rd. east 2 miles, bear right onto Jordan Rd., and follow 3 miles to park.

SMOKEY POINT RV PARK (Private)
97 units w/hookups for water/elec./sewer plus 1 tent site, reservations (800)662-7275, showers, laundry, rec room, trailer waste disposal, nearby store & restaurant, pets okay, $$$-$$$$$.
Located in Arlington, at 17019 28th Dr. NE.

SQUIRE CREEK PARK (County)
34 campsites, trailers to 70', wheelchair access, old growth trees, trailer waste disposal, pets okay, open mid May thru Sept., $$.
Take State 530 northeast 26 miles - located just off highway.

GRANITE FALLS

(East of Granite Falls)

BEAVER CREEK (Mt. Baker-Snoqualmie NF)

4 group sites, no water, reservations (360)436-1155, fishing, elev. 1600', groups $40/night.
Take Mountain Loop Hwy. east 24.4 miles.

COAL CREEK BAR (Mt. Baker-Snoqualmie NF)
5 group sites, no water, reservations (360)436-1155, trailers to 18', fishing, elev. 1600', groups $40/night.
Take Mountain Loop Hwy. east 23.5 miles.

ESSWINE CAMP (Mt. Baker-Snoqualmie NF)
Group site, no water, reservations (360)436-1155, fishing, groups $40/night.
Take Mountain Loop Hwy. east 16 miles.

GOLD BASIN (Mt. Baker-Snoqualmie NF)
128 units, 3 group sites - reservations (800)280-2267, trailers to 32', wheelchair access, river, fishing, elev. 1100', groups $43/night - individuals $$.
Take Mountain Loop Hwy. east 13.4 miles.

MARTEN CREEK (Mt. Baker-Snoqualmie NF)
4 group sites, no water, reservations (360)436-1155, trailers to 18', fishing, elev. 1400', groups $40/night.
Take Mountain Loop Hwy. east 20.6 miles.

TULALIP MILLSITE (Mt. Baker-Snoqualmie NF)
12 group sites, no water, reservations (360)436-1155, trailers to 32', elev. 1400', groups $50/night.
Take Mountain Loop Hwy. east 18.6 miles.

TURLO (Mt. Baker-Snoqualmie NF)
19 units, reservations (800)280-2267, trailers to 32', river, swimming, fishing, elev. 900', $$.
Take Mountain Loop Hwy. east 10.8 miles.

VERLOT (Mt. Baker-Snoqualmie NF)
26 units, trailers to 32', flush toilets, handicap access, river, fishing, swimming, elev. 900', $$.
Take Mountain Loop Hwy. east 11 miles.

WILEY CREEK (Mt. Baker-Snoqualmie NF)
3 group tent sites, no water, reservations (360)436-1155, shelters, fishing, elev. 1200', groups $50/night.
Take Mountain Loop Hwy. east 15 miles.

PORT TOWNSEND

FORT WORDEN (Washington State Park)
110 campsites - 80 w/hookups for water/elec./sewer plus 30 w/water & elec., reservation information (360)385-4730, trailers to 50', flush toilets, showers, wheelchair access, community kitchen, snack bar, groceries, trailers waste disposal, boat launch, scuba diving area, fishing, $-$$$$.
Located in Port Townsend, at the north end of town.

JEFFERSON COUNTY FAIRGROUNDS (County)
70 tent/trailer sites - some w/water & elec., information
(360)385-1013, trailers to 70', showers, horse track, $-$$.
Located in Port Townsend, at the north end of town.

POINT HUDSON RESORT (Private)   RV
18 units w/hookups for water/elec./sewer, no tents, reservations
(800)826-3854, showers, laundry, wheelchair access, fishing,
boat launch, marina, restaurant, open year round, $$$-$$$$.
Located at the docks - follow Water St. to the end.

(South of Port Townsend)

CHIMACUM PARK (County)
18 tent/trailer sites, picnic facilities, $$.
Take US 20 southwest 6 miles, Four Corners Rd. east 1 mile, and
Chimacum-Beaver Valley Rd. south 3 miles.

FORT FLAGLER (Washington State Park)   A RV
14 units w/water & elec., 102 standard sites, plus group area,
trailers to 50', flush toilets, showers, disabled access, trailer
waste disposal, boat launch, fishing, scuba diving area, $-$$$$.
Take State 20 southwest about 5 miles to the road marked
Hadlock/Fort Flagler State Park and follow signs.

OAK BAY PARK (County)   A RV
68 tent/trailer units - some w/elec., swimming beach, boat
launch, fishing, hiking, $$.
Take US 20 southwest 6 miles, Four Corners Rd. east 1 mile,
Chimacum-Beaver Valley Rd. south 2 miles, Hadlock Rd. east 2
miles, and Oak Bay Rd. south 2 miles.

OLD FORT TOWNSEND (Washington State Park)
40 units, trailers to 40', flush toilets, showers, community
kitchen, playfield, historic fort, trailer waste disposal, beach
access, fishing, clamming, open May thru mid Sept., $-$$.
Take State 20 southwest 4 miles and follow signs east.

PORT LUDLOW RV PARK (Private)   A RV
40 units w/hookups for water/elec./sewer, tents okay, reservations (360)437-9110, trailers to 40', pull thrus, showers, trailer
waste disposal, groceries, pets okay, open year round, $$-$$$.
Take US 20 southwest 6 miles, Four Corners Rd. east 1 mile,
Chimacum-Beaver Valley Rd. south 10 miles, Port Ludlow Rd.
east 1.5 miles, and Ludlow-Paradise Rd. east 2 miles to park.

SMITTY'S ISLAND RETREAT (Private)   RV
40 units w/hookups for water/elec./sewer, no tents, reservations
(360)385-2165, fishing, pets okay, open year round, $$$.
Take State 20 southwest about 5 miles to the road marked
Hadlock/Fort Flagler State Park and follow signs - Smitty's is 1
mile south of park.

EVERETT

LAKESIDE RV PARK (Private)
155 units w/full hookups plus 9 tent sites, reservations (800)468-7275, trailers to 60', pull thrus, showers, laundry, wheelchair access, propane, gas, trailer waste disposal, private lake, fishing, hiking, pets okay, open year round, $$$-$$$$$$.
Leave I-5 at exit #186, go west 1.3 miles, and turn left onto State 99S - located at 12321 Highway 99S.

SILVER SHORES RV PARK (Private)
87 units w/hookups for water/elec./sewer, 8 w/water & elec., plus 12 tent sites, reservations (206)337-8741, showers, laundry, rec room, tennis, trailer waste disposal, on Silver Lake, swimming, fishing, small pets okay, $$-$$$$.
Leave I-5 at exit #186, go west to 4th Ave., north to 112th St., over the freeway, and follow 14th Ave./Silver Lake Rd. south to 11621 W. Silver Lake Rd.

SNOHOMISH

FERGUSON PARK (City)
11 units w/hookups for water & elec. plus tent area, trailers to 34', showers, wheelchair access, playground, trailer waste disposal, lake - no motors, swimming, fishing, boat launch, no pets, open year round - no water in winter, $$-$$$.
Located in Snohomish, near junction of US 2 and State 9.

FLOWING LAKE COUNTY PARK (County)
30 units w/hookups for water/elec./sewer plus 10 tent sites, flush toilets, picnic area/shelters, trailer waste disposal, boat launch, swimming, fishing, pets okay, open year round, $$-$$$.
Head east on Three Lakes Rd. - park is about 4 miles.

LAKE ROESIGER PARK (County)
10 walk-in tent sites, wheelchair access, on lake - no motors, swimming, fishing, trail, pets okay, open mid May thru Sept., $$.
Head east on Three Lakes Rd., after about 8 miles you'll see signs pointing north to lake and park.

QUILCENE

FALLS VIEW CAMPGROUND (Olympic NF)
35 campsites, reservations (800)280-2267, trailers to 21', flush toilets, picnic area, fishing, hiking trails, elev. 500', $.
Take US 101 southwest 3.5 miles.

LAKE LELAND PARK (County)
22 tent/trailer sites, on lake, boat launch, fishing, swimming, $$.
Take US 101 north 6 miles and follow signs to east side of lake.

QUILCENE PARK (County)
8 tent/trailer sites, picnic facilities, play area, $$.
Located just south of town on US 101.

TRANQUILCENE TRAILER PARK (Private)
5 trailer sites w/hookups for water/elec./sewer, no restrooms, reservations (360)765-3409, trailers to 35', on Hood Canal, fishing, pets okay, open year round, $$.
Take US 101 south .7 mile.

BOTHELL

LAKE PLEASANT RV PARK (Private)
167 units w/full hookups, 12 w/water & elec., plus 11 tent sites, reservations (800)742-0386, pull thrus, showers, laundry, fishing, hiking, open year round, $$$-$$$$.
Leave I-405 at exit #26 and take Bothell Highway 1 mile south.

SEATTLE

AQUA BARN RANCH (Private)
105 units w/hookups for water/elec./sewer, 65 w/water & elec., plus 25 tent sites, reservations (206)255-4618, trailers to 35', showers, pool, hot tub, restaurant, trailer waste disposal, horse rentals, hiking, pets okay, open year round, $$$-$$$$.
Leave I-405 on State 169 and go east 3.5 miles.

BLAKE ISLAND (Washington State Park)
54 boat-in units, group area - reservations advised (360)731-0770, floats & buoys, marine pump out station, scuba diving area, fishing, nature trail, hiking, open year round, $-$$$.
Located on Blake Island, in Puget Sound, 3 miles west of Seattle.

RIVER BEND RV PARK (Private)
42 units w/hookups for water/elec./sewer, no tents, reservations (206)255-2613, trailers to 40', showers, laundry, on Cedar River, fishing, hiking, small pets okay, open year round, $$$$.
Leave I-405 on State 169 and go east 4.5 miles.

SEATTLE SOUTH KOA (Private)
133 units w/hookups for water/elec./sewer plus 18 w/water & elec., tents okay, reservations (206)872-8652, trailers to 50', showers, laundry, wheelchair access, playground, pool, rec room, groceries, propane, pets okay, open year round, $$$$-$$$$$.
Leave I-5 south at exit #152 and go east on Orillia Rd.

WILLOW VISTA MH/RV PARK (Private)
25 units w/hookups for water/elec./sewer, information (206) 872-8264, trailers to 40', showers, laundry, wheelchair access, pool, trailer waste disposal, pets okay, open year round, $$$$.

Leave I-405 on State 167, go south to 84th Ave., then north to 21740 84th Ave.

(North of Seattle)

TWIN CEDARS RV PARK (Private)
70 trailer sites w/hookups for water/elec./sewer, no tents, reservations (206)742-5540, trailers to 40', showers, laundry, wheelchair access, club house w/pool table, trailer waste disposal, pets okay, open year round, $$$$$.
Take I-5 north to Lynnwood exit #183, 164th St. west 1.3 miles to State 99, and go south to 17826 Highway 99N.

BELLEVUE

TRAILER INNS RV PARK (Private)
100 trailer sites w/hookups for water/elec./sewer, reservations (800)659-4684, trailers to 40', showers, laundry, pool, sauna, rec room, playground, pets okay, open year round, $$$$-$$$$$.
Located at 15531 SE 37th.

VASA PARK RESORT (Private)
6 units w/hookups for water/elec./sewer plus 16 w/water, tents okay, reservations (206)746-3260, trailers to 45',showers, playground, trailer waste disposal, on Sammamish Lake, fishing, swimming, pets okay, open mid May thru early Oct., $$$-$$$$.
Leave I-90 on Lake Rd. and follow signs north to resort.

WINSLOW

FAY BAINBRIDGE (Washington State Park)
26 units w/hookups for water only, trailers to 30', flush toilets, showers, disabled access, trailer waste disposal, on Puget Sound, boat launch, scuba diving area, fishing, open year round, $-$$$.
Take Madison Ave. north 5 miles and follow signs.

(Northwest of Winslow)

CAPTAINS LANDING (Private)
22 units w/hookups for water/elec./sewer, tents okay, reservations (360)638-2257, trailers to 70', showers, gas, groceries, restaurant, fishing, pets okay, $$$-$$$$$.
Take State 305 northwest 7 miles, cross bridge, and follow Millers Bay/Hansville Rd. north 15 miles.

KITSAP MEMORIAL (Washington State Park)
43 units, group area - reservations (360)779-3205, trailers to 30', flush toilets, showers, disabled access, playfield, trailer waste disposal, on Hood Canal, fishing, open year round, $$.
Take State 305 northwest 13 miles, and State 3 north 4 miles.

POINT-NO-POINT RESORT (Private)
38 units w/hookups for water/elec./sewer plus tent area, reservations (360)638-2233, trailers to 32', showers, laundry, ice, fishing, boat rental, no dogs, open April thru Oct., $$-$$$.
Take State 305 northwest 7 miles, cross bridge, and follow Millers Bay/Hansville Rd. north 15 miles.

BRINNON

COVE TRAILER PARK (Private) [RV]
25 RV sites w/water/elec./sewer, reservations (360) 796-4723, showers, laundry, trailer waste disposal, fishing. no dogs, $$.
Take US 101 north 3 miles.

DOSEWALLIPS (Washington State Park) [A] [RV]
40 units w/hookups for water/elec./sewer plus 87 standard sites, group area - reservations (360)796-4415, trailers to 60', flush toilets, showers, disabled access, trailer waste disposal, on Dosewallips River & Hood Canal, fishing, clamming, $-$$$.
Take US 101 south 1 mile.

SEAL ROCK (Olympic NF) [A] [RV]
35 units, trailers to 21', reservations (800)280-2267, flush toilets, wheelchair access, on Hood Canal, swimming, fishing, trail, $$.
Take US 101 north 2 miles.

(West of Brinnon)

COLLINS (Olympic NF) [A] [RV]
16 units, trailers to 21', river, fishing, nearby trails, elev. 200', $.
Take US 101 south 2 miles, and FSR 2510 west 4.8 miles.

ELKHORN (Olympic NF) [A] [RV]
18 units, trailers to 21', river, fishing, hiking, elev. 600', $.
Take US 101 north 1 mile, and FSR 2610 west 10 miles.

ELDON

HAMMA HAMMA (Olympic NF)
15 units, trailers to 21', river, swimming, fishing, hiking, bicycling, elev. 600', $.
Take US 101 north 1.7 miles, FSR 25 west 6.5 miles.

BREMERTON

ERLAND POINT MOTOR HOME PARK (Private)
2 trailer sites w/hookups for water/elec./sewer, no restrooms, adults only, reservations (360)373-8060, trailers to 32', no dogs, open year round, $$$.

Leave State 3 on Austin Dr., go past the hospital and turn onto Erland Point Rd. - located at 2800 Erland Point Rd.

ILLAHEE (Washington State Park)
33 units, group site - reservations (360)478-6460, trailers to 30', flush toilets, showers, wheelchair access, community kitchen, trailer waste disposal, on bay, boat launch, pier fishing, $-$$.
Take State 306 east 3 miles to park.

MANCHESTER (Washington State Park)
50 units, trailers to 42', flush toilets, showers, disabled access, picnic shelter, trailer waste disposal, historic site, scuba diving area, fishing, open year round - weekends only in winter, $-$$.
Leave State 3 south of town on State 160, follow to Port Orchard, and take the road around the point 6 miles to park.

ROCKY POINT MOBILE/RV PARK (Private)
25 trailer sites w/full hookups, no restrooms, reservations (360) 377-2885, trailers to 35', some pets okay, open year round, $$$.
Take Marine Drive to Rocky Point Rd. and 2115 Rocky Point Rd.

(West of Bremerton)

SCENIC BEACH (Washington State Park)
50 units, group area - reservations (360)830-5079, trailers to 40', flush toilets, showers, wheelchair access, community kitchen, trailer waste disposal, on Hood Canal, fishing, open year round - weekends only Oct. thru March, $-$$$.
Take Seabeck Hwy. northwest 12 miles.

BELFAIR

BELFAIR (Washington State Park)
47 units w/hookups for water/elec./sewer plus 134 standard sites, mail reservations available, trailers to 60', flush toilets, showers, wheelchair access, picnic shelter, trailer waste disposal, open play area, fishing, clamming, $-$$$$.
Take State 300 southwest 3 miles.

NORSELAND MOBILE ESTATES/RV (Private)
21 trailer sites w/hookups for water/elec./sewer, reservations (360)674-2874, showers, laundry, rec room, pets okay, $$$.
Take State 3 northeast 4 miles.

SHERWOOD HILLS ADULT RV PARK (Private)
33 trailer sites w/hookups for water/elec./sewer, adults only, reservations (360)275-3155, trailers to 40', showers, laundry, groceries, trailer waste disposal, small pets okay, $$$.
Take State 3 south 2.2 miles to Allyn city center and park.

SNOOZ JUNCTION RV PARK (Private)
18 units w/hookups for water/elec./sewer plus 18 w/water & elec., tents okay, reservations (360)275-2381, trailers to 70', showers, wheelchair access, trailer waste disposal, propane, on Hood Canal, fishing, pets okay, open year round, $$$$.
Take State 300 southwest 2.5 miles.

(South of Belfair)

JARRELL COVE (Washington State Park)
20 units, group area - reservations (360)426-9226, trailers to 30', flush toilets, showers, wheelchair access, fishing, $$.
Take State 3 southwest 17 miles and follow park road east 7 miles to campground.

PENROSE POINT (Washington State Park)
83 units, group area - reservations (206)884-2514, trailers to 35', flush toilets, showers, wheelchair access, community kitchen, trailer waste disposal, on Carr Inlet, fishing, clamming, open year round - weekends only in winter, $-$$$.
Take State 3 south 4 miles, State 302 southeast 12 miles, and Longbranch Rd. south 7 miles to park.

(Southwest of Belfair)

ROBIN HOOD VILLAGE (Private)
14 trailer sites w/hookups for water & elec., reservations (360)898-2163, showers, laundry, fishing, $$$.
Take State 3 south 1 mile, and State 106 southwest 13.5 miles.

SUMMERTIDE RV PARK & MARINA (Private)
25 units w/full hookups, tents okay, reservations (206)925-9277, trailers to 36', showers, laundry, play area, propane, on beach, boat launch/moorage/dock & rentals, fishing, pets okay, open year round, $$$-$$$$.
Take State 300 southwest 15.5 miles.

TWANOH (Washington State Park)
9 units w/hookups for water/elec./sewer plus 38 standard sites, group area - reservations (360)275-2222, trailers to 35', flush toilets, showers, community kitchen, wheelchair access, on Hood Canal, boat launch, fishing, swimming, water skiing, tennis court, open mid April thru Sept., $-$$$$.
Take State 3 south 1 mile, and State 106 southwest 8 miles.

FALL CITY

SNOQUALMIE RIVER CAMPGROUND (Private)
80 units w/hookups for water & elec. plus 100 w/out hookups, tents okay, reservations (206)222-5545, some group sites, showers, pavilion, playground, on the Snoqualmie River, fishing,

swimming, boating, pets okay, open April thru Oct., $$$-$$$$.
Located in Fall City, on SE 44th St.

TOLT MACDONALD PARK (County)
17 units plus 12 walk-in tent sites, hike-in group sites - reservations (206)296-2966, trailers okay, showers, wheelchair access, on river, swimming, fishing, pets okay, open year round, $$.
Take State 203 north 6 miles, head west on NE 32nd St., and follow signs.

ISSAQUAH

BLUE SKY RV PARK (Private) [RV]
51 units w/full hookups, no tents, reservations (206)222-7910, trailers to 40', showers, laundry, wheelchair access, covered pavilion, pets okay, open year round, $$$$.
Leave I-90 at exit #22 - located at 9002 302nd Ave. SE.

ISSAQUAH HIGHLANDS CAMPING CLUB (Private)
100 non-member units w/water & elec., tents okay, reservations (206)392-4596, trailers to 70', showers, laundry, pool, trailer waste disposal, pets okay, open year round, $$$-$$$$.
Take the Renton-Issaquah Rd. south of town 3.5 miles.

ISSAQUAH VILLAGE RV PARK (Private) [RV]
128 RV units w/water/elec./sewer, reservations (800)258-9223, trailers to 40', showers, laundry, wheelchair access, playground, trailer waste disposal, pets okay, open year round, $$$$$$.
Leave I-90 at exit #17, go north 1 block, and take 2 quick right turns - located at 650 First Ave. N.E.

NORTH BEND

DENNY CREEK (Mt. Baker-Snoqualmie NF)
39 units, 3 group areas - reservations (800)280-2267, trailers to 22', handicap access, fishing, elev. 2200', groups $38 - others $$.
Take I-90 southeast 17 miles, and FSR 58 northeast 2.2 miles.

TINKHAM (Mt. Baker-Snoqualmie NF)
48 units, reservations (800)280-2267, trailers to 22', river, waterfall, fishing, nature trail, elev. 1520', $$.
Take I-90 southeast 10 miles, and FSR 55 southeast 1.5 miles.

HOODSPORT

GLEN AYR RV PARK & MOTEL (Private)
49 units w/hookups for water/elec./sewer, adults only, no tents, reservations (360)877-9522, trailers to 42', showers, laundry, propane, therapy pool, rec room, lounge, on Hood Canal,

swimming, fishing, hiking, pets okay, open year round, $$$.
Take US 101 north 1 mile.

MIKE'S BEACH RESORT (Private)
25 sites, tents okay, information (360)877-5324, trailers to 30',
showers, laundry, store, beach, boat ramp & gas, surf fishing,
hiking, pets okay, open Feb. thru Nov., $$-$$$.
Take US 101 north about 8 miles to Lilliwaup and resort.

MINERVA BEACH (Private)
40 units w/hookups for water/elec./sewer, 10 pull thrus w/out
hookups, plus 20 tent sites, reservations (360)877-5145,
showers, laundry, wheelchair access, trailer waste disposal,
store, propane, on Hood Canal, scuba diving area, diving center,
fishing, clamming, pets okay, open year round, $$$.
Take US 101 south 3.2 miles.

POTLATCH (Washington State Park) 🅰️ RV
18 units w/hookups for water/elec./sewer plus 17 standard
sites, trailers to 60', flush toilets, showers, trailer waste disposal,
on Hood Canal, scuba diving area, fishing, clamming, $-$$$.
Take US 101 south 3 miles.

REST A WHILE RV PARK (Private) 🅰️ RV
92 units w/full hookups plus 2 tent sites, reservations (360)877-
9474, trailers to 45', showers, laundry, wheelchair access,
propane, groceries, drive-in restaurant, swimming, fishing, boat
launch & rental, pets okay, open year round, $$$-$$$$.
Take US 101 north 2.5 miles.

(Northwest of Hoodsport)

BIG CREEK (Olympic NF) 🅰️ RV
23 units, trailers to 30', swimming, fishing, hiking, elev 700', $.
Take Lake Cushman Rd. northwest 8 miles, and FSR 24 south .1
mile.

LAKE CUSHMAN RESORT (Private) 🅰️ RV
25 units w/hookups for water & elec. plus 25 tent sites,
reservations (800)588-9630, trailers to 40', showers, wheelchair
access, meeting hall, groceries, on lake, swimming, fishing, boat
launch & rental, hiking, pets okay, open year round, $$-$$$.
Take Lake Cushman Rd. northwest 5 miles.

LAKE CUSHMAN (Washington State Park)
30 units w/hookups for water/elec./sewer plus 51 standard
sites, group area - reservations (360)877-5491, trailers to 60',
flush toilets, showers, community kitchen, disabled access,
trailer waste disposal, on lake, boat launch, fishing, hiking trails,
$-$$$$.
Take Lake Cushman Rd. northwest 7 miles.

STAIRCASE CAMPGROUND (Olympic Nat'l Park)
59 units, trailers to 21', handicap access, on Elk Creek, swimming, fishing, hiking, open year round, elev. 765', $$.
Take Lake Cushman Rd. northwest 16 miles.

SHELTON

WE & YOU MOBILE HOME & RV PARK (Private)
16 units w/full hookups plus 10 tent sites, reservations (360) 426-3169, trailers to 40', showers, laundry, bicycle rental, small pets okay, open year round, $$-$$$.
Take the first Shelton exit off US 101 and head north - located at 261 SE Craig Rd.

(East of Shelton)

JARRELL'S COVE MARINA (Private)
4 units w/hookups for elec. plus 3 tent sites, reservations (360) 426-8823, trailers to 27', showers, laundry, playground, swimming, fishing, hiking, pets okay, open year round, $$-$$$.
Take State 3 northeast 8 miles, Spencer Lake Rd. east 4 miles, North Island Dr. north 3 miles, and Haskell Hill Rd. west 1 mile.

SPENCER LAKE RESORT & RV (Private)
25 RV units w/full hookups, no restrooms, reservations (360) 426-2505, trailers to 40', trailer waste disposal, on lake, fishing, pets okay, open year round, $$$$.
Take State 3 northeast 8 miles and Spencer Lake Rd. east 1 mile.

(West of Shelton)

BROWN CREEK (Olympic NF)
19 units, trailers to 21', swimming, fishing, hiking, elev. 600', $.
Take US 101 north 7.5 miles, Skykomish Valley Rd. northwest 5.3 miles, FSR 23 north 8.7 miles, and FSR 2353 east .5 mile.

LAKE NAHWATZEL RESORT (Private)
18 units w/hookups for water/elec./sewer plus 5 w/water & elec., no tents, reservations (360)426-8323, trailers to 35', showers, wheelchair access, restaurant, trailer waste disposal, on lake, fishing, pets extra, open year round, $$$-$$$$.
Follow Shelton Matlock Rd. west 10.5 miles.

TACOMA

FIR ACRES MOTOR HOME/RV PARK (Private)
14 trailer sites w/hookups for water/elec./sewer, reservations (206)588-7894, trailers to 40', showers, laundry, wheelchair accessible, pets okay, open year round, $$$.
Leave I-5 at exit #125 and go east .1 mile on Bridgeport Way SW.

KARWAN VILLAGE MH/RV PARK (Private)
6 trailer sites w/hookups for water/elec./sewer, adults only, reservations (206)588-2501, trailers to 40', showers, laundry, no pets, open year round, $$$.
Leave I-5 south at exit #129 (north #128) and go west on 84th St.

OAKNOLL RV PARK (Private) [RV]
36 RV units w/hookups for water/elec./sewer plus 2 w/water & elec., reservations (206)588-8867, trailers to 40', showers, laundry, trailer waste disposal, pets okay, open year round, $$-$$$.
Leave I-5 at exit #125 - located at 110404 S. Tacoma Way.

(North of Tacoma)

DASH POINT (Washington State Park)
136 units - 28 w/hookups for water & elec., trailers to 35', group area - reservations (206)593-2206, flush toilets, showers, trailer waste disposal, on sound, fishing, open year round, $-$$$.
Leave State 99 just north of Federal Way on State 509 and drive west 5 miles to park.

SALT WATER (Washington State Park) [A] [RV]
52 units, group area - reservations (206)764-4128, trailers to 60', flush toilets, showers, disabled access, trailer waste disposal, on sound, scuba diving area, hiking, open year round, $$-$$$.
Follow State 509 north of Federal Way following State 509 when they split - park is northwest 3 miles.

(West of Tacoma)

GIG HARBOR RV RESORT (Private) [A] [RV]
65 units w/full hookups, 37 w/water & elec., plus 15 tent sites, reservations (206)858-8138, trailers to 40', showers, laundry, pool in summer, playground & courts, groceries, propane, trailer waste disposal, pets okay, open year round, $$$-$$$$.
Take State 16 over the Narrows Bridge plus 6 miles, and head north on Burnham Dr. 1 mile to resort.

KOPACHUCK (Washington State Park)
41 standard units, trailers to 35', flush toilets, showers, disabled access, picnic shelter, trailer waste disposal, on Henderson Bay, scuba diving area, clamming, open year round, $-$$$.
Take State 16 north of the bridge 6 miles and follow signs.

PUYALLUP

MAJESTIC MOBILE MANOR/RV PARK (Private) [A] [RV]
118 units w/full hookups plus 12 tent sites, reservations (206) 845-3144, trailers to 40', showers, wheelchair access, pool, trailer waste disposal, pets okay, open year round, $$$-$$$$.
Follow State 167/River Rd. west 3 miles.

174

T-J'S RV PARK (Private)
20 trailer sites w/hookups for water/elec./sewer, adults only, reservations (206)847-7153, trailers to 60', showers, laundry, trailer waste disposal, pets okay, open year round, $$$-$$$$. Follow State 161 south 3 miles.

(South of Puyallup)

CAMP BENBOWS LAKE TANWAX RETREAT (Private)
50 units w/water/elec./sewer plus 100 w/water & elec., reservations (360)879-5426, trailers to 40', showers, laundry, wheelchair access, fishing, pets okay, open year round, $$$-$$$$. Take State 161 south 20 miles and watch for signs.

HENLEY'S SILVER LAKE RESORT (Private)
20 units w/hookups for water & elec., 12 w/elec. only, plus tent area, reservations (360)832-3580, trailers to 70', fishing dock, boat launch & rental, pets okay, open April thru Oct., $$-$$$. Take State 161 south 26 miles, 352nd Ave. west 4 miles, State 7 south 3 miles, and follow signs.

MERIDIAN TERRACE MOBILE MANOR (Private)
4 RV units w/full hookups, no restrooms, adults only, reservations (206)847-1443, trailers to 70', small pets okay, open year round, $$$. Take State 161 south 5 miles - located at 9816 193rd St.

RAINBOW RESORT (Private)
52 units w/hookups for water/elec./sewer plus 7 w/elec., tents okay, reservations (360)879-5115, trailers to 40', showers, laundry, wheelchair access, rec room, playground, trailer waste disposal, groceries, propane, on lake, swimming, fishing, boat rental, pets okay, open year round, $$-$$$. Take State 161 south 15 miles and Tanwax Dr. east .5 mile.

SIERRA-RAINIER RV PARK (Private)
8 RV units w/hookups for water/elec./sewer, no restrooms, reservations (360)893-6422, trailers to 38', playground, trailer waste disposal, stream, fishing, hiking, mini-railroad, small pets okay, open year round, $$$. Take State 161 south 12 miles, 264th St. east 5 miles, and Orville Rd. north to 25916 Orville Rd. E.

ENUMCLAW

KANASKAT-PALMER (Washington State Park)
19 units w/hookups for elec. plus 31 standard sites, trailers to 30', group area - reservations (360)886-0148, flush toilets, showers, disabled access, community kitchen, trailer waste disposal, on Green River, boating, fishing, $-$$$. Take State 410 east 1 mile and Palmer Rd. northeast 9 miles.

(Southeast of Enumclaw)

SILVER SPRINGS (Mt. Baker-Snoqualmie NF)
56 units, trailers to 22', reservations (800)280-2267, picnic area, wheelchair access, fishing, elev. 2600', $$.
Follow State 410 southeast 31.3 miles - located 1 mile north of Mt. Rainier Nat'l Park boundary.

THE DALLES (Mt. Baker-Snoqualmie NF)
44 units, trailers to 22', group area - reservations (800)280-2267, fishing, hiking, elev. 2200', groups $43/night - others $$.
Follow State 410 southeast 25.4 miles - located 7 miles north of Mt. Rainier Nat'l Park boundary.

WHITE RIVER (Mt. Rainier Nat'l Park)
117 campsites, trailers to 20', on White River, hiking, $$.
Follow State 410 southeast 36 miles - located 5 miles west of White River Entrance for Mt. Rainier Nat'l Park.

(Southwest of Enumclaw)

IPSUT CREEK (Mt. Rainier Nat'l Park)
29 units, trailers to 20', hiking, elev. 4400', $$.
Take State 165 south 12 miles to Carbonado - located 5 miles east of Mt. Rainier Nat'l Park's Carbon River Entrance.

SOUTH PRAIRIE CREEK RV PARK (Private)
105 units w/full hookups plus 70 w/out hookups, no tents, no restrooms, reservations (360)897-8465, trailers to 40', trailer waste disposal, creek, pets okay, open year round, $$-$$$$.
Take State 410 west 3 miles, State 165 south 2 miles, and State 162 west to South Prairie and park.

UNCLE JOHN'S RV PARK (Private)
3 RV sites w/water & elec., reservations (360)862-1003, trailers to 40', showers, laundry, small playground, propane, pets okay, open year round, $$$.
Take State 410 west about 6 miles to 26306 Highway 410.

OLYMPIA

ALDERBROOK ESTATES (Private)
14 units w/hookups for water/elec./sewer plus grassy tent area, reservations (360)357-9448, pull thrus, showers, laundry, wheelchair access, club house, pets okay, open year round, $$$.
Leave I-5 south at exit #102 and go 7 blocks to 2110 54th Ave.

BLACK LAKE RV PARK (Private)
28 units w/hookups for water/elec./sewer, 16 w/water & elec., plus 11 w/out hookups, tents okay, reservations (360)357-6775, pull thrus, showers, groceries, propane, trailer waste disposal, on

176

lake, swimming, fishing, boat launch & dock, motor & row boat rentals, pets okay, open year round, $$-$$$.
Leave I-5 on US 101, go west 2 miles, and take Black Lake Blvd. south 2 miles.

COACH POST (Private)
7 units w/out hookups, no tents, reservations (360)754-7580, trailers to 70', showers, laundry, wheelchair access, pets okay, open year round, $$$.
Leave US 101 north on the Evergreen College exit, turn right at the fire station, go up the hill, turn onto Kaiser for a few blocks and take 7th Ave. to 3633 7th Ave.

COLUMBUS PARK (Private)
48 units w/hookups for water/elec./sewer, 31 w/water & elec., plus 2 tent sites, reservations (360)786-9460, trailers to 35', showers, laundry, wheelchair access, playground, trailer waste disposal, on Black Lake, swimming, fishing, boat launch & docks, paddle boat rental, pets okay, open year round, $$-$$$.
Leave I-5 on US 101, go west 2 miles, and take Black Lake Blvd. south 3.5 miles.

SALMON SHORE RESORT (Private)
30 units w/hookups for water/elec./sewer, 15 w/water & elec., 10 w/elec., plus tent area, reservations (360)357-8618, trailers to 40', showers, laundry, picnic shelter, playfield, playground, groceries, trailer waste disposal, lake, swimming, fishing, boat launch & rental, pets okay, open year round, $$-$$$.
Leave I-5 to on US 101, go west 2 miles, and take Black Lake Blvd. south 3.3 miles.

(North of Olympia)

LAKESIDE RV PARK & CAMPGROUND (Private)
8 units w/hookups for water/elec./sewer plus 42 w/water & elec., tents okay, reservations (360)491-3660, showers, laundry, wheelchair access, groceries, boat launch/dock & rental, pets okay, open year round, $$$-$$$$.
Take I-5 north 6 miles - located at 7225 14th Ave. SE.

MARTIN WAY MH/RV PARK (Private)
10 units w/hookups for water/elec./sewer plus 4 w/water & elec., no tents, reservations (360)491-6840, trailers to 40', showers, laundry, no pets, open year round, $$$-$$$$.
Take I-5 north to exit #111, State 510 east .8 mile, and Martin Way south .1 mile.

NISQUALLY PLAZA RV PARK (Private)
27 RV units w/full hookups, 21 w/water & elec., plus 7 w/out hookups, no tents, reservations (360)491-3831, showers, laundry, wheelchair access, groceries, pool, playground, trailer waste disposal, gas, propane, river, fishing, boat launch, pets

okay, open year round, $$-$$$$.
Take I-5 north to exit #114 and campground.

RIVERBEND CAMPGROUND (Private)
30 units w/hookups for water/elec./sewer, 20 w/water & elec.,
10 w/water, plus tent sites, reservations (360)491-2534, trailers
to 40', trailer waste disposal, on Nisqually River, boat launch,
fishing, swimming, hiking, pets okay, $$-$$$.
Take I-5 north to exit #116 and follow signs - it's 4 miles.

(South of Olympia)

AMERICAN HERITAGE CAMPGROUND (Private)
24 units w/hookups for water/elec./sewer, 52 w/water & elec.,
plus 29 tent sites, reservations (360)943-8778, trailers to 35',
showers, laundry, groceries, pool, playground, propane, trailer
waste disposal, pets okay, open summer only, $$$$-$$$$$.
Take exit #99 off I-5, go east .3 mile, and turn south to 9610
Kimmie St. SW.

DEEP LAKE RESORT (Private)
13 units w/hookups for water/elec./sewer, 30 w/water & elec.,
plus 6 tent sites, reservations (360)352-7388, trailers to 35',
showers, laundry, playground, trailer waste disposal, swimming,
fishing, boat launch, boat & bicycle rentals, $$$-$$$$.
Take exit #95 off I-5, Maytown Rd. east 2.5 miles, and Tilley Rd.
north .5 mile.

MILLERSYLVANIA (Washington State Park)
52 units w/hookups for water & elec. plus 135 standard sites,
group sites - reservations (360)753-1519, trailers to 45', flush
toilets, showers, wheelchair access, community kitchen, trailer
waste disposal, boat launch, fishing, swimming, $-$$$$.
Take I-5 south of Olympia about 10 miles.

OLYMPIA CAMPGROUND (Private)
28 units w/full hookups, 45 w/water & elec., plus 32 tent sites,
reservations (360)352-2551, trailers to 40', 28 pull thrus,
showers, laundry, pool, playground, groceries, propane, gas,
trailer waste disposal, pets okay, open year round, $$$$-$$$$$.
Take exit #99 off I-5, go east .3 mile to Kimmie Rd., and north 1
mile to 83rd Ave. - located at 1441 83rd Ave. SW.

(West of Olympia)

THURSTON COUNTY ORV PARK (County)
Lots of tent/trailer & group sites, no hookups, information (360)
495-3243, trailer waste disposal, ORV trails/all levels, children's
motocross-style riding area, access to Capitol Forest Multi-use
Rec. Area, meeting hall, pets okay, open April thru Sept., $$.
US 101 to State 8, then west 11 miles to county line and park.

ELMA

ELMA RV PARK (Private)
60 units w/full hookups plus 2 grassy tent areas, reservations (360)482-4053, trailers to 40', showers, laundry, propane, trailer waste disposal, river, fishing, pets okay, open year round, $-$$$. Located in Elma, at 4730 Highway 12.

TRAVEL INN RESORT (Private) [RV]
180 units w/full hookups, no tents, reservations (360)482-3877, trailers to 40', showers, laundry, wheelchair access, swimming pool, trailer waste disposal, pets okay, open year round, $$$. Located in Elma, at 801 E. Main St.

EATONVILLE

ALDER LAKE PARK (Private) [A] [RV]
37 units w/hookups for water/elec./sewer, 45 w/water & elec., plus 16 tent sites, reservations (360)569-2778, trailers to 40', showers, wheelchair access, trailer waste disposal, fishing, boat launch & moorage, pets okay, open Jan. thru mid Dec., $$-$$$. Located in Eatonville, at 50324 School Rd.

MILL VILLAGE RV PARK (Private) [RV]
4 trailer sites w/hookups for water/elec./tv, no restrooms, no tents, reservations (360)832-4279, trailers to 40', showers, laundry, wheelchair access, trailer waste disposal, pets okay, open year round, $$. Located in town, at 220 Center St.

ELBE

COUGAR ROCK (Mt. Rainier Nat'l Park) [A] [RV]
200 campsites, trailers to 30', group area - information (360)569-2211, trailer waste disposal, hiking, closes in mid Oct., elev. 3100', $$. Take State 706 east 22.2 miles - located .8 mile east of Nisqually Entrance to Mt. Rainier Nat'l Park.

EAGLE'S NEST MOTEL & RV PARK (Private) [RV]
10 RV units w/hookups for water/elec./sewer, no restrooms, reservations (360)569-2533, trailers to 35', laundry, on Alder Lake, fishing, hiking, small pets okay, open year round, $$$. Take State 7 northwest 3 miles.

SUNSHINE POINT (Mt. Rainier Nat'l Park) [A] [RV]
18 campsites, trailers to 25', on Nisqually River, fishing, elev. 2000', $$. Take State 706 east 22.6 miles - located .5 mile east of Nisqually Entrance to Mt. Rainier Nat'l Park.

ASHFORD

ASHFORD VALLEY GROCERY & RV PARK (Private)
23 pull thrus w/hookups for water/elec./sewer, no tents, reservations (360)569-2560, trailers to 70', restrooms in store, trailer waste disposal, propane, no pets, open year round, $$$. Located in Ashford, right on State 706.

CENTRALIA

HARRISON RV PARK (Private)
35 units w/water/elec./sewer, 9 w/water & elec., plus grassy tent area, reservations (360)330-2167, trailers to 70', showers, laundry, wheelchair access, pets okay, open year round, $$-$$$. Leave I-5 at exit #82 and take Harrison Ave. west 2 miles.

PEPPERTREE WEST INN/RV PARK (Private)
28 units w/hookups for water/elec./sewer, 14 w/water & elec., plus grassy tent area, reservations (360)736-1124, trailers to 50', showers, laundry, wheelchair access, trailer waste disposal, restaurant/lounge, pets okay, open year round, $-$$$$. Leave I-5 at exit #81 - located on east side of freeway.

ROTARY RIVERSIDE PARK (City)
16 units w/hookups for water & elec. plus 15 tent sites, trailers to 36', showers, wheelchair access, trailer waste disposal, pets okay, open year round, $-$$. Leave I-5 at exit #82 - park is 2 blocks east.

TRAILER VILLAGE RV PARK (Private)
16 RV sites w/water/elec./sewer, reservations (360)736-9260, trailers to 40', showers, pets okay, open year round, $$$. Leave I-5 at exit #82 and take Harrison St. west .5 mile.

(Northeast of Centralia)

OFFUT LAKE RESORT & RV PARK (Private)
35 units w/water/elec./sewer, 16 w/elec., plus 9 tent sites, reservations (360)264-2438, showers, laundry, playground, trailer waste disposal, swimming, fishing, boat rental, $$$-$$$$. Take State 507 north 12 miles to Tenino, Pacific Hwy. north 4 miles, and Offut Lake Rd. east 1 mile to lake and resort.

CHEHALIS

RAINBOW FALLS (Washington State Park)
47 units, trailers to 32', group area - reservations (360)291-3767, flush toilets, showers, wheelchair access, community kitchen, trailer waste disposal, on Chehalis River, old growth trail, $-$$. Take State 6 west approximately 17 miles - located near Doty.

STAN HEDWALL PARK (City)
29 units w/water & elec., reservations (360)748-0271, trailers to 64', wheelchair access, showers, playground, trailer waste disposal, swimming, fishing, hiking, pets okay, $$.
Leave I-5 at Chehalis exit #76 and take Rice Rd. west .5 mile.

MARYS CORNER

LEWIS & CLARK (Washington State Park)
25 units, trailers to 60', flush toilets, showers, nature trail, $$.
Leave US 12 at Marys Corner and follow signs south to park.

SCOTTS U-FISH & RV PARK (Private)
30 units w/water/elec./sewer plus 20 dry sites, reservations (360)262-9220, trailers to 37', wheelchair access, showers, hot tub, groceries, propane, fishing, pets okay, open year round, $$$.
Take US 12 west 2 miles.

MOSSYROCK

BARRIER DAM CAMPGROUND (Private)
26 units w/hookups for water & elec. plus 14 tent sites, reservations (360)985-2495, trailers to 44', showers, playground, groceries, trailer waste disposal, open year round, $$-$$$.
Take US 12 west 6 miles and Fuller Rd. south 1 mile.

HARMONY LAKESIDE RV PARK (Private)
48 units w/water/elec./sewer plus 32 w/water & elec., tents okay, reservations (360)983-3804, trailers to 40', showers, wheelchair access, playfield, trailer waste disposal, on Mayfield Lake, fishing, boat launch, pets okay, open year round, $$$$.
Take Harmony Rd. northwest 2.5 miles at flashing light.

IKE KINSWA (Washington State Park)
41 units w/water/elec./sewer plus 60 w/out, trailers to 60', mail reservations, flush toilets, showers, disabled access, trailer waste disposal, boat launch, fishing, swimming, horse trails, $-$$$$.
Take US 12 west 6 miles and follow signs north to park.

LAKE MAYFIELD RESORT/RV/MARINA (Private)
60 units w/water & elec. plus tent sites, reservations (360)985-2357, trailers to 38', showers, swimming, fishing, boat launch & rental, pets okay, open year round, $$-$$$$.
Take US 12 west 5 miles and follow signs.

MAYFIELD LAKE COUNTY PARK (County)
54 units, group area, reservations (360)985-2364, showers, wheelchair access, playground, trailer waste disposal, swimming, fishing, boat launch, hiking, open May thru Sept., $$$-$$$$.
Take US 12 west 3 miles, turn at the dam and drive .3 mile.

MOSSYROCK PARK (Private)
105 units w/water & elec., tents okay, trailers to 36', (360)983-3900, showers, wheelchair access, trailer waste disposal, on lake, fishing, pets okay, open year round, $-$$$.
Take US 12 east 2 miles and follow signs.

MOUNTAIN ROAD MOBILE & RV PARK (Private)
7 units w/water/elec./sewer, dry/tent camp, (360)983-3094, trailers to 40', showers, disabled access, trailer waste disposal, pets okay, open year round, $$-$$$.
Located west of town, at 262 Mossyrock.

WINSTON CREEK RV PARK (Private)
15 units w/water/elec./sewer, dry/tent camp, (360)985-2003, showers, trailer waste disposal, pets okay, year round, $$-$$$.
Located at 132 Winston Creek Rd.

MORTON

BACKSTROM PARK (City)
10 units w/full hookups, 17 w/water & elec., plus tent area, trailers to 36', showers, pets okay, open year round, $$-$$$.
Located in Morton, at 715 Main Ave.

GLENOMA/RIFFE LAKE RV PARK (Private)
20 units w/water/elec./sewer, 5 w/water & elec., plus tent area, (360)498-5385, trailers to 70', showers, wheelchair access, trailer waste disposal, pool, pets/horses okay, open year round, $$-$$$.
Take US 12 east 8 miles to Glenoma and park.

ROADHOUSE INN RV (Private) [RV]
16 RV sites - 8 w/hookups for elec., no tents, reservations (360)496-5029, trailers to 36', pets okay, open year round, $.
Located 1 mile west of Morton, on US 12.

ROY'S MOTEL & RV PARK (Private) [RV]
7 units w/hookups for water/elec./sewer, no tents, reservations (360)496-5000, no restrooms, no pets, open year round, $$$.
Located in Morton, at 161 N. Second St.

TAIDNAPAM PARK (Private) [A] [RV]
19 units w/water/elec./sewer, 33 w/water & elec., plus 16 tent sites, (360)497-7707, trailers to 70', showers, wheelchair access, trailer waste disposal, on Riffe Lake, fishing, $-$$$.
Take US 12 east of town and follow signs to east end of lake.

RANDLE

COWLITZ FALLS PARK (County) [A] [RV]
12 units w/water & elec., 73 w/out hookups, plus group area,

tents okay, reservations (360)497-7175, trailers to 36', showers, wheelchair access, trailer waste disposal, on Lake Scanwa, boat ramp & dock, fishing, pets okay, open May thru Oct., $$-$$$.
Take US 12 west 2 miles and follow Peters Rd. south to park.

SHADY FIRS CAMPGROUND/RV PARK (Private)
17 units w/water & elec., 20 w/out hookups, plus tent area, reservations (360)497-6108, trailers to 70', showers, laundry, playground, horses & pets okay, open year round, $$-$$$.
Take US 12 east 3 miles - located at 107 Young Rd.

(Southeast of Randle)

ADAMS FORK (Gifford Pinchot NF)
24 units, trailers to 22', swimming, fishing, elev. 2600', $.
Take State 131 south 3 miles, FSR 23 southeast 15.7 miles, FSR 21 southeast 4.7 miles, and FSR 56 east .2 mile.

BLUE LAKE CREEK (Gifford Pinchot NF)
11 units, trailers to 32', on river, fishing, hiking, elev. 1900', $.
Take State 131 south 3 miles and FSR 23 southeast 13.2 miles.

IRON CREEK (Gifford Pinchot NF)
98 units, trailers to 32', on river, fishing, hiking, old-growth trees, open mid May thru mid Oct., elev. 1200', $$-$$$.
Take State 131 south 3 miles and FSR 25 southwest 9 miles.

NORTH FORK (Gifford Pinchot NF)
33 units, 3 group sites - reservations (800)280-2267, trailers to 32', fishing, hiking, on river, bicycling, open mid May thru mid Oct., elev. 1500', individual sites $$-$$$.
Take State 131 south 3 miles and FSR 23 southeast 8.7 miles.

TAKHLAKH (Gifford-Pinchot NF)
54 units, trailers to 22', lake - speed limits, boating, fishing, swimming, hiking, nearby lava flow, elev. 4500', $.
Take State 131 south 3 miles, FSR 23 southeast 28.9 miles, and FSR 2329 north 1.6 miles.

TOWER ROCK (Gifford Pinchot NF)
22 units, reservations (800)280-2267, trailers to 22', on river, fishing, open mid May thru early Oct., elev. 1100', $$-$$$.
Take State 131 south 3 miles, FSR 23 southeast 6.8 miles, and FSR 2306 west 1.8 miles.

TOWER ROCK U-FISH RV PARK (Private)
9 units w/water/elec./sewer, 20 w/water & elec., plus tent area, reservations (360)497-7680, restaurant, trailer waste disposal, trout ponds, horses & pets okay, open year round, $$-$$$.
Take State 131 south 3 miles, FSR 23 southeast 6.8 miles, and follow signs - located 2 miles past Cispus Learning Center.

CASTLE ROCK

DREWS TRAILER PARK (Private)
14 RV units w/water/elec./sewer, no restrooms, reservations (360)274-8920, trailers to 40', no pets, open year round, $$$.
Take State 504 east 10 miles to Toutle and park.

MT. ST. HELENS RV PARK (Private)
88 units w/full hookups plus tent sites, (360)274-8522, trailers to 70', showers, disabled access, pets okay, year round, $$$$.
Take State 504 east 2 miles - located on hill behind grocery store.

SEAQUEST (Washington State Park)
16 units w/water/elec./sewer plus 76 standard sites, group reservations (360)274-8633, trailers to 50', flush toilets, showers, wheelchair access, trailer waste disposal, fishing, $-$$$.
Take State 504 east 5 miles.

SILVER LAKE MOTEL & RESORT (Private)
7 units w/water/elec./sewer, 14 w/water & elec., plus tent sites, (360)274-6141, trailers to 35', showers, groceries, playground, rec room, swimming, fishing, boat launch/rental, pets okay, $$$.
Take State 504 east 6 miles.

TOUTLE VILLAGE RV PARK (Private)
10 units w/water/elec./sewer plus 2 tent sites, reservations (360)274-9315, trailers to 35', showers, laundry, wheelchair access, trailer waste disposal, pets okay, $$-$$$.
Take State 504 east 10 miles.

VOLCANO VIEW RESORT (Private)
29 units w/water/elec./sewer plus 15 tent sites, reservations (360)274-7087, trailers to 35', showers, wheelchair access, boat rental, fishing, hiking, pets okay, open year round, $$-$$$$.
Take State 504 east 8 miles to east end of Silver Lake.

(North of Castle Rock)

COWLITZ RESORT & RV PARK (Private)
25 units w/water/elec./sewer, reservations (360)864-6611, showers, trailer waste disposal, river, boat launch, fishing, $$$.
Take I-5 north to exit #59 - in Toledo, at 162 Cowlitz Loop.

FROST ROAD TRAILER PARK (Private)
21 units w/water/elec./sewer, tents okay, reservations (360)785-3616, showers, laundry, rec room, trailer waste disposal, $$-$$$.
I-5 to exit #63, go east .8 mile, north 1.5 mile, and west .5 mile.

MERMAC RV PARK & STORE (Private)
55 trailer sites w/full hookups, reservations (360)274-6785, showers, handicap facilities, laundry, groceries, $$$.
Leave I-5 just north of Castle Rock on exit #52 - park is .6 mile.

KELSO

BROOKHOLLOW RV PARK (Private)
133 RV units w/full hookups, trailers to 70', reservations (360) 577-6474, showers, laundry, pets extra, open year round, $$$$. Leave I-5 at exit #39 and head east .8 mile on Allen.

LONGVIEW

MARV'S RV PARK (Private)
20 units w/full hookups plus tent area, (360)795-3453, trailers to 40', showers, wheelchair access, rec room, propane, trailer waste disposal, fishing, pets okay, open year round, $$-$$$. Take State 4 west 20 miles.

OAKS TRAILER & RV PARK (Private)
94 RV units w/full hookups, reservations (360)425-2708, trailers to 40', pull thrus, showers, wheelchair access, play area, pets okay, open year round, $$$-$$$$. Located at 636 California Way in Longview.

COUGAR

BEAVER BAY CAMP (Pacific Power)
63 campsites, group area - reservations required (503)464-5035, flush toilets, showers, handicap access, trailer waste disposal, playground, on Yale Reservoir, boat launch, fishing, swimming, water skiing, open May thru Oct., groups $120/night - others $$. Follow State 503 east 2 miles.

COUGAR CAMP (Pacific Power)
45 tent sites, group area - reservations required (503)464-5035, flush toilets, showers, handicap access, playground, on Yale Reservoir, boat launch, fishing, swimming, water skiing, open summer only, groups $120/night - others $$. Follow State 503 east 1 mile.

COUGAR RV PARK (Private)
14 units w/hookups for water/elec./sewer plus 7 tent sites, reservations (360)238-5224, trailers to 70', showers, pets okay, open year round, $$-$$$. Located at 16730 Lewis River Rd.

LONE FIR RESORT (Private)
32 units w/hookups for water/elec./sewer, tents okay, reservations (360)238-5210, trailers to 40', showers, laundry, ice, swimming pool, pets okay, $$$-$$$$. Located on Lewis River Rd. - follow signs.

LOWER FALLS REC. AREA (Nat'l Volcanic Mon.)

42 campsites, trailers to 32', on Lewis River, waterfalls, pets okay, open when no snow, $-$$.
Take State 503 east 18 miles, and FSR 90 north 12 miles - located at monument headquarters.

SWIFT CAMP (Pacific Power)

93 campsites, trailers okay, flush toilets, handicap access, trailer waste disposal, on Swift Reservoir, boat launch, fishing, swimming, water skiing, open May thru Oct., $$.
Take State 503 east 18 miles and FSR 90 a short distance to campground.

YALE

CRESAP BAY CAMP (Pacific Power)

58 campsites, group site - reservations required (503)464-5035, flush toilets, showers, handicap access, trailer waste disposal, on Lake Merwin, boat ramp & moorage, swimming, fishing, water skiing, interpretive trail, open summer only, groups $120/night - others $$.
Take State 503 east 2 miles, and Lewis River Highway south 4 miles to camp.

SADDLE DAM (Pacific Power)

14 tent/trailer units, flush toilets, showers, handicap access, trailer waste disposal, on Lake Merwin, boat ramp, swimming, fishing, water skiing, open late April thru early Nov., $$.
Take State 503 east 2 miles, and Lewis River Highway south 4 miles to campground.

KALAMA

CAMP KALAMA RV PARK (Private)

65 units w/full hookups plus 20 w/water & elec., tents okay, reservations (360)673-2456, pull thrus, showers, laundry, wheelchair access, groceries & tackle, game room, playground, trailer waste disposal, on Kalama River, swimming, fishing, boat launch, pets okay, open year round, $$$-$$$$$.
Leave I-5 at exit #32 and follow Kalama River Rd. east .1 mile.

LOUIS L. RASMUSSEN RV PARK (Private)

22 units w/hookups for water/elec/sewer, 5 dry sites, plus tent area, reservations (360)673-2626, trailers to 40', showers, wheelchair access, trailer waste disposal, on Columbia River, fishing, nature trail, pets okay, open year round, $$-$$$.
Leave I-5 northbound at exit #27 (southbound exit #30) - located at 268 Hendrickson Dr.

PORT OF KALAMA RV PARK (Port)

22 pull thrus w/hookups for water/elec./sewer plus tent area, reservations (360)673-2325, showers, wheelchair access, playfield, playground, trailer waste disposal, river, fishing, boat launch, gas, diesel, pets okay, open year round, $$-$$$.
Leave I-5 at exit #32 - park is 1 block west.

WOODLAND

COLUMBIA RIVERFRONT RV PARK (Private)

75 units w/full hookups plus tent area, reservations (800)845-9842, trailers to 40', showers, laundry, wheelchair access, heated pool, volleyball & basketball courts, propane, on Columbia River, fishing, hiking, pets okay, open year round, $-$$$$.
Leave I-5 at exit #22 and follow the dike access road for 2 miles - located at 1881 Dike Rd.

YACOLT

SUNSET (Gifford Pinchot NF)

16 units, trailers to 22', wheelchair access - inc. trail, stream, fishing, hiking, pets okay, elev. 1000', $.
Take County Rd. 16 south 3 miles, County Rd. 12 east 8 miles, and FSR 42 to campground.

VANCOUVER

GOLDEN WEST MOBILE MANOR (Private)

23 units w/full hookups, no tents, reservations (360)892-7463, trailers to 31', showers, laundry, playground, rec hall, trailer waste disposal, small pets okay, open year round, $$$-$$$$.
Leave I-205 at Orchards exit and take Fourth Plain Blvd. to 131st Ave. - located at 6816 NE 131st Ave.

99 MOBILE LODGE & RV PARK (Private)

60 units w/hookups for water/elec./sewer, no tents, reservations (360)573-0351, showers, laundry, pets extra, $$$.
Take I-5 north to 134th St. exit - located on State 99 at 129th St.

(North of Vancouver)

BATTLE GROUND LAKE (Washington State Park)

35 units plus 15 primitive horse campsites, group area - reservations (360)687-4621, trailers to 50', flush toilets, showers, disabled access, community kitchen, snack bar, trailer waste disposal, on lake, boat launch, scuba diving area, fishing, swimming, horse trails, open year round, $-$$$.
Take I-5 north 9 miles, State 502 east 10 miles, and follow signs northeast 4 miles to park.

BIG FIR CAMPGROUND (Private)
37 units w/water/elec./sewer plus 38 tent sites, (360)887-8970, trailers to 70', showers, pets okay, open year round, $$-$$$.
Take I-5 north to exit #14 and go east 4 miles to campground.

LEWIS RIVER RV PARK (Private)
25 units w/water/elec./sewer, 45 w/water & elec., 15 tent sites, (360)225-9556, trailers to 60', showers, laundry, wheelchair access, pool, trailer waste disposal, fishing, pets okay, $$$$.
Take I-5 north 20 miles to exit #21 and State 503 east 5 miles.

PARADISE POINT (Washington State Park)
70 units, trailers to 45', flush toilets, showers, trailer waste disposal, on E. Fork Lewis River, boat launch, fishing, hiking trail, open year round - weekends only Oct. thru March, $-$$.
Take I-5 north 15 miles.

VOLCANO VIEW CAMPGROUND (Private)
23 units w/water/elec./sewer, 25 w/water & elec., 27 tent sites, (360)231-4329, showers, groceries, playfield, pets okay, $$-$$$.
Take I-5 north 20 miles to exit #21, State 503 northeast 24 miles to Ariel, and go south 1 mile to campground.

(East of Vancouver)

BEACON ROCK TRAILER & RV PARK (Private)
50 units w/full hookups plus tent area, (509)427-8473, trailers to 60', showers, laundry, wheelchair access, on Columbia River, propane, boat launch/dock & moorage, fishing, hiking, pets okay, open year round, $$-$$$.
Take State 14 east about 32 miles to the town of Skamania - located at 62 Moorage Rd.

BEACON ROCK (Washington State Park)
33 units, group area - reservations (360)427-8265, trailers to 50', flush toilets, showers, disabled access, community kitchen, trailer waste disposal, on Columbia River, boat launch, fishing, trail to top of monolith, pets okay, open April thru Oct., $-$$.
Take State 14 east 35 miles to Beacon Rock and campground.

NORTHWEST FISHING GUIDE/RV PARK (Private)
4 units w/water/elec./sewer, 5 w/water & elec., plus 3 dry sites, tents okay, reservations (509)427-4625, trailers to 40', showers, trailer waste disposal, pets okay, open March thru Dec., $-$$$.
Take State 14 east to milepost #33 and turn onto Woodard Creek Rd. - located at 202 Woodard Creek Rd.

REED ISLAND (Washington State Park)
5 primitive boat-in sites, no water, on Columbia River, picnic facilities, fishing, open year round, $.
Take State 14 east 16 miles to the Camas/Washougal Marina and boat to campground - located 1 mile east of Washougal.

CENTRAL WASHINGTON CAMPGROUNDS

See Page

191
191
191-192
192-194

194
195
195-197
197-199

200
200-201
202

202

202-204
204-205
205-206
206-207

207-209
209-210
210

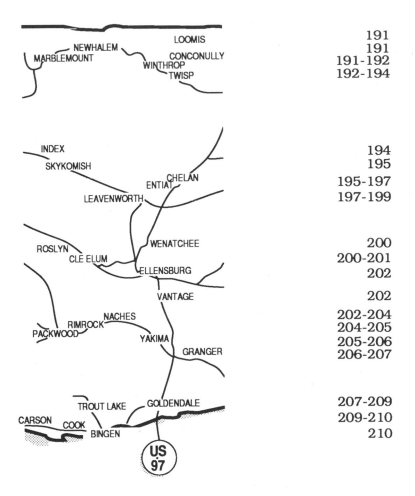

LOOMIS

THE STAGE STOP AT SULLY'S (Private)
18 units w/hookups for water/elec./sewer, tents okay, reservations (509)223-3275, wheelchair access, groceries, restaurant, pets okay, open year round, $-$$.
Located right in Loomis, on Main St.

NEWHALEM

DEVIL'S PARK (Okanogan NF)
Dispersed hike-in tent camping in the Pasayten Wilderness, creek, horse trails - meager grazing & scarce water in late summer, $.
Take State 20 approximately 15 miles east of Newhalem to Devil's Park Trailhead #738, and follow trail 3.5 miles to campground.

McMILLAN PARK (Okanogan NF)
Dispersed hike-in tent camping in the Pasayten Wilderness, creek, horse trails - meager grazing & scarce water in late summer, $.
Take State 20 approximately 15 miles east of Newhalem to Devil's Park Trailhead #738, and follow trail 2 miles to campground.

MARBLEMOUNT

COLONIAL CREEK (N. Cascades Nat'l Park)
164 units, trailers to 22', flush toilets, wheelchair access, picnic area, summer program, trailer waste disposal, at Diablo Lake, boat launch, fishing, hiking, pets okay, $$.
Take State 20 east of Marblemount 24 miles.

GOODELL CREEK (N. Cascades Nat'l Park)
22 units, small trailers okay, on Skagit River, raft/canoe launch, fishing, hiking, $$.
Take State 20 east 13 miles.

NEWHALEM CREEK (N. Cascades Nat'l Park)
129 units, trailers to 22', flush toilets, wheelchair access, trailer waste disposal, on Skagit River, fishing, hiking, $$.
Take State 20 east 14 miles.

CONCONULLY

CONCONULLY (Washington State Park)
75 units, trailers to 60', flush toilets, showers, community kitchen, trailer waste disposal, boat launch, fishing, swimming, trail, open year round - weekends only Oct. thru March, $-$$.
Follow signs - at south end of town.

JACK'S RV PARK & MOTEL (Private)
66 units w/hookups for water/elec./sewer, tents okay, reservations (509)826-0132, trailers to 40', showers, laundry, pool, trailer waste disposal, propane, on Conconully Reservoir, fishing, hiking, mountain biking, pets okay, open year round, $$-$$$.
Located in town, 1 block east of Main St.

KOZY CABINS & RV PARK (Private)
12 units w/full hookups, tents okay, reservations (509)826-6780, showers, stream, fishing, $$-$$$.
Located in town, at 111 Broadway.

LAZE DAZE RV PARK (Private)
43 RV sites w/hookups for water/elec./sewer, reservations (509)826-0326, trailers to 38', showers, laundry, wheelchair access, on reservoir, pets okay, open April thru Sept., $$-$$$.
Located in town, 1 block east of Main St.

LIARS COVE RESORT (Private)
30 units w/hookups for water/elec./sewer, tents okay, reservations (509)826-1288, showers, lake, swimming, fishing, boat launch & rental, $$$.
Located at the east end of town.

SHADY PINES RESORT (Private)
23 units w/water/elec./sewer, tents okay, reservations (509)826-2287, showers, swimming, fishing, boat rental, $$$-$$$$.
Located 1 mile out of town, on west shore of Conconully Res.

'THE OTHER PLACE' RV PARK (Private)
25 units w/full hookups, no tents, reservations (509)826-4231, wheelchair access, showers, laundry, nearby lake & fishing, $$$.
Located just east of Main, on A St.

(North of Conconully)

ORIOLE (Okanogan NF)
10 units, stream, fishing, elev. 2900', $.
Take Salmon Creek N. Fork Rd. northwest 1.8 miles and FSR 38 northwest an additional .8 mile.

SALMON MEADOWS (Okanogan NF)
7 units, stream, hiking trails, horse corral, elev. 4500', $.
Take Salmon Creek N. Fork Rd. northwest 1.8 miles and FSR 38 northwest an additional 6.9 miles.

WINTHROP

BIG TWIN LAKE CAMPGROUND (Private)
20 units w/hookups for water/elec./sewer, 26 w/water & elec., 40 w/out hookups, plus tent area, reservations (509)996-2650,

pull-thrus, showers, laundry, playground, trailer waste disposal, on lake, swimming, fishing, boat rentals, no large dogs, $$$.
Take State 20 south 3 miles and Twin Lake Rd. west 2.3 miles.

DERRY'S RESORT ON PEARRYGIN LAKE (Private)
64 units w/hookups for water/elec./sewer plus 90 tent sites, reservations (509)996-2322, showers, laundry, groceries, trailer waste disposal, swimming, fishing, boat launch, pets okay, $$$.
Take Riverside north .5 mile, Bluff St. east 2 miles, and Pearrygin Lake Rd. east 1 mile.

METHOW RIVER/WINTHROP KOA (Private)
16 units w/hookups for water/elec./sewer, 72 w/water & elec., plus 42 tent sites, reservations (509)996-2258, trailers to 70', showers, laundry, playground, pool, groceries, trailer waste disposal, on river, boat launch, fishing, hiking, bicycle rental, horse tie up area, pets okay, open mid April thru Oct., $$$$-$$$$$.
Follow State 20 south 1 mile.

PEARRYGIN LAKE (Washington State Park)
30 units w/water/elec./sewer plus 53 standard sites, mail reservations, trailers to 60', group area - reservations (509)996-2370, flush toilets, showers, wheelchair access, trailer waste disposal, boat launch, fishing, open April thru mid Nov., $-$$$$.
Take Riverside north .5 mile, Bluff St. east 2 miles, and follow Pearrygin Lake Rd. to campground.

PINE-NEAR TRAILER PARK (Private)
28 units w/hookups for water/elec./sewer plus 25 tent sites, reservations (509)996-2391, showers, laundry, trailer waste disposal, pets okay, $$-$$$.
Take Riverside north .5 mile and Bluff St. east .1 mile.

(North of Winthrop)

FALLS CREEK (Okanogan NF)
7 units, trailers to 18', fishing, swimming, short hike to waterfall, elev. 2300', $.
Take W. Chewack Rd. north 6.6 miles and FSR 51 north 5.3 miles.

(West of Winthrop)

EARLY WINTERS (Okanogan NF)
13 units, trailers to 16', wheelchair access, river, fishing, elev. 2160', $$.
Follow State 20 northwest 16 miles.

KLIPCHUCK (Okanogan NF)
46 units, trailers to 32', flush toilets, wheelchair access, stream, fishing, hiking, rattlesnake area, elev. 2920', $$.
Take State 20 northwest 17.2 miles and FSR 300 north 1 mile.

LONE FIR (Okanogan NF)
27 units, trailers to 22', wheelchair access, creek, fishing, hiking, views of Silver Star Glacier, elev. 3640', $$.
Follow State 20 northwest 26.8 miles.

TWISP

(East of Twisp)

J R (Okanogan NF)
6 units, trailers to 25', wheelchair access, stream, bicycling, elev. 3900', $.
Follow State 20 east 12.1 miles.

LOUP LOUP (Okanogan NF)
25 units, trailers to 22', stream, access to mountain bike trails, elev. 4200', $.
Follow State 20 east 13 miles and FSR 42 north .6 mile.

RIVER BEND RV PARK (Private)
69 units w/hookups for water/elec./sewer plus 35 tent sites, reservations (509)997-3500, showers, laundry, groceries, playground, trailer waste disposal, fishing, pets okay, $$$-$$$$.
Follow State 20 southeast 6 miles.

(West of Twisp)

BLACK PINE LAKE (Okanogan NF)
23 units, trailers to 25', lake - non-electric motors, wheelchair access - includes trail, boat launch & docks, fishing, hiking, pets okay, elev. 4200', $$.
Take Poorman Creek Rd. west 11 miles, FSR 43 south 8 miles.

POPLAR FLAT (Okanogan NF)
16 units, trailers to 22', wheelchair access, river, fishing, hiking trails, elev. 2900', $.
Take Poorman Creek Rd. west 10.8 miles, FSR 44 northwest 9.4 miles.

WAR CREEK (Okanogan NF)
12 units, trailers to 25', fishing, hiking trails, elev. 2400', $.
Take Poorman Creek Rd. west 10.8 miles, FSR 44 west 3.3 miles.

INDEX

WALLACE FALLS (Washington State Park)
6 tent units, picnic shelter, disabled access, on Wallace River, waterfalls, $$.
Take US 2 west 6 miles - located 2 miles northeast of Gold Bar.

SKYKOMISH

BECKLER RIVER (Mt. Baker-Snoqualmie NF)
27 units, trailers to 22', reservations (800)280-2267, fishing, swimming, on site caretaker, elev. 900', $$.
Take US 2 east 1 mile and FSR 65 north 2 miles.

MILLER RIVER (Mt. Baker-Snoqualmie NF)
Group sites - reservations required (800)280-2267, trailers to 22', swimming, fishing, elev. 1000', $32.50 small group/$84.50 large.
Take US 2 west 2.5 miles, FSR 64 southeast 1 mile, and FSR 6410 south 1 mile.

MONEY CREEK (Mt. Baker-Snoqualmie NF)
24 units plus group sites, reservations (800)280-2267, trailers to 22', wheelchair access, swimming, fishing, on site caretaker, pets okay, elev. 900', $$.
Take US 2 west 2.5 miles and FSR 64 southeast .1 mile.

CHELAN

LAKESHORE RV PARK (Private)
141 units w/full hookups plus 20 w/water & elec., tents okay, reservations (509)682-5031, trailers to 70', showers, playground, trailer waste disposal, on lake, swimming, fishing, bumper & paddleboat rentals, no dogs in summer, $$$-$$$$$.
Located right in Chelan, on State 150.

(West of Chelan)

KAMEI RESORT (Private)
10 units w/hookups for water/elec./sewer plus 45 w/water & elec., tents okay, reservations (509)687-3690, trailers to 34', showers, snack bar, on Wapato Lake, fishing, boat launch/rental & dock, pets okay, open May thru July, $$$.
Take State 150 along the north shore of Lake Chelan 5 miles and follow Swartout/Wapato Lake Rd. an additional 5 miles to resort.

LAKE CHELAN (Washington State Park)
17 units w/water/elec./sewer, 127 standard sites, plus group area, mail reservations, trailers to 30', flush toilets, showers, disabled access, snack bar, trailer waste disposal, boat launch, scuba diving area, fishing, swimming, water skiing, $-$$$$.
Follow the road leading around south side of Lake Chelan - campground is 9 miles west of city.

PARADISE RESORT (Private)
25 units w/hookups for water & elec. plus 15 tent sites, reservations (509)687-3444, showers, store, on Wapato Lake, boat launch & rental, fishing, hiking, pets okay, open April thru Labor Day, $$$.

Take State 150 along the north shore of Lake Chelan 5 miles, follow Swartout/Wapato Lake Rd. an additional 3 miles, take a right and go 2 blocks to resort.

TWENTYFIVE MILE CREEK (Washington State Park)
23 units w/hookups for water/elec./sewer plus 63 standard sites, trailers to 30', group area - reservations (509)687-3710, flush toilets, showers, trailer waste disposal, lake, boat launch & dock, swimming, $$-$$$$.
Follow the road leading around south side of Lake Chelan - campground is 20 miles west of city.

(North of Chelan)

ALTA LAKE (Washington State Park)
16 units w/hookups for water & elec. plus 149 standard sites, trailers to 40', group area - reservations (509)923-2473, flush toilets, showers, wheelchair access, community kitchen, trailer waste disposal, boat launch, fishing, swimming, trail, $-$$.
Take US 97 northeast 17 miles, State 153 west 2 miles, and follow campground road south 2 miles.

(Southeast of Chelan)

DAROGA (Washington State Park)
25 units w/hookups for water & elec. plus 17 walk-in/boat-in tent sites, group area - reservations (509)884-8702, showers, wheelchair access, playfield & ball courts, trailer waste disposal, swimming beach, boat launch & moorage, fishing, windsurfing, hiking, open April thru Oct., $-$$$.
Take State 150 southeast 2 miles to where it meets US 97, cross the Columbia River and continue south 15 miles.

ORONDO RIVER PARK (Port)
12 units w/hookups for water & elec., tents okay, reservations (509)784-1796, wheelchair accessible restrooms, showers, on Columbia River, boat launch/moorage/dock & gas, fishing, pets okay, open mid April to mid Oct., $$$.
Take State 150 southeast 2 miles to where it meets US 97, cross the Columbia River and continue south 20 miles.

ENTIAT

ENTIAT CITY PARK (City)
31 RV units w/hookups for elec. plus 50 tent sites, information (509)784-1500, showers, wheelchair access, playground, trailer waste disposal, lake, swimming, fishing, boat launch & moorage, no pets, open year round - no hookups Nov. to March, $$$-$$$$.
Leave US 97 in Entiat on Lakeshore Dr., and follow to park.

COTTONWOOD (Wenatchee NF)
25 campsites plus group area, trailers to 22', river, fishing, hiking, elev. 3100', $.
Take US 97 southwest 1.4 miles and Entiat Valley Rd. northwest 39 miles.

FOX CREEK (Wenatchee NF)
9 campsites, some trailers, fishing, elev. 2300', $.
Take US 97 southwest 1.4 miles and Entiat Valley Rd. northwest 27 miles.

LAKE CREEK (Wenatchee NF)
18 campsites, trailers to 18', fishing, hiking, elev. 2400', $.
Take US 97 southwest 1.4 miles and Entiat Valley Rd. northwest 28.2 miles.

NORTH FORK (Wenatchee NF)
9 units - 1 trailer to 22', river, fishing, trail, elev. 2700', $.
Take US 97 southwest 1.4 miles and Entiat Valley Rd. northwest 33.5 miles.

PINE FLAT GROUP CAMP (Wenatchee NF)
1 group site - information (509)784-1511, no water, on Mad River, fishing, hiking, elev. 1900', groups $30/night.
Take US 97 southwest 1.4 miles, Entiat Valley Rd. northwest 9 miles, and FSR 5700 northwest 3 miles.

SILVER FALLS (Wenatchee NF)
29 campsites, trailers to 22', group area - reservations (509)784-1511, limited handicap access, stream, fishing, hiking, waterfall, pets okay, elev. 2400', $.
Take US 97 southwest 1.4 miles and Entiat Valley Rd. northwest 30.4 miles.

LEAVENWORTH

CHALET RV PARK (Private)
16 units w/full hookups, 12 w/water & elec., 1 w/elec. only, plus 12 tent sites, reservations (509)548-4578, showers, laundry, nearby fishing & stores, pets okay, $$$-$$$$$.
At east end of Leavenworth, on US 2.

PINE VILLAGE KOA (Private)
46 units w/hookups for water/elec./sewer, 60 w/water & elec., plus 29 tent sites, reservations (509)548-7709, showers, laundry, groceries, picnic shelter, playground, trailer waste disposal, swimming pool, hot tub for adults, river, swimming, fishing, hiking, pets okay, $$$$-$$$$$.
Take US 2 east .3 mile and River Bend Dr. north .5 mile.

(North of Leavenworth)

GOOSE CREEK (Wenatchee NF)

29 campsites - some okay for trailers, fishing, elev. 2200', $$.
Take US 2 east of town .3 mile, State 209 north 17.5 miles, and
FSR 6100 north 3.2 miles.

(Northwest of Leavenworth)

COUGAR INN RV (Private)

50 units, tents okay, trailers to 70', reservations (509)763-3354,
showers, disabled access, restaurant, on lake, pedal/row boat
rentals, boat launch, fishing, hiking, pets okay, year round, $$.
Take US 2 northwest 16 miles and follow State 207 north to the
head of Lake Wenatchee.

COVE RESORT (Private)

10 units w/water/elec./sewer, 25 w/water & elec., plus 65 tent
sites, (509)763-3130, trailers to 34', showers, on Fish Lake, boat
rentals/launch, fishing, hiking, pets okay, year round, $$-$$$$.
Take US 2 northwest 16 miles, State 207 north 5 miles, and
Chiwawa Loop Rd east 1 mile.

GLACIER VIEW (Wenatchee NF)

23 tent units plus 16 walk-in sites on Lake Wenatchee shore,
boat launch, swimming, fishing, water skiing, elev. 1900', $$.
Take US 2 northwest 15.9 miles, State 207 northeast 3.4 miles,
South Shore Rd. west 3.9 miles, and FSR 290 west 1.5 miles.

LAKE WENATCHEE (Washington State Park)

197 units, group area - reservations (509)763-3101, trailers to
60', flush toilets, showers, disabled access, trailer waste disposal,
boat launch, swimming, horse trails & rental, pets okay, $-$$$.
Take US 2 northwest 16 miles and State 207 north 6 miles.

MIDWAY VILLAGE & GROCERY (Private)

14 RV sites w/full hookups, reservations (509)763-3344, trailers
to 40', pets okay, open year round, $$$.
Take US 2 northwest 16 miles, State 207 north 5 miles, and
Chiwawa Loop Rd east .5 mile.

NASON CREEK (Wenatchee NF)

73 units plus group site, trailers to 32', flush toilets, river,
fishing, Nason Ridge Trailhead, pets okay, elev. 1800', $$.
Take US 2 northwest 16 miles, State 207 north 3.4 miles, and
South Shore Rd. west .1 mile.

TUMWATER (Wenatchee NF)

84 units, trailers to 20', group site - reservations (800)280-2267,
flush toilets, handicap access, stream, fishing, hiking, elev.
2000', groups $50/night - individuals $$.
Follow US 2 northwest 9.9 miles to campground.

(Southwest of Leavenworth)

BLACKPINE CREEK HORSECAMP (Wenatchee NF)
10 units, trailers to 22', horse ramp, elev. 3000', $.
Take US 2 west .5 mile and Icicle Rd. southwest 19.2 miles.

BRIDGE CREEK (Wenatchee NF)
6 units, trailers to 18', fishing, hiking, elev. 1900', $$.
Take US 2 west .5 mile and Icicle Rd. southwest 9.4 miles.

CHATTER CREEK (Wenatchee NF)
12 units, trailers to 22', group area - reservations (800)280-2267,
fishing, hiking, elev. 2800', $$.
Take US 2 west .5 mile and Icicle Rd. southwest 16.1 miles.

EIGHTMILE (Wenatchee NF)
45 units, trailers to 20', group area - reservations (800)280-2267,
handicap access, stream, fishing, hiking, elev. 1800', $$.
Take US 2 west .5 mile and Icicle Rd. southwest 8 miles.

ICICLE RIVER RANCH (Private)
52 units w/full hookups plus 12 tent sites, (509)548-5420,
showers, spa, river, swimming, fishing, pets okay, $$$$-$$$$$.
Take US 2 west .5 mile and Icicle Rd. southwest 3 miles.

IDA CREEK (Wenatchee NF)
10 units, trailers to 20', handicap access, fishing, hiking, $$.
Take US 2 west .5 mile and Icicle Rd. southwest 14.2 miles.

JOHNNY CREEK (Wenatchee NF)
65 units, trailers to 20', handicap access, fishing, hiking, elev.
2300', $$.
Take US 2 west .5 mile and Icicle Rd. southwest 12.4 miles.

ROCK ISLAND (Wenatchee NF)
22 units, trailers to 22', handicap access, stream, fishing, hiking,
elev. 2900', $$.
Take US 2 west .5 mile and Icicle Rd. southwest 17.7 miles.

(Southeast of Leavenworth)

BLUE SHASTIN TRAILER & RV PARK (Private)
75 units w/hookups for water/elec./sewer plus 5 tent sites,
reservations (509)548-4184, showers, laundry, lounge, pool,
trailer waste disposal, river, fishing, hiking, pets okay, $$$-$$$$.
Take US 2 southeast 4 miles and US 97 south 7 miles.

VALLEY COTTAGE MOTEL RV (Private)
5 RV units w/hookups for water/elec./sewer, no restrooms,
reservations (509)548-5731, trailers to 40', on river, fishing,
hiking, no pets, open year round, $$.
Follow US 2 east 7 miles to Dryden - located at 8912 Motel Rd.

WENATCHEE

BEEBE BRIDGE PARK (PUD)
27 units w/water & elec., tents okay, reservations (800)424-3526, trailers to 30', showers, wheelchair access, trailer waste disposal, river, boat launch, fishing, hiking, no pets, open May thru Oct., $$$-$$$$.
Take State 28 north 5 miles and US 2/97 north 34 miles.

LINCOLN ROCK (Washington State Park)
32 units w/water/sewer/elec., 35 w/water & elec., plus 27 tent sites, mail reservations, trailers to 65', flush toilets, showers, disabled access, trailer waste disposal, boat launch, fishing, water skiing, open year round, $$-$$$$.
Take State 28 north 4 miles and US 2 north 2 miles.

SQUILCHUCK (Washington State Park)
Group campsites - reservations required (509)664-6373.
Follow Squilchuck Rd southwest 9 miles.

WENATCHEE CONFLUENCE (Washington State Park)
51 units w/water/elec./sewer plus 8 tent sites, trailers to 65', showers, wheelchair access inc. trail, playground, trailer waste disposal, Columbia & Wenatchee Rivers, boat launch, fishing, swimming, water skiing, year round, $$-$$$$.
North of town take Euclid Ave. south .8 mile and follow signs.

ROSLYN

CLE ELUM RIVER (Wenatchee NF)
35 units, trailers to 22', fishing, hiking, elev. 2200', $$.
Take State 903 northwest 8 miles and CR 903 northwest 7 miles.

SALMON LA SAC (Wenatchee NF)
127 units, trailers to 22', flush toilets, handicap access, picnic shelter, fishing, hiking, horse ramp/corrals, trailhead to Cascade Crest Trail & Alpine Lakes Wilderness, elev. 2400', $-$$.
Take State 903 northwest 8 miles, CR 903 northwest 10.7 miles.

THE LAST RESORT (Private)
8 units w/water & elec., tents okay, reservations (509)649-2222, restaurant, propane, on Lake Cle Elum, fishing, hiking, $$$.
Take State 903 northwest 4 miles and follow signs to resort road - it's approximately 1 mile.

WISH POOSH (Wenatchee NF)
39 units, trailers to 22', flush toilets, on Cle Elum Lake, boat launch, swimming, fishing, water skiing, occasionally closes late in season due to low water, elev. 2400', $$.
Take State 903 northwest 7 miles and FSR 112 west .1 mile.

CLE ELUM

TRAILER CORRAL RV PARK (Private)
15 units w/hookups for water/elec./sewer, 11 w/water & elec., plus 4 w/out hookups, reservations (509)674-2433, showers, trailer waste disposal, open year round, $$$.
Take I-90 east to exit #85 and follow State 970 east 1 mile.

(West of Cle Elum)

CRYSTAL SPRINGS (Wenatchee NF)
20 units, trailers to 22', picnic shelter, fishing, berry & mushroom picking, elev. 2400', $.
Take I-90 west 20.7 miles and FSR 212 northwest .4 mile.

KACHESS (Wenatchee NF)
180 units, trailers to 32', group area - reservations (800)280-2267, flush toilets, on Lake Kachess, boat launch, swimming, fishing, water skiing, hiking, interpretive trail, occasionally closes late in season due to low water, elev. 2300', $$.
Take I-90 west 20.7 miles and FSR 49 northeast 5.4 miles.

LAKE EASTON (Washington State Park)
45 units w/hookups for water/elec./sewer plus 92 standard sites, trailers to 60', group area - reservations (509)656-2230, flush toilets, showers, disabled access, trailer waste disposal, boat launch, fishing, swimming, $-$$$$.
Take I-90 west to exit# 70 - located 1 mile west of Easton.

RV TOWN INC. (Private)
20 units w/hookups for water/elec./sewer plus 52 w/water & elec., tents okay, reservations (509)656-2360, trailers to 40', showers, laundry, playground, pool, restaurant, trailer waste disposal, stream, fishing, hiking, pets & horses okay, $$$$.
Take I-90 west to exit #70 - located in Easton.

(East of Cle Elum)

MINERAL SPRINGS (Wenatchee NF)
12 units, fishing, elev. 2700', $$.
Take US 97 east 12 miles and US 97 north 9 miles.

MINERAL SPRINGS RESORT & RV (Private)
8 units w/hookups for water & elec. plus 7 w/elec., reservations (509)857-2361, restaurant, hiking, gold panning, agate beds, $$.
Take US 97 east 12 miles and US 97 north 9 miles.

TANEUM (Wenatchee NF)
13 units, picnic area, hiking, horse & motorcycle trails, stream, fishing, elev. 2400', $$.
Take I-90 east 12 miles, Taneum Rd. west 3 miles, and FSR 33 northwest 4.2 miles.

ELLENSBURG

ELLENSBURG KOA (Private)

12 units w/hookups for water/elec./sewer, 88 w/water & elec., plus 40 tent sites, reservations (509)925-9319, showers, wheelchair access, laundry, groceries, rec room, playground, swimming pool, trailer waste disposal, on river, boat launch, rafting, fishing, nearby restaurant & horse facilities, open April thru mid Oct., $$$$-$$$$$.
Leave I-90 at exit #106 and follow signs to campground.

RIVERVIEW CAMPGROUND (Private)
34 units w/water & elec. plus 76 tent sites, reservations (509) 952-6043, trailers to 35', showers, propane, on river, boat rental, fishing, hiking, pets okay, open March thru mid Oct., $-$$$.
Located on State 821, between mileposts 14 & 15.

VANTAGE

VANTAGE KOA (Private)
114 units w/hookups for water/elec./sewer plus 36 tent sites, reservations (509)856-2230, showers, laundry, groceries, rec room, playground, pool, hot tub, trailer waste disposal, on Columbia River, swimming, fishing, pets okay, $$$-$$$$.
Leave I-90 on exit #136 - located 2 blocks north.

WANAPUM (Washington State Park)
50 units w/hookups for water/elec./sewer, trailers to 60', flush toilets, showers, on reservoir, boat launch, fishing, swimming, trail, open year round, pets okay, $$$.
Take Huntzinger Rd south 3 miles.

NACHES

WINDY POINT (Wenatchee NF)

15 units, trailers to 22', on Tieton River, fishing, elev. 2000', $.
Take US 12 west 12.7 miles.

(Northwest of Naches)

BUMPING LAKE (Wenatchee NF)
45 units, trailers to 30', boat launch, swimming, fishing, water skiing, elev. 3400', $.
Take US 12 west 4.3 miles, State 410 northwest 27.8 miles, and FSR 1800 southwest 11.4 miles.

CEDAR SPRINGS (Wenatchee NF)

15 units, trailers to 22', on Bumping River, fishing, elev. 2800', $.
Take US 12 west 4.3 miles, State 410 northwest 27.8 miles, and FSR 1800 southwest .5 mile.

COTTON WOOD (Wenatchee NF)
16 units, trailers to 22', on Naches River, fishing, elev. 2300', $.
Take US 12 west 4.3 miles and State 410 northwest 17.7 miles.

COUGAR FLAT (Wenatchee NF)
12 units, trailers to 20', on Bumping River, fishing, elev. 3100', $.
Take US 12 west 4.3 miles, State 410 northwest 27.8 miles, and FSR 1800 southwest 6 miles.

EAGLE ROCK RESORT (Private)
10 units w/water/elec./sewer, tents okay, trailers to 35', (509) 658-2905, disabled access, propane, groceries, restaurant, on Naches River, fishing, hiking, pets okay, year round, $$-$$$.
Take US 12 west 4.3 miles and State 410 northwest 7.7 miles.

HELLS CROSSING (Wenatchee NF)
18 units, trailers to 20', picnic area, on American River, fishing, elev. 3200', $.
Take US 12 west 4.3 miles and State 410 northwest 33.7 miles.

INDIAN FLAT (Wenatchee NF)
11 units, trailers to 20', on Bumping River, fishing, elev. 2600', $.
Take US 12 west 4.3 miles and State 410 northwest 26.6 miles.

KANER FLAT (Wenatchee NF)
41 units, trailers to 30', near Little Naches River, fishing, historic wagon train camp on Old Naches Trail, elev. 2700', $.
Take US 12 west 4.3 miles, State 410 northwest 24.9 miles, and FSR 1900 northwest 2.5 miles.

LITTLE NACHES (Wenatchee NF)
21 units plus 3 group areas, trailers to 20', on Little Naches River, fishing, elev. 2600', $.
Take US 12 west 4.3 miles, State 410 northwest 24.9 miles, and FSR 1900 northwest .1 mile.

LODGEPOLE (Wenatchee NF)
33 units, trailers to 20', picnic area, river, fishing, elev. 3500', $.
Take US 12 west 4.3 miles and State 410 northwest 40.6 miles.

PLEASANT VALLEY (Wenatchee NF)
16 units, trailers to 22', river, fishing, hiking, elev. 3300', $.
Take US 12 west 4.3 miles and State 410 northwest 37 miles.

SAWMILL FLAT (Wenatchee NF)
25 units, trailers to 24', wheelchair access, on Naches River, fishing, elev. 2500', $.
Take US 12 west 4.3 miles and State 410 northwest 23.7 miles.

SODA SPRINGS (Wenatchee NF)
26 units, trailers to 30', on Bumping River, fishing, natural mineral springs, elev. 3100', $.

Take US 12 west 4.3 miles, State 410 northwest 27.8 miles, and FSR 1800 southwest 4.8 miles.

SQUAW ROCK RESORT (Private)
28 units w/hookups for water/elec./sewer plus 36 w/water & elec., tents okay, reservations (509)658-2926, trailers to 35', showers, playground, game room, swimming pool, hot tub, groceries, restaurant, trailer waste disposal, on Naches River, fishing, hiking, most dogs okay, open year round, $$$.
Take US 12 west 4.3 miles and State 410 northwest 15 miles.

RIMROCK

COVE RESORT (Private)
3 RV sites w/hookups for water/elec./sewer, reservations (509)672-2470, no restrooms, trailers to 35', on Rimrock Lake, boat launch & moorage, fishing, hiking, swimming, pets okay, open April thru Oct., $$$$.
Located west of Rimrock, near milepost #164 on US 12.

GAME RIDGE MOTEL & RV (Private)
2 RV sites w/hookups for water/elec./sewer, reservations (509)672-2212, no restrooms, trailers to 28', hot tub, game room, playground, on Tieton River, fishing, hiking, pets extra, open year round, $$$$$.
Located in Rimrock, at 27350 US 12.

INDIAN CREEK (Wenatchee NF)
39 units, trailers to 30', near 2 lakes, elev. 3000', $$.
Take US 12 west of Rimrock 6.8 miles.

US 12 WEST RESORT (Private)
30 RV sites w/water & elec., reservations (509)672-2460, showers, propane, restaurant, on Rimrock Lake, boat launch & rental, fishing, hiking, pets okay, open year round, $$$.
Located west of Rimrock, past Cove Resort, at 37590 US 12.

(East of Rimrock)

HAUSE CREEK (Wenatchee NF)
42 units, trailers to 30', flush toilets, wheelchair access, on Tieton River, fishing, elev. 2500', $$.
Take US 12 east of Rimrock 6.9 miles.

RIVER BEND (Wenatchee NF)
6 units, trailers to 20', on Tieton River, fishing, elev. 2500', $.
Take US 12 east of Rimrock 3.2 miles.

WILLOWS (Wenatchee NF)
16 units, trailers to 20', on Tieton River, fishing, elev. 2400', $.
Take US 12 east of Rimrock 5 miles.

PACKWOOD

PACKWOOD RV & MOBILE HOME PARK (Private)
27 units w/full hookups, 36 w/ water/elec./sewer, 12 w/water & elec, plus 20 tent sites, reservations (360)494-5145, trailers to 70', 18 pull thrus, showers, laundry, trailer waste disposal, pets extra, open year round, $$$.
Located in Packwood, at city center.

(Northeast of Packwood)

LA WIS WIS (Gifford Pinchot NF)
100 units - a few trailers to 18', flush toilets, limited wheelchair access, river, fishing, hiking, elev. 1400', $$.
Take US 12 east 7 miles and follow campground road.

OHANAPECOSH (Mt. Rainier Nat'l Park)
205 units, trailers to 30', trailer waste disposal, hiking, old growth trees, on Ohanapecosh River, fishing, closes in late Oct., elev. 2000', $$.
Take US 12 east 8 miles and State 123 north 4 miles - located 1.5 miles south of Mt. Rainier Nat'l Park entrance.

(South of Packwood)

WALUPT LAKE (Gifford Pinchot NF)
43 units, trailers to 22', wheelchair access, lake - speed limits, fishing, horse facilities, trail into Goat Rocks Wilderness, elev. 3900', $$.
Take US 12 west 2.7 miles, FSR 21 southeast 16.4 miles, and FSR 2160 east 4.5 miles.

YAKIMA

CIRCLE H RV RANCH (Private)
57 units w/full hookups, tents okay, reservations (509)457-3683, trailers to 60', showers, laundry, wheelchair access, playground, pool, spa, lounge, pets okay, open year round, $$$$.
Leave I-82 at exit #34 and take 18th St. north .3 mile.

TRAILER INNS RV PARK (Private)
101 units w/full hookups plus 7 tent sites, reservations (509)452-9561, trailers to 60', showers, laundry, wheelchair access, playground, fireside lounge, arcade room, indoor pool, sauna, therapy pools, trailer waste disposal, pets okay, open year round, $$$-$$$$.
Leave I-82 at exit #31 - located at 1610 N. First St.

WOODLAND PARK (Private)
30 units w/hookups for water/elec./sewer, no tents, reservations (509)453-9353, trailers to 60', no restrooms, playground, on lake

- no motors, boat launch/moorage & dock, paddle boat rental, fishing, hiking, bicycle path, pets okay, open year round, $$.
Leave I-82 at exit #31 - located at 2008 N. First St.

(East of Yakima)

YAKIMA KOA (Private)
50 units w/full hookups, 30 w/water & elec., plus 120 tent sites, reservations (509)248-5882, trailers to 40', showers, laundry, wheelchair access, playground, game room, groceries, propane, trailer waste disposal, 2 ponds, fishing, canoe rentals, pets okay, open year round, $$$$.
Take State 24 east 1 mile and Keyes Rd. north .3 mile.

YAKIMA SPORTSMAN (Washington State Park)
36 units w/hookups for water/elec./sewer plus 28 standard sites, trailers to 60', flush toilets, showers, community kitchen, trailer waste disposal, on Yakima River, fishing, children's fishing pond, $-$$$$.
Take State 24 east 1 mile and Keyes Rd. north to park.

(South of Yakima)

WHITE DOVE MOBILE HOME PARK (Private) [RV]
13 trailer sites w/hookups for water/elec./sewer, no restrooms, reservations (509)457-4555, trailers to 26', pets okay, open year round, $$$.
Leave I-82 south of town on the Union Gap exit, take Rudkin Rd north and watch for signs - located at 1702 Rudkin Rd.

GRANGER

GRANGER RV PARK (Private) [RV]
45 units w/hookups for water/elec./sewer, reservations (509) 854-1300, trailers to 36', pull thrus, showers, laundry, propane, trailer waste disposal, pets okay, open year round, $$-$$$.
Leave I-82 on State 223 and go south .3 mile.

LAMPLIGHTER VILLAGE RV PARK (Private) [RV]
10 RV units w/full hookups, reservations (509)882-1076, trailers to 40', no restrooms, pets okay, open year round, $$$.
Located at 300 Wilson Highway 18.

SMITTY'S RV OVERNIGHTER (Private) [RV]
16 RV units w/hookups for water/elec./sewer, reservations (509)882-5858, trailers to 70', pull thrus, no restrooms, trailer waste disposal, pets okay, open year round, $$$.
Leave I-82 on exit #82 - located at 608 W. Wine Country Rd.

YAKIMA NATION RV PARK (Tribal)
95 units w/hookups for water/elec./sewer plus tent area, reservations (800)874-3087, trailers to 60', showers, laundry, wheelchair access, swimming pool, hot tub, game room, playground, basketball court, restaurant, propane, trailer waste disposal, pets okay, open year round, $$-$$$$.
Take State 223 west 3 miles, State 22 northwest 6 miles to Toppenish, and follow signs.

GOLDENDALE

BROOKS MEMORIAL (Washington State Park)
23 units w/hookups for water/elec. plus 22 standard sites, trailers to 30', group area - reservations (509)773-5382, flush toilets, showers, community kitchen, trailer waste disposal, fishing, hiking trails, $-$$$.
Take State 97 north 15 miles.

PEACH BEACH (Private)
6 units w/hookups for water/elec./sewer, 46 w/water & elec., plus 30 tent sites, reservations (509)773-4698, showers, trailer waste disposal, river, fishing, swimming, hiking, pets okay, $$-$$$.
Take US 97 north to Park exit, and drive 1 mile to Peach Beach.

PINE SPRINGS RESORT (Private)
3 units w/hookups for water/elec./sewer, 10 w/water & elec., plus 12 tent sites, reservations (509)773-4434, play area, trailer waste disposal, restaurant, store, propane, fishing, hiking, pets okay, $-$$$.
Take US 97 north 12 miles.

SUNSET RV PARK (Private)
17 units w/hookups for water/elec./sewer, 15 w/water, plus tent area, reservations (509)773-3111, showers, wheelchair access, heated pool, mini-golf, play area, trailer waste disposal, near observatory, pets okay, open April thru Nov., $$-$$$.
Located right in Goldendale, at the corner of US 97 & Simcoe Dr.

(Southeast of Goldendale)

CROW BUTTE (Washington State Park)
50 campsites w/hookups for water/elec./sewer, trailers to 60', group area - reservations (509)875-2644, flush toilets, showers, disabled access, picnic shelter, trailer waste disposal, boat launch, fishing, water skiing, $-$$$.
Take US 97 south 10 miles and State 14 east 49 miles.

MARYHILL (Washington State Park)

50 units w/hookups for water/elec./sewer, trailers to 50', flush toilets, showers, disabled access, community kitchen, trailer waste disposal, on Columbia River, boat launch, scuba diving area, fishing, swimming, windsurfing, water skiing, hiking, pets okay - not on beach, $-$$$$.
Take US 97 south 10 miles and State 14 east 2 miles.

(Southwest of Goldendale)

HORSETHIEF LAKE (Washington State Park)

12 campsites, trailers to 30', flush toilets, trailer waste disposal, boat launch, on Columbia River & Horsethief Lake, scuba diving area, fishing, swimming, windsurfing, hiking, pets okay, $-$$.
Take US 97 south 10 miles and State 14 west 18 miles.

TROUT LAKE

ELK MEADOWS RV PARK (Private)

24 units w/hookups for water/elec./sewer, 24 w/water & elec., 10 tent sites, plus group area, reservations (509)395-2400, trailers to 40', showers, laundry, wheelchair access, trailer waste disposal, fishing, hiking, pets okay, open year round, $$-$$$.
Take State 141 north of town to milepost #25 and follow the signs to Elk Meadows - it's about 1 mile.

GULER-MT. ADAMS PARK (County)

10 units w/hookups for water & elec., plus 40 w/water, trailers to 40', tents okay, group area - reservations (509)773-3900, showers, trailer waste disposal, pets okay, $-$$.
Follow the signs - located just south of Trout Lake.

(West of Trout Lake)

ATKISSON GROUP CAMP (Gifford Pinchot NF)

Group site, trailers okay, no drinking water, elev. 2700', $$$$.
Take State 141 north out of Trout Lake and follow it southwest 4 miles to this Sno-Park campground.

CULTUS CREEK (Gifford Pinchot NF)

51 units, trailers to 32', wheelchair access, stream, trailhead to Indian Heaven Backcountry, elev. 4000', $-$$.
Take State 141 north out of Trout Lake, follow this southwest 5.5 miles to FSR 24, and go northwest 12.6 miles.

PETERSON GROUP CAMP (Gifford Pinchot NF)

Group site, trailers to 22', reservations required - (509)395-2501, wheelchair access, hiking, elev. 2800', $$$$.
Take State 141 north out of Trout Lake, follow this southwest 5.5 miles to FSR 24, and go west 2.5 miles.

PETERSON PRAIRIE (Gifford Pinchot NF)
30 units, trailers to 32', wheelchair access, hiking, berry picking, elev. 2800', $-$$.
Take State 141 north out of Trout Lake, follow this southwest 5.5 miles to FSR 24, and go west 2.5 miles.

CARSON

BIG FOOT PARK (Private)
19 RV sites plus grassy tent area, reservations (509)427-4441, trailers to 70', showers, laundry, wheelchair access, near Columbia River, fishing, hiking, pets okay, $-$$.
Located in Carson, at 184 Metzger Rd.

CARSON HOT SPRINGS (Private)
14 units w/full hookups plus 11 tent sites, reservations (509) 427-8292, showers, handicap access, hot springs, therapy baths, trailer waste disposal, fishing, hiking, pets okay, $-$$$.
Go up the hill, past the golf course, take a left and go down the hill to resort.

(Northwest of Carson)

BEAVER (Gifford Pinchot NF)
27 units, trailers to 25', group area - reservations (800)280-2267, flush toilets, wheelchair access, hiking, fishing, near Trapper Creek Wilderness, pets okay, elev. 1100', $$-$$$$.
Take Wind River Rd. northwest 12.2 miles.

PANTHER CREEK (Gifford Pinchot NF)
33 units, trailers to 25', near Pacific Crest Trail, stream, fishing, hiking, horse trails & loading ramp, pets okay, elev. 1000', $$-$$$$.
Take Wind River Rd. northwest 9 miles, FSR 6517 east 1.5 miles, and FSR 65 south .1 mile.

PARADISE CREEK (Gifford Pinchot NF)
42 campsites, trailers to 25', river, wheelchair access, fishing, hiking, Lava Butte Trailhead, pets okay, elev. 1500', $$-$$$$.
Take Wind River Rd. northwest 13.8 miles and Meadow Creek Rd. north 6.3 miles.

(Southwest of Carson)

LEWIS & CLARK CAMP/RV PARK (Private)
20 units w/hookups for water/elec./sewer, 40 w/water & elec., plus 10 tent sites, reservations (509)427-5559, showers, laundry, rec room, trailer waste disposal, river, fishing, hiking, 9 hole golf course next to park, $$$.
Take State 14 west to milepost #37 - park is about 1 mile west of North Bonneville, on Evergreen Dr.

COOK

HOME VALLEY PARK (County)
23 units, showers, picnic area, play area, wheelchair access, on Columbia River, swimming, fishing, wind surfing, $$$.
Take State 14 west of Cook to milepost #50 and park.

OKLAHOMA (Gifford Pinchot NF)
23 units, trailers to 22', on Little White Salmon River, wheelchair access, fishing, pets okay, elev. 1700', $$.
Just east of town, take the road to Willard 7 miles north, and follow Oklahoma/FSR 18 north another 8 miles to campground.

MOSS CREEK (Gifford Pinchot NF)
18 units, trailers to 32', on Little White Salmon River, wheelchair access, fishing, pets okay, elev. 1400', $$.
Just east of town, take the road to Willard north 7 miles, and follow Oklahoma/FSR 18 north 1 mile to the campground.

BINGEN

WIND RANCH (Private)
6 units w/hookups for water & elec. plus open camp area, tents okay - no ground fires, information (509)493-2312, showers, near Columbia River & windsurfing, pets extra, open mid April to mid Sept., $$-$$$$.
Located 2 miles east of the Hood River Bridge, in Bingen, just off State 14.

EASTERN WASHINGTON CAMPGROUNDS

See Page

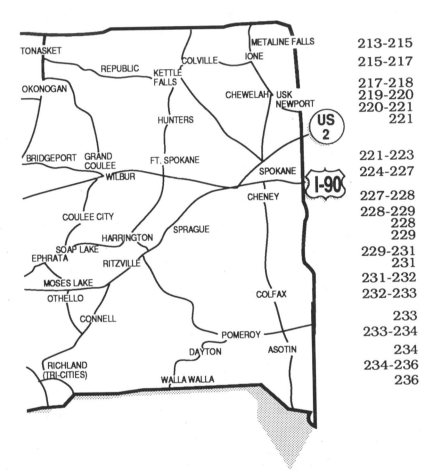

Location	See Page
METALINE FALLS	213-215
COLVILLE / IONE	215-217
CHEWELAH / USK	217-218
NEWPORT	219-220
	220-221
	221
SPOKANE	221-223
	224-227
CHENEY	227-228
	228-229
	228
	229
	229-231
	231
	231-232
COLFAX	232-233
	233
POMEROY	233-234
ASOTIN	234
	234-236
WALLA WALLA	236

RIVERVIEW TRAILER COURT (Private)

4 trailer sites w/hookups for water/elec./sewer, no tents, reservations (509)486-2491, no restrooms, trailers to 40', on Okanogan River, fishing, hiking, pets okay, open year round, $$. Located just off US 97, in Tonasket, at 1305 W. Fourth.

SHANNON'S (Private)

5 RV sites w/full hookups plus tent area, reservations (509)486-2259, trailers to 40', pets okay, open year round, $-$$$. Located at 626 S. Whitcomb, in Tonasket.

(North of Tonasket)

ORCHARD RV PARK (Private)

41 units w/hookups for water/elec./sewer, 12 w/out hookups, plus grassy tent area, reservations (509)476-2669, trailers to 60', pull thrus, showers, wheelchair access, on Lake Osoyoos, boat ramp, fishing, swimming beach, hiking, pets okay, open March thru mid Oct., $$-$$$.
Take State 97 north 18.5 miles, Eastside Osoyoos Lake Rd. around the lake, and Thorndyke Loop Rd. to the park.

OSOYOOS LAKE (Washington State Park)

80 units, trailers to 45', flush toilets, showers, snackbar, trailer waste disposal, boat launch, fishing, swimming, water skiing, open year round - weekends only Nov. thru March, $-$$$.
Take State 97 north 18.5 miles - located just north of Oroville.

OSOYOOS RV PARK (Private)

11 units w/hookups for water/elec./sewer, 30 w/water & elec., plus 14 tent sites, reservations (509)476-3781, showers, laundry, trailer waste disposal, lake, swimming, fishing, boat launch, $$-$$$
Take US 97 north 25 miles - located at the US/Canada border.

RAINBOW RESORT (Private)

26 units w/hookups for water/elec./sewer, 14 w/water & elec., plus tent area, reservations (509)223-3700, trailers to 35', wheelchair access, showers, on Spectacle Lake, swimming, fishing, boat launch & rental, pets okay, open April thru Oct., $$$.
Take US 97 north approximately 7 miles and Loomis Rd. west 6 miles to resort.

SPECTACLE FALLS RESORT (Private)

20 units w/hookups for water/elec./sewer, 10 w/water & elec., plus small tent area, reservations (509)223-4141, showers, ice, trailer waste disposal, on Spectacle Lake, swimming, fishing, boat launch/rental & gas, pets okay, $$$.
Take US 97 north approximately 7 miles and Loomis Rd. west 8 miles to resort.

SPECTACLE LAKE RESORT (Private)

34 units w/hookups for water/elec./sewer plus 6 tent sites, reservations (509)223-3433, trailers to 40', showers, laundry, ice, swimming pool, playfield, playground, on lake, swimming, fishing, boat launch & rental, pets okay, open year round, $$$.
Take US 97 north approximately 7 miles and Loomis Rd. west 5 miles to resort.

SUN COVE RESORT (Private)

20 units w/hookups for water/elec./sewer, 7 w/water & elec., plus 15 w/out hookups, reservations (509)476-2223, trailers to 35', showers, laundry, rec room, heated pool, trailer waste disposal, groceries, tavern, lake, boat ramp, canoeing, fishing, hiking, pets okay, open April thru Oct., $$$$.
Take US 97 north 16 miles to Oroville, Wannacut Lake Rd. west 10 miles, and resort road north 1 mile.

(East of Tonasket)

BETH LAKE (Okanogan NF)

15 units, boating, swimming, fishing, hiking, elev. 2900', $.
Take State 20 east 20 miles, Bonaparte Lake Rd. north 6 miles, FSR 32 northeast 6 miles, and head northwest 1 mile.

BONAPARTE LAKE (Okanogan NF)

26 units plus group area, trailers to 32', flush toilets, wheelchair access, boat launch, swimming, fishing, hiking, elev. 3600', $$.
Take State 20 east 20 miles, Bonaparte Lake Rd. north 3 miles, and FSR 32 north .7 mile - located south of the resort.

BONAPARTE LAKE RESORT (Private)

32 units w/water/elec./sewer, tents okay, reservations (509)486-2828, trailers to 35', showers, laundry, cafe, groceries, propane, trailer waste disposal, fishing dock, swimming, boat launch & rental, pets extra, open mid April thru Oct., elev. 3500', $$.
Take State 20 east 20 miles, Bonaparte Lake Rd. north 6 miles.

LOST LAKE (Okanogan NF)

18 units, trailers to 32', group area - reservations (509)486-2186, flush toilets, wheelchair access, boat launch, swimming, fishing, hiking, elev. 3800', groups $40 to $70/night - individuals $$.
Take State 20 east 20 miles, Bonaparte Lake Rd. north 6 miles, FSR 32 northeast 3 miles, FSR 33 northwest 3.5 miles, and FSR 50 south .5 mile to campground.

METALINE FALLS

MILLPOND (Colville NF)

10 units, trailers to 28', stream, fishing, elev. 2600', $.
Take State 31 northeast 1.5 miles and Sullivan Lake Rd. east 3.5 miles.

MT. LINTON RV PARK (Private)
26 units w/full hookups plus tent area, reservations (509)446-4553, trailers to 40', pull thrus, showers, wheelchair access, laundry, nearby river & fishing, pets okay, seasonal, $$-$$$.
Take State 31 south 2 miles to the town of Metaline and park.

SULLIVAN LAKE (Colville NF)
34 units, trailers to 28', group area - reservations (509)446-2681, on lake, fishing, swimming, water skiing, hiking, elev. 2600', groups $75/night - individuals $$.
Take State 31 northeast 1.5 miles and Sullivan Lake Rd. east 5 miles.

IONE

IONE MOTEL & RV PARK (Private)
16 units w/hookups for water/elec./sewer plus 2 w/water & elec., tents okay, reservations (509)442-3213, showers, laundry, on Pend Oreille River, boat launch, paddle boat rentals, fishing, swimming, water skiing, pets okay, open year round, $-$$$.
Located at the south end of town.

NOISY CREEK (Colville NF)
19 units, trailers to 28', boat launch, swimming, fishing, water skiing, hiking trails, elev. 3200', $$.
State 31 south 1 mile, Sullivan Lake Rd. northeast 9 miles.

COLVILLE

COLVILLE FAIRGROUNDS RV PARK (County)
40 units w/hookups for water & elec., 40 w/elec., plus 20 tent sites, information (509)684-2585, trailers to 70', showers, wheelchair access, trailer waste disposal, playfield, pets okay, open April thru Nov., $-$$.
Take US 395 to Colville's Fairgrounds exit and follow signs.

WILDERNESS WEST RESORT (Private)
27 units w/hookups for water/elec./sewer, 18 w/water & elec., plus 5 tent sites, reservations (509)732-4263, trailers to 32', showers, wheelchair access, laundry, rec room, playfield, groceries, gas, on Deep Lake, swimming, fishing, boat launch & rental, hiking, no pets, elev. 2200', $$-$$$$.
Take State 20 east 1 mile to Aladdin Rd. and go north 30 miles to Deep Lake - located on northeast shore.

(East of Colville)

BEAVER LODGE RV PARK (Private)
8 units w/hookups for water/elec./sewer, 4 w/water & elec., plus 28 w/out hookups, tents okay, reservations (509)684-5657,

showers, laundry, groceries, propane, on lake, boat launch, fishing, swimming, canoe & paddle boat rental, elev. 3300', $$-$$$.
Take State 20 east 25 miles.

LAKE GILLETTE (Colville NF)
43 units, trailers to 32', some multi-family sites, flush toilets, wheelchair access, trailer waste disposal, on lake, hiking, nearby motorcycle trails, bicycling, elev. 3200', $$.
Take State 20 east 25 miles.

LAKE LEO (Colville NF)
8 units, trailers to 18', on lake, boat launch, swimming, fishing, elev. 3200', $.
Take State 20 east 29 miles.

LAKE THOMAS (Colville NF)
15 tent sites, on lake, boating, swimming, fishing, water skiing, nearby motorcycle trails, bicycling, elev. 3200', $.
Take State 20 east 25.5 miles and campground road east 1 mile.

REPUBLIC

FERRY LAKE (Colville NF)
18 units, trailers to 22', boat ramp, fishing, elev. 3300', $.
Take State 21 south 7 miles, FSR 53 southwest 6 miles, FSR 5330 north 1 mile, and lake road north .5 mile.

LONG LAKE (Colville NF)
24 units, trailers to 22', lake - no motors, fly fishing, swimming, elev. 3300', $$.
Take State 21 south 7 miles, FSR 53 southwest 8 miles, and FSR 400 south 1.5 miles.

SWAN LAKE (Colville NF)
32 units, trailers to 32' in 25 sites, community kitchen, boat ramp, swimming, fishing, hiking trails, elev. 3700', $$.
Take State 21 south 7 miles and FSR 53 southwest 8 miles.

(North of Republic)

BLACK BEACH RESORT (Private)
60 units w/hookups for water/elec./sewer, reservations (509) 775-3989, showers, laundry, wheelchair access, playground, trailer waste disposal, groceries, on Lake Curlew, swimming, fishing, boat launch & rental, $$-$$$.
Take State 21 east and north 6 miles, West Curlew Lake Rd. north 8 miles, and Black Beach Rd. east 1 mile.

CURLEW LAKE (Washington State Park)
18 units w/hookups for water/elec./sewer, 7 w/water & elec., plus 57 standard sites, trailers to 30', flush toilets, showers,

wheelchair access, trailer waste disposal, boat launch, fishing, hiking, open April thru Oct., $-$$$.
Take State 21 east and north 10 miles.

PINE POINT RESORT (Private)
32 units w/hookups for water/elec./sewer, tents okay, reservations (509)775-3643, showers, laundry, playground, groceries, trailer waste disposal, on Curlew Lake, swimming, fishing, boat launch & rental, pets okay, open late April thru Oct., $$-$$$.
Take State 21 east and north 10 miles.

TIFFANY'S RESORT (Private)
14 units w/hookups for water/elec./sewer, 2 w/water & elec., plus 3 tent sites, reservations advised (509)775-3152, trailers to 70', showers, laundry, playground, groceries, propane, gas, on Curlew Lake, swimming, fishing, boat launch & rental, pets okay, open mid April thru Oct., $$$.
Take State 21 east and north 6 miles, West Curlew Lake Rd. north 10 miles.

KETTLE FALLS

CIRCLE-UP RV PARK (Private)
10 units w/hookups for water/elec./sewer, 10 w/water & elec., plus 6 tent sites, reservations (509)738-6617, trailers to 40', showers, store, trailer waste disposal, nearby fishing, hiking, bicycling, pets okay, open April thru Oct., $$-$$$.
Take US 395 south 2 miles.

GRANDVIEW INN MOTEL & RV PARK (Private)
28 units w/hookups for water/elec./sewer plus grassy tent area, reservations (509)738-6733, trailers to 40', showers, laundry, wheelchair access, groceries, propane, on Lake Roosevelt, fishing, hiking, horses & pets okay, open April thru Nov., $$$.
Located at the intersection of US 395 & State 25, in Kettle Falls.

KETTLE FALLS (Coulee Dam Rec. Area)
89 units plus group sites, trailers okay, wheelchair access, boat & trailer waste disposal, boat ramp & dock, swimming, summer programs, elev. 1234', $$-$$$.
Take Kettle Park Rd. towards the river and campground.

LOCUST GROVE (Coulee Dam Rec. Area)
2 group sites, reservations (509)738-6266, tents okay, trailers to 70', wheelchair access, picnic shelter w/elec., on Lake Roosevelt, fishing, trail, pets okay, $1.00/person - $10.00 minimum.
Take Kettle Park Rd. towards the river and campground.

YELLOW PINE RV PARK (Private)
32 units w/full hookups plus 10 tent sites, reservations (509)738-6757, trailers to 40', pull thrus, showers, laundry,

wheelchair access, deli/store, propane, gas, trailer waste disposal, pets okay, open year round, $$-$$$.
Located in Kettle Falls, at 950 US Highway 395.

(North of Kettle Falls)

EVANS (Coulee Dam Rec. Area)
34 units, trailers okay, trailer waste disposal, summer programs, boat ramp & dock, swimming, elev. 1285', $$.
Follow State 25 north approximately 9 miles to campground.

MARCUS ISLAND (Coulee Dam Rec. Area)
27 units, trailers okay, boat dock & ramp, elev. 1281', $$.
Follow State 25 north approximately 5 miles to campground.

WHISPERING PINES RV PARK (Private)
44 units w/hookups for water/elec./sewer plus tent area, reservations (509)738-2593, pull thrus, showers, laundry, game room, playground, basketball court, store, ice, walk to river, lake, fishing, hiking, pets okay, open year round, $$-$$$.
Take US 395 north 6.5 miles and follow signs.

OKANOGAN

COUNTY FAIRGROUNDS Okanogan County)
52 units w/hookups for water/elec./sewer plus 36 w/water & elec., tents okay, reservations (509)422-1621, trailers to 30', showers, wheelchair access, on Okanogan River, fishing, horse corral & stalls, pets okay, open March thru Sept., $$.
Located on east shore of Okanogan River, 1 mile north of town.

CARL PRECHT MEM. RV PARK (City)
65 units w/hookups for water/elec./sewer plus 5 tent sites, trailers to 36', showers, wheelchair access, tennis, city swimming pool, playfield, trailer waste disposal, Okanogan River, boat launch, fishing, pets okay, open March to Oct., $$.
Take State 20 north 5 miles to Omak - located on the east side of town, near the fairgrounds.

LEGION PARK (City)
49 units, information (509)422-3600, trailers to 40', flush toilets, showers, wheelchair access, on Okanogan River, nearby boat launch, fishing, pets okay, open mid April thru Oct., $.
Located in Okanogan, on State 215, at the north end of town.

PONDEROSA MOTOR LODGE & RV PARK (Private)
10 units w/hookups for water/elec./sewer plus grassy tent area, reservations (509)422-0400, trailers to 30', showers, laundry, wheelchair access, swimming pool, deli, nearby river & fishing, small pets okay, open year round, $$-$$$.
Located in Okanogan, at 1034 Second St.

CHEWELAH

FORTYNINER CAMPGROUND & MOTEL (Private) `RV`
24 units w/hookups for water/elec./sewer, reservations (509)935-8613, showers, laundry, ice, indoor pool, jacuzzi, rec room, trailer waste disposal, $$$.
Located on US 395 at the south edge of town.

(South of Chewelah)

GRANITE POINT PARK (Private) `RV`
53 units w/hookups for water/elec./sewer plus 6 w/water & elec., no tents, trailers to 35', reservations (509)233-2100, showers, laundry, groceries, rec room, playground, lake, swimming, fishing, boat launch & rental, no pets, $$$-$$$$.
Take US 395 southeast 17.5 miles - located about 1.5 miles south of Loon Lake.

SHORE ACRES RESORT (Private) `A` `RV`
17 units w/hookups for water/elec./sewer, 5 w/water & elec., plus 13 tent sites, reservations (509)233-2474, trailers to 30', showers, groceries, playground, lake, swimming, fishing, boat launch & rental, $$$.
Take US 395 southeast 16 miles, State 292 west 1.8 miles, and Shore Acres Rd. south 1.8 miles.

SILVER BEACH RESORT (Private) `RV`
33 units w/hookups for water/elec./sewer, 14 w/water & elec., plus 6 w/elec. only, no tents, reservations (509)937-2811, trailers to 35', showers, laundry, wheelchair access, playground, restaurant, groceries, propane, trailer waste disposal, lake, boat launch/rental & moorage, swimming, fishing, pets okay, open April thru Sept., $$$-$$$$.
Take US 395 south 4 miles, State 231 south 2 miles, and Waitts Lake Rd. west 3 miles.

USK

KEO'S KORNER (Private) `A` `RV`
10 units w/hookups for water/elec./sewer plus tent area, reservations (509)445-1294, trailers to 30', groceries, deli, propane, on Pend Oreille River, boat launch & dock, fishing, hiking, pets okay, open year round, $-$$.
Located in Usk, at 111 Fifth St.

(North of Usk)

BLUESLIDE RESORT (Private) `A` `RV`
31 units w/hookups for water/elec./sewer, 29 w/elec., plus tent area, reservations (509)445-1327, trailers to 60', group area, showers, laundry, wheelchair access, playground, heated pool,

trailer waste disposal, on river, boat launch, fishing, propane, groceries, hiking, pets okay, open Mem. Day thru Sept., $$-$$$.
Take State 20 north 21 miles.

BROWNS LAKE (Colville NF)
18 units, trailers to 22', lake - no motors, boat ramp, fly fishing only, elev. 3400', $$.
Take Kings Lake Rd. northeast 6.5 miles and FSR 5030 north 3 miles.

SKOOKUM CHINOOK CAMPGROUND (Private)
25 units - some w/elec., tents okay, reservations (509)447-4158, trailers to 26', showers, wheelchair access, on N. Skookum Lake, boat launch/moorage & dock, canoe & boat rentals, fishing, hiking, horses & pets okay, open mid April thru Oct., $$.
Take Kings Lake Rd. northeast 8.5 miles.

SOUTH SKOOKUM LAKE (Colville NF)
24 units, trailers to 22', lake - speed limits, boat launch, fishing, hiking, elev. 3600', $$.
Take Kings Lake Rd. northeast 7.5 miles.

NEWPORT

AUDREY'S RV PARK (Private)
23 units w/water/elec./sewer, no restrooms, reservations (509)447-3220, trailers to 32', trailer waste disposal, restaurant, river, fishing, hiking, pets okay, open year round, $-$$.
Located at south end of Newport - 332391 N. Highway 2.

MARSHALL LAKE RESORT (Private)
15 units w/hookups for water/elec./sewer, 20 w/water & elec., 7 w/water, plus tent area, reservations (509)447-4158, trailers to 36', showers, small store, canoe & paddleboat rentals, boat launch & dock, horse corral, pets okay, open year round, $$-$$$.
Cross the Pend Oreille River bridge on US 2, turn left and travel along the river for 2.5 miles, turn right onto Bead Lake Rd. for 2.5 miles, turn right onto Marshall Lake Rd. and follow 1.5 miles.

OLD AMERICAN KAMPGROUND (Private)
64 units w/full hookups plus tent area, reservations (509)447-3663, trailers to 40', wheelchair accessible restroom, showers, laundry, propane, trailer waste disposal, on Pend Oreille River, boat launch/dock, fishing, pets okay, open year round, $$-$$$$.
Located in Newport, at 701 N. Newport Ave.

PIONEER PARK (Colville NF)
14 units, trailers to 22', on Box Canyon Reservoir, fishing, elev. 2000', $$.
Cross the Pend Oreille River bridge on US 2, turn left and go 2 miles.

DIAMOND LAKE RESORT (Private)

25 units w/hookups for water/elec./sewer plus 25 w/water & elec., tents okay, reservations (509)447-4474, trailers to 70', pull thrus, showers, cafe, groceries, propane, gas, trailer waste disposal, boat launch/moorage/dock & rental, swimming beach, fishing, pets okay, open year round, $$$.
Take US 2 southwest 10 miles.

JERRY'S LANDING RV PARK (Private)

24 units w/hookups for water/elec./sewer plus 10 w/water & elec., reservations (509)292-2337, trailers to 35', showers, wheelchair access, groceries, trailer waste disposal, on lake, swimming, fishing, boat launch & rental, small pets okay, open April thru Sept., $$$.
Take US 2 southwest approximately 19 miles and Oregon Rd. west 1 mile to Eloika Lake and RV park.

PEND OREILLE PARK (County)

40 units, trailers to 20', reservations (509)447-4821, flush toilets, showers, wheelchair access, old growth trees, hiking & horse trails, horses & pets okay, open Mem. Day thru Labor Day, $$.
Take US 2 southwest 16 miles.

HUNTERS

GIFFORD (Coulee Dam Rec. Area)

47 units, trailers okay, picnic area, trailer waste disposal, boat ramp & dock, elev. 1249', $$.
Take State 25 north - located just south of Gifford.

HUNTERS (Coulee Dam Rec. Area)

39 units plus 3 small group sites, trailers okay, picnic facilities, trailer waste disposal, swimming beach, boat ramp & dock, elev. 1233', $$.
Leave State 25 at Hunters and head west toward the water and campground.

BRIDGEPORT

BIG RIVER RV PARK (Private)

16 units w/full hookups, tents okay, reservations (509)686-2121, trailers to 40', showers, laundry, propane, on Columbia River, fishing, no pets, open year round, $$-$$$.
Located in Bridgeport, at 1415 Jefferson.

ROCK GARDEN RV PARK (Private)

12 units w/hookups for water/elec./sewer, 8 w/water & elec., plus lots of tent sites, reservations (509)686-5343, showers,

laundry, playfield, playground, trailer waste disposal, river, fishing, pets okay, $-$$$.
Take State 173 northwest 2.5 miles.

WATERFRONT MARINA (City)
34 units w/hookups for water & elec. plus 14 w/out hookups, reservations (509)686-7231, showers, covered picnic area, playground, trailer waste disposal, river, fishing, boat launch, pets okay, $$$-$$$$.
Located in Bridgeport, at Columbia and 7th St.

(Northeast of Bridgeport)

BRIDGEPORT (Washington State Park)
20 units w/hookups for water/elec. plus 14 tent sites, group area - reservations (509)686-7231, trailers to 45', flush toilets, showers, disabled access, community kitchen, trailer waste disposal, on Lake Rufus Woods, boat launch, fishing, open April thru Oct., $$-$$$$.
Take State 173 northeast to State 17 and go north 1.5 miles.

GRAND COULEE

COULEE PLAYLAND RESORT & RV PARK (Private)
40 units w/hookups for water/elec./sewer, 13 w/water & elec., plus 12 tent sites, reservations (509)633-2671, showers, laundry, snack bar, groceries, playground, trailer waste disposal, on Banks Lake, swimming, fishing, boat launch & rental, pets okay, $$$-$$$$.
Follow State 155 west 1 mile to resort.

CURLY'S CAMPGROUND (Private)
16 units w/hookups for water/elec./sewer plus 6 tent sites, information (509)633-0750, showers, pets okay, $$-$$$.
Follow State 174 northwest 2 miles.

KING'S COURT RV PARK (Private)
22 units w/full hookups, 10 w/water & elec., plus 2 tent sites, reservations (800)759-2608, trailers to 40', pull thrus, showers, wheelchair access, laundry, trailer waste disposal, store, pets okay, open year round, $$$-$$$$.
Located in Grand Coulee - right on State 174.

(East of Grand Coulee)

LAKEVIEW TERRACE RV PARK (Private)
25 units w/hookups for water/elec./sewer plus 10 tent sites, reservations (509)633-2169, showers, laundry, picnic tables, shade, playfield, playground, $$-$$$.
Take State 174 southeast 3 miles.

SPRING CANYON (Coulee Dam Rec. Area)
87 units plus group area, trailers okay, picnic area, handicap access, groceries, trailer & boat waste disposal, boat dock & ramp, swimming, summer programs, pets okay, elev. 1234', $$.
Take State 174 southeast 5 miles to campground road, then head 1.1 miles north.

(South of Grand Coulee)

BANKS LAKE GOLF & COUNTRY CLUB (Private)
13 RV sites w/out hookups, no tents, no restrooms, reservations (509)633-0163, trailers to 40', pets okay, open March thru Oct., free w/golf - others $$$$.
Follow State 155 3 miles south of town to golf course.

STEAMBOAT ROCK (Washington State Park)
100 units w/hookups for water/elec./sewer, 5 tent sites, plus group area, mail reservations available, trailers to 60', flush toilets, showers, disabled access, snackbar, trailer waste disposal, on Banks Lake, boat launch, fishing, water skiing, scuba diving area, hiking & horse trails, pets okay, $-$$$$.
Take State 155 southwest 7.2 miles, and head northwest on campground road.

SUN BANKS RESORT (Private)
20 units w/full hookups, 100 w/water & elec., plus 130 tent sites, reservations (509)633-3786, trailers to 70', pull thrus, showers, laundry, wheelchair access, store, on Banks Lake, boat & jet ski rental, boat launch/moorage & dock, swimming beach, fishing, hiking, horse corral, pets okay, open year round, $$$$$.
Take State 155 south 3.5 miles.

FORT SPOKANE

FORT SPOKANE (Coulee Dam Rec. Area)
67 units plus group area, trailers okay, handicap access, trailer waste disposal, boat ramp, swimming, elev. 1247', $$.
Located just north of historic Fort Spokane on State 25.

PORCUPINE BAY (Coulee Dam Rec. Area)
31 units, trailers okay, trailer waste disposal, boat dock & ramp, swimming, elev. 1238', $$.
Take State 25 south 8 miles, Porcupine Bay Rd. north 4.3 miles.

SEVEN BAYS MARINA (Tribal)
36 units w/hookups for water/elec./sewer, 18 w/water, plus 40 tent sites, information (509)725-1676, trailers to 40', showers, laundry, wheelchair access, casino, groceries, restaurant, propane, gas, on Lake Roosevelt, boat launch/moorage & dock, fishing, hiking, pets okay, open Easter thru Oct., $$-$$$.
Located south of Fort Spokane - follow signs off State 25.

WILBUR

BELLS TRAILER PARK (Private) RV
30 trailer sites w/hookups for water/elec./sewer, reservations (509)647-5888, showers, laundry, ice, pets okay, $$$.
Located in Wilbur, one block off US 2, at east edge of town.

KELLER FERRY (Coulee Dam Rec. Area) 🅰 RV
55 units, trailers okay, group sites - reservations (509)725-2751, trailer & boat waste disposal, boat ramp, swimming - lifeguard in summer, elev. 1229', $$.
Take State 21 14 miles north to Keller Ferry Landing.

THE RIVER RUE RV PARK (Private) 🅰 RV
19 units w/hookups for water/elec./sewer, 21 w/water & elec., plus 21 tent sites, reservations (509)647-2647, showers, wheelchair access, playfield, playground, groceries, snack bar, propane, trailer waste disposal, pets okay, $$-$$$.
Take State 21 north 14 miles.

SPOKANE

CEDAR VILLAGE RV PARK (Private) 🅰 RV
35 units w/full hookups plus tent area, reservations (509)838-8558, trailers to 35', showers, wheelchair access, propane, trailer waste disposal, pets extra, open year round, $$-$$$$.
Located in Spokane, 2 miles off the I-90 Airport/Business Loop, at W. 5415 Sunset Hwy.

EL RANCHO RV PARK (Private) RV
6 RV units w/out hookups, no tents, no restrooms, reservations (509)455-9400, trailers to 35', pets okay, open year round, $$$.
Leave I-90 at exit #280 - located at W. 3000 Sunset Blvd.

OVERLAND STATION (Private) 🅰 RV
32 units w/hookups for water/elec./sewer plus tent area, reservations (509)747-1703, trailers to 65', pull thrus, showers operate April thru Sept., laundry, wheelchair access, groceries, playground, pets okay, open year round, $$$-$$$$.
Leave I-90 at exit #272 and look for signs.

PARKLANE MOTEL & RV PARK (Private) RV
17 trailer sites w/hookups for water/elec./sewer, reservations (800)533-1626, no restrooms, trailers to 40', laundry, ice, play area, pets okay - refundable deposit, open year round, $$$$$.
Leave I-90 at exit #283-B, go .8 mile to Havana St., north .03 mile to Sprague Ave., and east to 4412 Sprague Ave.

PONDEROSA HILLS RV PARK (Private) 🅰 RV
168 units w/full hookups plus 50 tent sites, reservations (800)494-7275, trailers to 40', pull thrus, showers, laundry,

playground, trailer waste disposal, propane, basketball court, pets okay, open year round, $$$-$$$$$.
Leave I-90 at exit #272, take Hallet Rd. east 1 mile, and Mallon Rd. south .5 mile.

SHADOWS RV PARK & CAMPGROUND (Private)
20 units w/hookups for water/elec./sewer, 40 w/water & elec., plus tent area, reservations (509)467-6951, trailers to 40', showers, laundry, trailer waste disposal, pets okay, open April thru Sept., $$$-$$$$.
Follow US 395 north of city center to its junction with US 2 and take the Division St. exit to campground.

TRAILER INNS RV PARK (Private)
98 RV units w/full hookups plus 6 tent sites, reservations (800)659-4864, trailers to 65', showers, laundry, wheelchair access, playground, pets okay, open year round, $$$-$$$$.
Leave I-90 at exit #285 and follow signs - located at 6021 East Fourth Ave.

(North of Spokane)

AL'S RESTAURANT & RV PARK (Private)
20 units w/hookups for water/elec./sewer, no tents, reservations (509)292-8015, no restrooms, trailers to 40', trailer waste disposal, propane, lounge, some pets, open year round, $$$.
Take US 2 north 12 miles beyond its junction with US 395 - located near Chattaroy.

KIRK'S LODGE - MT. SPOKANE (Private)
21 units w/hookups for water & elec. plus 20 tent sites, reservations (509)238-9114, trailers to 40', showers, game room, playground, trailer waste disposal, groceries, restaurant, kids fishing area, horses & pets okay, open year round, $$-$$$.
Take US 2 northeast 10 miles and State 206 northeast 18 miles.

MOUNT SPOKANE (Washington State Park)
12 units, trailers to 30', group area - reservations (509)456-4169, disabled access, picnic shelter, hiking, horse trails, $-$$.
Take US 2 northeast 10 mile and State 206 northeast 19 miles.

RIVERSIDE (Washington State Park)
101 units, trailers to 45', flush toilets, showers, community kitchen, trailer waste disposal, on rivers, boat launch, fishing, horse trails & rental, ORV area, open year round, $-$$$$.
Located 6 miles northwest of Spokane.

WILD ROSE RV PARK (Private)
32 units w/hookups for water/elec./sewer plus 10 tent sites, reservations (509)276-8853, trailers to 45', showers, laundry, small pets okay, open year round, $$-$$$$.
Located on US 395, 10 miles north of its junction with US 2.

WILLOW BAY RESORT & TAVERN (Private)
15 units w/hookups for water & elec. plus lots of tent sites, reservations (509)276-2350, trailers to 40', showers, laundry, wheelchair access, small store, trailer waste disposal, on Long Lake, boat launch & dock, row boat rentals, fishing, pets extra, open year round, $$-$$$.
Follow State 291 northwest to Nine Mile Falls - located at 6607 Highway 291, near milepost #20.

(East of Spokane)

ALPINE MOTEL RV PARK (Private)
70 pull thrus w/hookups for water/elec./sewer plus 40 sites w/water & elec., tents okay, reservations (509)928-2700, trailers to 50', showers, laundry, wheelchair access, swimming pool, restaurant, groceries, play area, horses & pets okay, open year round, $$$$-$$$$$.
Take I-90 east to exit #293 - located at 18815 Cataldo.

KOA OF SPOKANE (Private)
180 units w/full hookups plus 20 tent sites, reservations (509) 924-4722, trailers to 50', showers, laundry, wheelchair access, groceries, swimming pool, game room, playground, trailer waste disposal, pets okay, open March thru Oct., $$$$-$$$$$.
Take I-90 east to exit #293 and Barker Rd. north 1.3 miles.

LIBERTY LAKE PARK (County)
21 RV sites w/hookups for water & elec. plus tent area, information (509)456-4730, trailers to 35', showers, wheelchair access, playground, on lake, swimming, fishing, hiking, no pets, open Mem. Day to Labor Day, $-$$.
Take I-90 east to exit #296 and Liberty Lake Rd., south 4 miles.

SUTTON BAY RESORT (Private)
8 units w/hookups for water & elec. plus 12 tent sites, reservations (509)226-3660, trailers to 30', showers, wheelchair access, playground, on Newman Lake, boat launch/moorage & dock, boat & canoe rentals, fishing, hiking, small pets okay, open Mem. Day to Labor Day, $$$.
Take I-90 east to exit #296 and head north 8 miles.

(Southwest of Spokane)

BARBERS RESORT (Private)
50 units w/hookups for water & elec. plus tent area, reservations (509)299-3830, trailers to 40', pull thrus, showers, playground, trailer waste disposal, propane, lake, swimming, fishing, boat launch/dock & rental, pets okay, open April thru Sept., $$$.
Take I-90 southwest to exit #264 and follow Salnaive Rd. north 2 miles to resort.

BERNIE'S LAST RESORT (Private)
8 units w/hookups for water/elec./sewer, 12 w/water & elec., plus 20 tent sites, reservations (509)299-7273, trailers to 32', showers, laundry, wheelchair access, rec room, trailer waste disposal, lake, swimming, fishing, boat rental, pets okay, open April thru Sept., $$$.
Take I-90 southwest 7 miles to exit #270, the Medical Lake turnoff northwest 3.2 miles, and Four Lakes Rd. to resort.

FISHTRAP LAKE RESORT (Private)
20 units w/hookups for water & elec., tents okay, reservations (509)235-2284, trailers to 30', wheelchair access, groceries, ice, trailer waste disposal, swimming, fishing, boat launch & rental, pets okay, open mid April thru Sept., $$.
Take I-90 southwest to exit #254 and Fishtrap Rd. southeast 3.5 miles to resort.

PICNIC PINES ON SILVER LAKE (Private)
30 units w/hookups for water/elec./sewer plus 12 tent sites, reservations (509)299-3223, trailers to 30', wheelchair accessible restrooms, restaurant/lounge, rec room, playground, swimming, fishing, boat launch & rental, pets okay, open year round, $$.
Take I-90 southwest to exit #270, the Medical Lake turnoff northwest 3.5 miles, and Silver Lake Rd. to campground.

RAINBOW COVE (Private)
3 units w/hookups for water/elec./sewer, 10 w/water & elec., 3 w/elec. only, plus 3 tent sites, reservations (509)299-3717, trailers to 36', showers, wheelchair access, picnic area, cafe, tackle shop, lake, boat launch/dock & rental, fishing, swimming, pets okay, open year round, $$$-$$$$.
Take I-90 southwest to exit #270, the Medical Lake turnoff northwest 3.5 miles, and Clear Lake Rd. south 3 miles.

CHENEY

PEACEFUL PINES RV PARK (Private)
10 units w/hookups for water/elec./sewer, 6 w/water & elec., plus 14 w/out hookups, tents okay, reservations (509)235-4966, showers, wheelchair access, trailer waste disposal, open year round, $$$.
Located at 1231 W. 1st St.

(South of Cheney)

BADGER LAKE RESORT (Private)
10 units w/hookups for water/elec./sewer, no tents, reservations (509)235-2341, trailers to 40', showers, groceries, playground, lake, fishing, swimming, boat rental, no pets, $$$.
Follow Badger Lake Rd. south 9.5 miles to resort.

BUNKERS RESORT (Private)

15 units w/hookups for water/elec./sewer plus 15 w/water & elec., reservations (509)235-5212, trailers to 35', showers, wheelchair access, groceries, trailer waste disposal, restaurant, on Williams Lake, boat launch & rental, fishing, swimming, hiking, pets okay, open April thru Sept., $$-$$$.
Take Cheney Plaza Rd. south 11.5 miles and Williams Lake Rd. west .5 mile.

WILLIAMS LAKE RESORT (Private)

90 units w/hookups for water/elec./sewer, 50 w/water & elec., plus 10 tent sites, reservations (509)235-2391, trailers to 45', flush toilets, showers, wheelchair access, playground, propane, restaurant, groceries, trailer waste disposal, on lake, swimming, fishing, boat launch & rental, hiking, pets okay, $$$-$$$$.
Take Cheney Plaza Rd. south 11.5 miles and Williams Lake Rd. west 3.5 miles.

SPRAGUE

FOUR SEASONS CAMPGROUND (Private)

24 units w/hookups for water/elec./sewer, 14 w/water or elec., plus grassy tent area, reservations (509)257-2332, trailers to 36', showers, wheelchair access, pool, groceries, trailer waste disposal, on Sprague Lake, boat launch/moorage/dock & rentals, fishing, pets okay, open mid March thru mid Oct., $$$.
Go west towards Sprague Lake and follow signs to campground.

LAST ROUNDUP MOTEL/RV/CAMP (Private)

13 units w/hookups for water/elec./sewer plus 10 tent sites, information (509)257-2583, showers, laundry, ice, playfield, pets okay, open April thru Sept., $$-$$$.
Located .5 mile east of I-90 Sprague exit #245.

SPRAGUE LAKE RESORT (Private)

30 units w/hookups for water/elec./sewer plus 30 tent sites, reservations (509)257-2864, trailers to 40', pull thrus, showers, laundry, wheelchair access, ice, playground, trailer waste disposal, on lake, swimming, fishing, boat launch & rental, pets okay, open April thru Sept., $$$.
Leave Sprague, and go west 2 miles to lake and resort.

COULEE CITY

COULEE CITY PARK (City)

34 units w/hookups for water/elec./sewer plus 106 tent sites, trailers to 24', reservations (509)632-5331, showers, playground, trailer waste disposal, on lake, swimming, fishing, boat launch, pets okay, $$.
Located in Coulee City, at north edge of town.

BLUE LAKE RESORT (Private)
23 units w/water/elec./sewer, 33 w/water & elec., plus 19 tent sites, (509)632-5364, showers, groceries, playground, swimming, fishing, boat launch & rental, pets okay, $$-$$$.
Take US 2 west 2 miles and State 17 south 10 miles.

COULEE LODGE RESORT (Private)
22 units w/hookups for water/elec./sewer, 11 w/water & elec., plus 12 tent sites, reservations (509)632-5565, disabled access, showers, laundry, groceries, trailer waste disposal, on lake, swimming, fishing, boat launch, jet ski & boat rental, $$-$$$.
Take US 2 west 2 miles and State 17 south 8 miles.

LAURENTS SUN VILLAGE RESORT (Private)
56 units w/water/elec./sewer, 40 w/water & elec., plus 4 tent sites, reservations (509)632-5664, showers, laundry, playground, rec room, store, gas, propane, on lake, swimming, water skiing, boat launch/dock & rentals, fishing, hiking, pets okay, $$$.
Take US 2 west 2 miles, State 17 south 8 miles, and State Park Rd. east 1 mile to resort.

SUN LAKES PARK RESORT (Private)
110 units w/water/elec./sewer, tents okay - no fire pits, reservations (509)632-5291, showers, laundry, pool, playfield, groceries, propane, trailer waste disposal, on lake, swimming, fishing, boat launch & rental, golf, hiking, pets okay, $$$-$$$$.
Take US 2 west 2 miles and State 17 south 7 miles.

SUN LAKES (Washington State Park)
18 units w/water/elec./sewer plus 175 standard sites, trailers to 50', group area - reservations (509)632-5583, flush toilets, showers, disabled access, groceries, trailer waste disposal, boat launch, fishing, swimming, boat & horse rental, horse trails, pets okay, $$-$$$$.
Take US 2 west 2 miles and State 17 south 5 miles.

HARRINGTON

COUNTRY CLUB COURT (Private)
17 units plus tent area, trailers to 70', showers, wheelchair access, trailer waste disposal, on golf course, pets okay, $$.
Located in Harrington, right next to the golf course.

SOAP LAKE

AMERICAN ADVENTURE RESORT (Private)
72 units w/hookups for water/elec./sewer plus 40 w/water & elec., tents okay, reservations (509)246-1103, trailers to 40', pull

thrus, showers, laundry, wheelchair access, pool, hot tub, game room, restaurant, store, propane, on Soap Lake, fishing, hiking, pets okay, open year round - no water in winter, $$$$.
Located at 22818 North State 17, in Soap Lake.

ROBBIE'S RV PARK (Private)
18 units w/full hookups plus 4 tent sites, reservations (509)246-0906, trailers to 50', showers, wheelchair access, pets okay, open year round, $$$.
Located at 428 S. Division.

SOAP LAKES SMOKIAM CAMPGROUND (City)
52 units w/hookups for water/elec./sewer, tents okay, information (509)246-1211, showers, laundry, Soap Lake mud baths, playground, groceries, trailer waste disposal, swimming, fishing, pets okay, $$.
Take State 17 north 3 miles to campground.

EPHRATA

OASIS PARK (Private)
31 units w/full hookups, 38 w/water & elec., plus big tent area, reservations (509)754-5102, showers, laundry, wheelchair access, covered picnic area, playfield, swimming pool, trailer waste disposal, groceries, mini golf, golf course, pond, fishing, hiking, pets okay, $$-$$$.
On State 28, about 1 mile south of its junction with State 282.

STARS & STRIPES RV PARK (Private)
37 units w/water/elec./sewer plus 14 tent sites, reservations (509)787-1062, trailers to 40', showers, laundry, wheelchair access, heated pool, game room, playground, propane, trailer waste disposal, pets & horses okay, open year round, $$$-$$$$.
Take State 28 south 5 miles to 5707 State Highway 28.

(Southwest of Ephrata)

QUINCY VALLEY GOLF & RV (Private)
15 units - most have full hookups, no tents, reservations (509)787-3244, trailers to 40', showers, laundry, wheelchair access, swimming pool, restaurant, golf course, trailer waste disposal, pets okay, open year round, $$$.
Take State 28 south and west 16 miles to Quincy, turn south on State 281 and go 5 miles.

SHADY TREE RV PARK (Private)
41 units w/full hookups plus tent area, reservations (509)785-2851, trailers to 40', showers, laundry, wheelchair access, outdoor amphitheater, pets okay, open year round, $$-$$$.
Take State 28 south 4 miles and State 283 southwest 15 miles - located near US 90.

VILLAGER INN MOTEL/RV PARK (Private)
11 units w/hookups for water/elec./sewer, no tents, reservations (509)787-3515, no restrooms, trailers to 40', swimming pool, no pets, open year round, $$$.
Take State 28 south and west 16 miles to Quincy - located at 711 Second Ave.

RITZVILLE

BEST WESTERN HERITAGE INN/RV PARK (Private)
30 units w/hookups for water/elec./sewer plus 10 tent sites, reservations (509)659-1007, showers, laundry, wheelchair access, swimming & therapy pool, pets okay, $$$$.
Located just off I-90 east at exit #221 - on frontage road.

COTTAGE RV PARK & MOTEL (Private)
19 units w/full hookups, no tents, reservations (509)659-0721, showers, laundry, trailer waste disposal, pets okay, $$$.
Located in Ritzville, at city center.

ODESSA GOLF & RV PARK (Private)
12 units w/hookups for water & elec., tents okay, reservations (509)982-0093, on golf course, pets okay, golfers stay for free - others $-$$.
Take I-90 west 14 miles, State 21 north 19 miles, and State 28 to the west end of Odessa and campground.

MOSES LAKE

BIG SUN RESORT & RV PARK (Private)
50 units w/full hookups plus 10 tent sites, reservations (509) 765-8294, showers, laundry, wheelchair access, ice, playground, on Moses Lake, fishing, boat launch & rental, pets okay, $$-$$$.
Leave I-90 at exit #176, take Broadway north .5 mile, and Marina Dr. west - located at 2300 W. Marina Dr.

CASCADE PARK CAMPGROUND (Private)
20 units w/hookups for water & elec. plus 27 tent sites, reservations (509)766-9240, trailers to 36', showers, on lake, boat launch & moorage, fishing, pets okay, open May thru Sept., $$$.
Leave I-90 at exit #176, at Broadway's third stoplight turn left onto Statford Rd., go around lake, turn left onto Valley Rd., and follow this down the hill to the lake and campground.

SUN CREST RESORT (Private)
44 units w/hookups for water/elec./sewer plus 15 tent sites, reservations (509)765-0355, trailers to 52', pull thrus, showers, laundry, wheelchair access, swimming pool, jacuzzi, game room, playground, pets okay, open year round, $$$-$$$$.
Take the Hansen Rd. exit off I-90 and go to 303 N. Hansen Rd.

WILLOWS TRAILER VILLAGE (Private)
38 units w/hookups for water/elec./sewer, 26 w/water & elec., plus large tent area, reservations (509)765-7531, showers, laundry, groceries, trailer waste disposal, pets okay, $$-$$$.
Take State 17 south 2 miles and CR M southeast .3 mile.

(South of Moses Lake)

MAR DON RESORT (Private)
160 units w/hookups for water/elec./sewer, 55 w/water & elec., 135 w/out hookups, plus beach tent area, information (509)765-5061, flush toilets, showers, playground, cafe/lounge, groceries, propane, gas, on Potholes Reservoir, swimming beach, 2 boat launches, marina, boat moorage, fishing dock, boat & motor rental, hiking, pets okay, $$$-$$$$.
Take State 17 southeast 10 miles and Potholes Reservoir Rd. west 8 miles.

POTHOLES (Washington State Park)
60 units w/hookups for water/elec./sewer plus 60 standard sites, trailers to 50', group area - reservations (509)765-7271, flush toilets, showers, wheelchair access - inc. trails, trailer waste disposal, on reservoir, boat launch, fishing, water skiing, pets okay, $-$$$$.
Take State 17 southeast 10 miles and Potholes Reservoir Rd. west 13 miles.

PHEASANT RUN RV (Private)
10 units w/hookups for water/elec./sewer, tents okay, restroom in store - wheelchair accessible, reservations (509)349-2514, trailers to 70', deli, pets okay, open year round, $$.
Take State 17 south 12 miles and go east on State 170 toward Warden - located at 17005 Highway 170.

OTHELLO

HUNTER HILL VINEYARD PARK (Private)
5 units w/hookups for water/elec./sewer plus grassy tent area, reservations (509)346-2736, trailers to 37', showers, laundry, hot tub, winery & tasting room, small store, trailer waste disposal, 60 nearby small lakes, pets okay, open year round, $$-$$$.
Head north out of Othello to McMananon Rd. - it's 9.5 miles to the vineyard park.

ROYAL CITY GOLF & RV PARK (Private)
12 units w/hookups for water & elec., tents okay - no restrooms, reservations (509)346-2052, trailers to 70', trailer waste disposal, golf course, pets okay, open March thru Oct., $$.
Take State 26 west of Othello 25 miles to Royal City.

COLFAX

HILLTOP MOBILE HOME PARK (Private)
8 trailer sites w/hookups for water/elec./sewer, no tents, reservations (509)397-3442, trailers to 35', showers, laundry, wheelchair access, trailer waste disposal, small pets okay, open year round, $$$.
Located on Highway 22, at the southwest edge of town.

TIFFANY'S RIVER INN @ BOYER PARK (Private)
14 units w/hookups for water/elec./sewer plus 14 w/water & elec., tents okay, reservations (509)397-3208, trailers to 38', showers, laundry, wheelchair access, seasonal restaurant, gas, trailer waste disposal, on Snake River, swimming, fishing, boat launch & moorage, hiking, pets okay, open year round, $$$.
Take State 26 west and follow Almota Rd. to the park - located 23 miles south of Colfax.

CITY OF PULLMAN RV PARK (City) [RV]
24 trailer sites w/hookups for water/elec./sewer, reservations (509)334-4555, swimming pool, playfield, $$.
Take US 195 southeast 13 miles to Pullman, follow Grand Ave. 2 blocks northeast to Paradise St., go east to Spring St., and follow signs to City Playfield - located at south end of Playfield.

CONNELL

CONNELL PARK ESTATES (Private) [RV]
9 units w/hookups for water/elec./sewer, no tents, reservations (509)234-2222, trailers to 30', showers, laundry, wheelchair access, trailer waste disposal, small pets okay, open year round, $$$-$$$$.
Located in Connell, just off Highway 395, at 200 W. Hawthorne.

POMEROY

CENTRAL FERRY (Washington State Park)
60 units w/hookups for water/elec./sewer, trailers to 45', group area - reservations (509)549-3551, flush toilets, showers, disabled access, picnic shelter, trailer & boat waste disposal, on Snake River, boat launch, fishing, water skiing, $-$$$.
Take US 12 northwest 13 miles and State 127 north 9 miles.

CHIEF TIMOTHY (Washington State Park) [A] [RV]
33 units w/hookups for water/elec./sewer plus 33 standard sites, trailers to 60', flush toilets, showers, wheelchair access, groceries, picnic shelter, trailer waste disposal, on Lower Granite Lake, boat launch, docks for boat campers, fishing, water sports, interpretive center - Lewis & Clark Expedition, $-$$$$.
Take US 12 east 22 miles.

LYON'S FERRY MARINA & RV PARK (Private)

18 units w/water/elec./sewer plus 38 w/out hookups, tents okay, reservations (509)399-2001, trailers to 40', showers, wheelchair access, restaurant, store, propane, on river, boat ramp & rental, swimming, fishing, pets okay, open year round, $$.
US 12 northwest 22 miles, State 261 northwest 18 miles.

LYON'S FERRY (Washington State Park)

50 units - some will hold trailers to 45', flush toilets, showers, picnic shelter, disabled access, trailer waste disposal, at confluence of Snake & Palouse Rivers, boat launch, fishing, swimming, open April thru Sept., $-$$.
US 12 northwest 22 miles, State 261 northwest 18 miles.

PALOUSE FALLS (Washington State Park)

10 units, trailers to 40', flush toilets, showers, picnic shelter, on Palouse River, 190' waterfall, hiking, open April thru Sept., $$.
US 12 northwest 22 miles, State 261 northwest 21 miles.

DAYTON

LEWIS & CLARK TRAIL (Washington State Park)

30 units, some trailers to 28', group sites - reservations (509)337-6457, flush toilets, showers, community kitchen, trailer waste disposal, campfire programs in summer, fishing, $-$$.
Take US 12 southwest 5 miles.

ASOTIN

FIELDS SPRING (Washington State Park)

20 primitive sites, some trailers to 30', community kitchen, wheelchair access, trailer waste disposal, Puffer Butte trail, $-$$.
Take State 129 southwest 23.5 miles.

RICHLAND

ARROWHEAD RV PARK (Private)

70 units w/full hookups, tents okay, reservations (509)545-8206, trailers to 70', pull thrus, showers, laundry, wheelchair access, pets extra, open year round, $$$$-$$$$$$.
Located southeast of Richland, in Pasco, at 3120 Commercial.

COLUMBIA MOBILE VILLAGE (Private)

20 units w/hookups for water/elec./sewer, reservations (509)783-3314, pets okay, open year round, $$$.
Located southeast of Richland, in Kennewick, take State 14 to Clearwater Ave. - campground is 1.3 miles west.

COLUMBIA PARK (City)

30 units w/hookups for water & elec., 22 w/out hookups, plus 26 tent sites, trailers to 70', showers, groceries, trailer waste disposal, near river, bike/hike trails, pets okay, open May thru Sept., $$-$$$.

Take US 12 southeast to Columbia Center exit and follow signs.

DESERT GOLD TRAILER PARK/MOTEL (Private)

85 units w/hookups for water/elec./sewer plus 15 tent sites, reservations (509)627-1000, showers, laundry, groceries, swimming & therapy pools, pets okay, open year round, $$-$$$$.

Take US 12 southeast to Columbia Dr. and follow signs.

GREEN TREE RV PARK (Private)

70 RV sites w/hookups for water/elec./sewer, reservations (509)547-6220, trailers to 45', showers, laundry, wheelchair access, trailer waste disposal, pets okay, open year round, $$$$.

Leave I-82 east on exit #13 - park is just north, on 4th Ave.

TRAILER CITY PARK (Private)

4 trailer sites w/full hookups, no tents, reservations (509)783-2513, no restrooms, trailers to 30', swimming pool, trailer waste disposal, no pets, open year round, $$$$.

Located southeast of Richland, in Kennewick, at 7120 W. Bonnie Ave.

(West of Richland)

BEACH RV PARK (Private)

36 units w/hookups for water/elec./sewer, reservations (509) 588-5959, trailers to 40', showers, laundry, wheelchair access, river, fishing, pets okay, open year round, $$$$.

Take I-82 west 11 miles to the Benton City exit - located in Benton City, on Abby Ave.

(East of Richland)

CHARBONNEAU PARK (Corps)

15 units w/water/elec./sewer plus 40 w/elec., tents okay, trailers to 70', showers, wheelchair access, playground, propane, gas, trailer waste disposal, lake, swimming, fishing, boat launch, open year round - limited facilities Nov. thru March, $$-$$$.

I-82 east 5 miles, State 14 northeast 4 miles, US 12 south 3 miles, State 124 east 8 miles, and Sun Harbor Dr. north 2 miles.

FISHHOOK PARK (Corps)

41 units w/hookups for water & elec. plus 20 tent sites, information (509)547-7781, trailers to 70', showers, wheelchair access, playground, trailer waste disposal, lake, swimming, fishing, boat launch, elev. 4500', open April thru Sept., $$-$$$.

I-82 east 5 miles, State 14 northeast 4 miles, US 12 south 3 miles, State 124 east 15 miles, and Page Rd. north 4 miles.

HOOD PARK (Corps)

69 units w/elec., tents okay, trailers to 70', showers, wheelchair access, playground, trailer waste disposal, lake, swimming, fishing, boat launch, elev. 3500', open April thru Sept., $$-$$$.
I-82 east 5 miles, State 14 northeast 4 miles, and US 12 south 3 miles - located at junction with State 124.

WINDUST PARK (Corps)

20 units, trailers to 70', wheelchair access, trailer waste disposal, on Lower Snake River, boat launch, fishing, pets okay, open year round - limited facilities Oct thru March, $$.
I-82 east 5 miles, State 14 northeast 4 miles, US 12 south 5 miles, Pasco/Kahlotus Hwy. northeast 28 miles, and Burr Canyon Rd. south 6 miles.

(South of Richland)

PLYMOUTH PARK (Corps)

17 units w/hookups for water/elec./sewer plus 15 tent sites, showers, wheelchair access, trailer waste disposal, lake, river, swimming, fishing, boat launch, $$$.
Take I-82 south 29 miles - park is 1 mile west of Umatilla Bridge.

WALLA WALLA

COUNTRY ESTATES (Private) RV

4 units w/hookups for water/elec./sewer, no tents, reservations (509)529-5442, trailers to 32', showers, laundry, wheelchair access, small pets okay, open year round, $$$.
Take State 125 southwest to Larch St. exit, after 2 blocks turn right on Scenic View Dr. and follow to 938 Scenic View Dr.

FORT WALLA WALLA CAMPGROUND (City)

21 units w/water & elec. plus 41 tent sites, reservations (509)527-4527, trailers to 70', showers, wheelchair access, playground, trailer waste disposal, 300 acre park w/museum, remote car & airplane track, nature trail, pets okay, open year round - no hookups or restrooms in winter, $$-$$$.
State 125 southwest 4 miles, Dalles Military Rd. west .7 mile.

GOLDEN WEST ESTATES (Private) RV

8 RV sites w/full hookups, adults only, reservations (509)529-4890, showers, laundry, wheelchair access, heated pool, club house w/game area, no pets, open year round, $$$.
Take West Rose Pl. to Jasper - located at 1424 Jasper.

RV RESORT FOUR SEASONS (Private) RV

90 RV sites w/full hookups, reservations (509)529-6072, trailers to 75', pull thrus, showers, laundry, wheelchair access, stream, fishing, hiking, small pets okay, open year round, $$$$.
State 125 southwest 4 miles and Dalles Military Rd. west .7 mile.

INDEX

Bicycle camps - 27, 34, 144, 155, 156

Bicycle paths - 19, 21, 40, 55, 59, 76, 76, 89, 90, 122, 178, 193, 206, 235

Boat access only - 13, 106, 107, 154, 156, 160, 166, 188, 196

Boat launch - 19, 21, 22, 23, 24, 26, 27, 28, 29, 30, 31, 32, 33, 34, 35, 36, 37, 39, 40, 43, 44, 45, 46, 51, 54, 55, 56, 58, 60, 61, 63, 65, 69, 70, 72, 73, 74, 75, 76, 77, 78, 79, 80, 81, 82, 83, 84, 87, 88, 89, 90, 91, 92, 93, 96, 98, 99, 100, 102, 104, 105, 107, 108, 109, 110, 111, 112, 113, 114, 117, 118, 120, 121, 122, 123, 124, 125, 131, 132, 133, 134, 136, 141, 147, 153, 154, 155, 156, 157, 158, 159, 160, 161, 162, 163, 164, 165, 167, 169, 170, 172, 175, 177, 178, 179, 181, 184, 185, 186, 187, 188, 191, 192, 193, 194, 195, 196, 198, 200, 201, 202, 204, 206, 207, 208, 213, 214, 215, 216, 217, 218, 219, 220, 221, 222, 223, 225, 226, 227, 228, 229, 231, 232, 233, 234, 235, 236

Boat rental - 23, 24, 26, 27, 29, 30, 31, 34, 35, 36, 37, 45, 51, 56, 64, 75, 77, 79, 81, 84, 88, 93, 95, 98, 99, 100, 104, 105, 106, 107, 108, 110, 113, 114, 118, 120, 122, 124, 131, 132, 133, 138, 141, 152, 153, 155, 156, 157, 159, 161, 162, 168, 170, 172, 175, 177, 178, 180, 181, 184, 192, 193, 195, 198, 202, 204, 206, 213, 214, 215, 216, 217, 219, 220, 221, 222, 223, 226, 227, 228, 229, 231, 232, 234

Canoe/kayak/rafting - 21, 24, 25, 72, 96, 134, 138, 159, 162, 191, 206, 220, 226

Fishing - 19, 20, 21, 22, 23, 24, 25, 26, 27, 28, 29, 30, 31, 32, 33, 34, 35, 36, 37, 38, 39, 40, 41, 42, 43, 44, 45, 46, 47, 48, 51, 52, 53, 54, 55, 56, 57, 58, 59, 60, 61, 62, 63, 64, 65, 66, 67, 68, 69, 70, 71, 72, 73, 74, 75, 76, 77, 78, 79, 80, 81, 82, 83, 84, 87, 88, 89, 90, 91, 92, 93, 94, 95, 96, 97, 98, 99, 100, 101, 102, 103, 104, 105, 106, 107, 108, 109, 110, 111, 112, 113, 114, 117, 118, 119, 120, 121, 122, 123, 124, 125, 126, 131, 132, 133, 134, 135, 136, 137, 138, 139, 104, 141, 142, 143, 144, 145, 146, 147, 148, 151, 152, 153, 154, 155, 156, 157, 158, 159, 160, 161, 162, 163, 164, 165, 166, 167, 168, 169, 170, 171, 172, 173, 174, 175, 176, 177, 178, 179, 180, 181, 182, 183, 184, 185, 186, 187, 188, 191, 192, 193, 194, 195, 196, 197, 198, 199, 200, 201, 202, 203, 204, 205, 206, 207, 208, 209, 210, 213, 214, 215, 216, 217, 218, 219, 220, 221, 222, 223, 225, 226, 227, 228, 229, 230, 231, 232, 233, 234, 235, 236

Full hookups - 12, 19, 20, 21, 22, 23, 24, 25, 26, 27, 28, 29, 30, 31, 32, 33, 34, 35, 36, 37, 38, 39, 40, 42, 43, 44, 46, 47, 48, 52, 53, 58, 59, 60, 61, 65, 66, 67, 68, 69, 72, 73, 74, 76, 77, 78, 79, 80, 81, 82, 84, 87, 89, 90, 92, 93, 95, 96, 97, 98, 101, 102, 103, 105, 106, 107, 110, 112, 118, 121, 122, 125, 131, 132, 133, 134, 135, 137, 138, 139, 140, 141, 142, 143, 144, 145, 146, 147, 151, 153, 157, 158, 159, 160, 161, 165, 166, 169, 170, 171, 172, 173, 174, 175, 176, 177, 178, 179, 182, 184, 185, 186, 187, 188, 192, 195, 197, 198, 199, 205, 206, 209, 213, 215, 217, 220, 221, 222, 223, 224, 225, 226, 230, 231, 234, 235, 236

Golf - 58, 87, 90, 95, 101, 143, 209, 223, 229, 230, 231, 232

Group campsites - 14, 19, 24, 25, 27, 29, 30, 32, 34, 35, 38, 39, 44, 45, 47, 48, 51, 55, 59, 60, 61, 64, 66, 70, 71, 72, 73, 74, 76, 80, 82, 83, 84, 87, 88, 95, 96, 97, 98, 99, 100, 102, 104, 105, 107, 108, 118, 119, 121, 122, 123, 126, 140, 142, 151, 153, 155, 157, 158, 160, 161, 162, 163, 164, 166, 167, 168, 169, 170, 171, 172, 174, 175, 176, 178, 179, 180, 181, 182, 183, 184, 185, 186, 187, 188;, 193, 195, 196, 197, 198, 199, 200, 201, 203, 207, 208, 209, 214, 215, 217, 219, 221, 222, 223, 224, 225, 229, 232, 233, 234

Hike-in access only - 12, 20, 21, 23, 55, 82, 83, 88, 106, 156, 165, 171, 191, 196, 198

Hiking - 19, 20, 21, 22, 23, 24, 25, 26, 27, 29, 30, 31, 32, 33, 34, 35, 36, 37, 38, 39, 40, 41, 42, 43, 44, 45, 47, 48, 51, 53, 54, 55, 56,

57, 59, 60, 61, 62, 63, 64, 65, 66, 68, 69, 70, 71, 72, 73, 74, 75, 76, 77, 78, 79, 80, 81, 82, 83, 84, 87, 88;, 89, 90, 91, 92, 94, 95, 96, 97, 98, 99, 100, 101, 102, 103, 104, 105, 106, 107, 108, 109, 110, 111, 112, 113, 114, 117, 118, 119, 120, 121, 122, 123, 124, 125, 126, 131, 132, 133, 134, 135, 136, 137, 138, 139, 140, 141, 142, 144, 145, 146, 147, 151, 152, 153, 154, 155, 156, 157, 158, 159, 164, 165, 166, 168, 172, 173, 174, 175, 176, 178, 179, 181, 183, 184, 187, 188, 191, 192, 193, 194, 195, 196, 197, 198, 199, 200, 201, 202, 203, 204, 205, 206, 207, 208, 209, 213, 214, 215, 216, 217, 218, 219, 220, 221, 223, 225, 226, 228, 229, 230, 232, 233, 234, 236

Horse trails or facilities - 21, 38, 40, 45, 55, 59, 62, 63, 79, 81, 84, 87, 90, 91, 97, 103, 108, 109, 110, 111, 113, 118, 119, 140, 144, 153, 155, 159, 161, 164, 181, 182, 183, 187, 209, 217, 218, 220, 221, 223, 225, 226, 229, 230

Lake - 13, 19, 20, 25, 27, 33, 34, 35, 36, 37, 38, 39, 41, 42, 44, 45, 52, 55, 56, 57, 60, 61, 63, 64, 65, 66, 69, 70, 71, 73, 74, 75, 77, 79, 81, 82, 83, 84, 88, 90, 91, 93, 96, 98, 99, 100, 101, 102, 103, 104, 105, 106, 107, 108, 109, 110, 112, 113, 114, 117, 118, 119, 120, 121, 122, 123, 124, 125, 126, 133, 134, 138, 140, 141, 146, 153, 155, 157, 158, 159, 161, 162, 165, 166, 167, 172, 173, 175, 176, 177, 178, 179, 180, 181, 182, 183, 186, 187, 191, 192, 193, 194, 195, 196, 198, 200, 201, 202, 204, 205, 206, 208, 213, 214, 215, 216, 217, 218, 219, 220, 221, 222, 223, 226, 227, 228, 229, 230, 231, 232, 233, 235, 236

Lake - no motors - 25, 33, 41, 56, 65, 69, 70, 73, 83, 88, 90, 93, 98, 101, 106, 117, 120, 121, 165, 206, 216, 220

Mountain biking - 21, 81, 87, 88, 162, 168, 183, 192, 194, 215

Off-road vehicles - 23, 26, 35, 36, 37, 38, 178, 216, 225

OR campgrounds - 15-126
    Abbott Creek - 76
    Ada Fishing Resort - 34
    Adel Store & RV Park - 126
    Agate Beach Trailer & RV - 29
    Agate Beach Trailer Park - 42

Agness RV Park - 43
Ainsworth State Park - 53
Airport Park - 51
Alameda Ave. Trailer Court - 73
Alder Glen - 25
Alder-Dune Lake - 33
Allen Springs - 96
Allingham - 96
Alpine - 90
Alsea Bay Trailer Park - 30
Alsea Falls - 64
Amacher Park - 73
American Adventure - 87
Anglers Trailer Village - 43
Anson Wright Park - 119
Antelope Flat Reservoir - 100
Anthony Lake - 120
Archie Knowles - 32
Arizona Beach - 43
Armstrong - 55
Ash Creek Mobile Park - 60
Asher's RV Park - 122
Aspen Point - 113
Astoria Koa - 19
Atrivers Edge RV Resort - 47
B & B RV Court - 60
Babe the Blue Ox RV Park - 62
Baker Bay - 70
Bandon RV Park - 40
Bandon-Port Orford KOA - 41
Bar View Jetty Park - 21
Barton Park - 55
Bastendorff Beach Park - 39
Bay City RV Park - 23
Bay Shore Trailer Park - 24
Beach Front RV Park - 46
Beachside State Park - 31
Bear Mountain RV Park - 80
Bear Springs - 94
Beaver Sulpher - 82
Beavertail - 92
Becker's High Chaparrel - 95
Bedrock - 68
Belknap Woods Resort - 64
Bellacres Mobile Estate - 53
Bend Campground - 102
Bend Keystone RV Park - 102
Bend O' the River - 78
Bennett Park - 41
Benton Cty. Fairgrounds - 63
Beverly Beach State Park - 29
Biak by the Sea MH Park - 22
Big Barn Marina/RV Park - 22
Big Eddy - 51
Big Elk - 29
Big Lake - 98
Big Lake West - 98
Big Meadows Horse Camp - 62
Big Pine - 78
Big Pines RV Park - 107
Big Pool - 68
Big Slide Lake - 55
Big Spruce Trailer Park - 24
Black Butte Motel/RV Park - 96
Black Canyon - 69

Blackberry - 30
Blackhorse - 119
Blair Lake - 69
Blue Bay - 98
Blue Hole - 93
Blue Jay Campground - 40
Blue Lake Resort - 98
Blue Pool - 69
Bluebill Campground - 38
Boardman Marina Park - 118
Bob's Budget RV Park - 89
Bogus Creek - 72
Breitenbush - 61
Bridge of the Gods RV Park - 87
Broadway MH Park - 125
Broken Arrow - 74
Broken Bowl - 68
Brooke Trailer Court - 118
Browns Camp - 23
Buck Lake MH & RV Park - 33
Bud's Camp & RV Park - 20
Bull Prairie - 122
Bullards Beach - 40
Bully Creek Reservoir - 124
Buttercreek Rec. Complex - 117
Camp Creek - 91
Camp Klamath River RV - 110
Camp Sherman - 97
Camp Wilkerson - 51
Camper Cove - 25
Campers Cove - 83
Campers Flat - 69
Canal Creek - 30
Canton Creek - 72
Cantrall-Buckley Park - 82
Cape Blanco State Park - 42
Cape Kiwanda RV Park - 26
Cape Lookout State Park - 24
Cape Perpetua - 32
Carberry - 82
Carl G. Washburne Park - 34
Carter Bridge - 55
Carter Lake - 34
Cascade Locks KOA - 87
Cascade Locks Marine - 87
Cascadia State Park - 63
Cascara - 68
Castle Rock - 99
Catherine Creek Park - 120
Cave Creek - 45
Caves Highway - 45
Cavitt Creek - 73
Chalet Village Annex - 66
Champoeg State Park - 55
Charles V. Stanton Park - 76
Charleston Marina/Park - 39
Chetco RV Park - 46
Chief Paulina Horse - 103
Chimney Rock Recreation - 99
Chinook Trailer Park - 30
Chinquapin Group Camp - 45
Chukar Park - 125
Cinder Hill - 104
Circle 5 Trailer Park - 97
Circle Creek Campground - 20

Circle W RV Park - 79
City Center Trailer Park - 28
Clackamas Lake - 90
Clay Creek - 32
Clear Lake - 90
Cleator Bend - 61
Clyde Holliday State Park - 122
Cobble Rock - 100
Coberg Hills RV Resort - 66
Coho Marina & RV Park - 36
Cold Spring - 97
Cold Springs Resort & RV - 96
Coldwater Cove - 64
Collier State Park - 111
Columbia Gorge RV Village - 53
Condon MH & RV Park - 93
Corvallis-Albany KOA - 62
Cottage Grove Lake - 71
Country Campgrounds - 124
County Fairgrounds - 95
Cove Palisades State Park - 95
Cow Creek RV Park - 76
Coyote Rock RV Park - 27
Crane Prairie - 104
Crane Prairie Resort - 105
Crater Lake Motel & RV - 109
Crater Lake Resort - 110
Crater Lake RV Park - 110
Crescent Creek - 108
Crescent Lake - 108
Crescent RV Park - 107
Crook County RV Park - 99
Crooked River Ranch RV - 101
Crown Point RV Park - 54
Crown Villa RV Park - 102
Crystal Corral Park - 99
Crystal Crane Hot Springs - 126
Cultus Lake - 105
Cushman RV & Boat Dock - 34
Cutsforth Park - 119
Cy Bingham Park - 107
Cypress Grove RV Park - 79
Daphne Grove - 41
Darlings Resort - 35
Delintment Lake - 125
Delta - 66
Depot Park - 123
Deschutes Bridge - 105
Deschutes River Resort - 96
Deschutes River State Park - 89
Desert Terrace - 101
Detroit Lake State Park - 60
Devil's Canyon - 94
Devil's Lake State Park - 27
Dexter Shores RV Park - 68
Diamond Lake - 75
Diamond Lake RV Park - 75
Digit Point - 109
Doe Point - 81
Dolly Varden - 68
Dovre - 25
Drift Creek Landing - 31
Driftwood II - 35
Driftwood RV Park - 38
Driftwood RV Park - 46

Dufur City Park - 92
Dufur RV Park - 92
Eagle Creek - 87
Eagle Rock - 72
Eagle Valley RV/MH Park - 121
East Bay - 109
East Davis Lake - 107
East Lake - 104
East Lake Resort & RV - 104
East Shore Recreation Site - 37
Ecola State Park - 20
Elk Creek - 23
Elk Lake - 102
Elk River RV Campground - 42
Elkhorn Valley - 59
Elkton RV Park - 71
Emigrant - 126
Emigrant Campground - 83
Emigrant Springs Park - 118
Eugene Kamping World - 66
Eugene Mobile Village - 67
Evergreen Park - 27
Evergreen Park - 42
Expo Lake RV Park - 81
Falls - 126
Fan Creek - 25
Farewell Bend - 77
Farewell Bend State Park - 123
Fern Ridge Shores - 67
Fernview - 63
Feyrer Park - 58
Fir Grove/El Rancho - 52
Firs Trailer Park - 38
Fish Creek - 56
Fish Lake - 65
Fish Lake - 81
Fish Lake - 126
Fish Lake Resort - 81
Fish Mill Lodges - 35
Fisherman's Point - 68
Fishermen's Bend - 60
Fishery - Coverts Landing - 54
Fishin' Hole Park & Marina - 31
Flamingo Mobile & RV Park - 57
Flumet Flat - 82
Flycasters RV Park - 80
Flying "M" Ranch - 54
Fogarty Creek RV Park - 27
Forest Glen - 59
Fort Henrietta RV Park - 117
Fort Klamath Lodge & RV - 110
Fort Stevens State Park - 19
Fossil Motel & Trailer Park - 94
Four Seasons RV Resort - 44
Fourbit Ford - 77
Fourmile Lake - 113
French Gulch Camp - 82
French Pete - 66
Frissell Crossing - 66
Frog Lake - 90
Frona Park - 41
Frontier Court - 118
Gales Creek - 23
Gerber Reservoir - 111
Get Canyon - 92

Glenyan KOA - 83
Gold Lake - 70
Gold'N Rogue KOA - 80
Gone Creek - 91
Goose Lake State Park - 112
Gorge - 97
Grande Ronde Lake - 121
Grants Pass Over-Niters - 78
Grants Pass/Redwood KOA - 44
Grayback - 45
Green Acres - 101
Green Acres Mobile & RV - 99
Greensprings RV/MH - 112
Griffin Park - 78
Grizzly Campground - 83
Gull Point - 105
H.B. VanDuzer Forest - 27
Hagelstein Park - 113
Ham Bunch Cherry Creek - 40
Hamaker - 77
Hampton - 69
Handy Haven RV Park - 30
Happy Camp - 24
Happy Landing RV/Marina - 31
Happy Place RV Park - 32
Harbor View Inn - 22
Harbor Village Trailer Park - 28
Harbor Vista Campground - 33
Harpham Flat - 94
Harris Beach State Park - 47
Hart-Tish Park - 82
Hat Rock Campground - 117
Have-A-Nice Day Camp - 80
Hawthorne Acres Mobile - 58
Haystack Reservoir - 96
Hebo Lake - 25
Heceta Beach RV Park - 33
Herman Creek Horse Camp - 87
Heron's Landing RV Park - 22
Hewitt Park - 121
Hi-Way Haven RV Park - 72
Hidden - 119
Hidden Pines RV Park - 105
Highlander Motel & RV - 103
Hilgard Junction Park - 120
Hitching Post Trailer - 122
Holiday RV Park - 28
Holiday RV Park - 82
Honey Bear Campground - 43
Hood View - 91
Hoover - 61
Hoover Group Camp - 61
Horse Creek Group Camp - 66
Horsefall Campground - 38
Horseshoe Bend - 72
Hot Lake RV Resort - 120
Hot Springs - 104
House Rock - 63
Howard Prairie Lake Resort - 84
Huckleberry Hill MH Park - 39
Hudson/Parcher Park - 51
Humbug - 61
Humbug Mountain Park - 42
Hunt Park/Fairgrounds - 92
Hunter Creek Mobile & RV - 43

Hunter's RV - 112
Hyatt Lake - 84
Hyatt Lake Resort - 84
Ice Cap Creek - 65
Idle Wheels Village - 124
Illahe - 42
Indian Creek Recreation - 44
Indian Crossing - 119
Indian Ford - 98
Indian Henry - 56
Indian Lake Campground - 118
Indian Mary Park - 78
Iseberg Park RV - 57
Island Park - 26
Jackman Park - 126
Jackson F. Kimball Park - 110
Jackson Hot Spring - 83
Jantzen Beach RV Park - 52
Jessie M. Honeyman Park - 35
Jetty Fishery - 23
Joe Graham Horse Camp - 91
John Day Trailer Park - 123
John Neal Memorial Park - 60
Jones Canyon - 92
Jones Creek - 24
Joseph P. Stewart Park - 76
Jubilee Lake - 117
Junipers Res. RV Resort - 112
Kah-Nee-Ta - 95
Kampers West Kamp/RV - 19
Kane's Hideaway Marina - 60
Kelley's RV Park - 38
Keno Camp - 114
Kerby Trailer Park - 45
Kilchis River Park - 23
Kimball Creek RV Resort - 44
King Silver RV Park - 31
Kingfisher - 56
Klamath Falls KOA - 113
Klum Landing - 84
Kozy Kove Marina & RV - 31
LaGrande Rendezvous RV - 120
Lagoon-Siltcoos - 35
Lake Fork - 121
Lake Harriert - 56
Lake in the Woods - 73
Lake of the Woods Resort - 113
Lake Owyhee Resort - 124
Lake Owyhee State Park - 124
Lake Selmac RV Resort - 44
Lake View Mobile & RV - 34
Lake's Edge RV Park - 35
Lakeshore RV Park & Store - 99
Lakeshore Travel Park - 35
Lampliter Motel & RV - 103
Lane County Harbor Vista - 33
Langlois Travel Park - 41
LaPine State Park - 105
Lariat Motel & RV Park - 121
Lava Lake - 105
Lava Lake RV/Camp - 105
Laverne Park - 40
Lazy Acres Motel & RV - 80
Lazy Bend - 56
Lazy Daze MH Park - 65

Lemolo Lake Resort - 75
Lepage Park - 89
LeRose RV Park - 52
Lily Glen Campground - 84
Lincoln City KOA - 27
Link Creek - 98
Little Crater - 104
Little Crater Lake - 91
Little Fawn - 102
Little Redwood - 47
Little Redwood Bar - 47
Lobster Creek - 44
Lockaby - 56
Lodgepole - 35
Loeb State Park - 48
Lone Pine - 100
Lone Pine RV Park - 89
Longbend - 94
Loon Lake - 36
Loon Lake Lodge Resort - 37
Lost Creek - 75
Lost Creek - 89
Lost Lake - 88
Lost Prairie - 63
Lower Bridge - 97
Lower Palisades - 100
Lucky Lodge RV Park - 44
Lucky Seven Trailer Park - 118
Ludlum Place - 48
Macks Canyon - 92
Maple-Lane Trailer/Marina - 32
Marion Forks - 62
Martin's Trailer Harbor - 28
Marys Peak - 64
Maupin City Park - 93
Mazama - 75
McKenzie Bridge - 64
McKenzie River RV Park - 65
McKinley's Marina & RV - 30
Meadow Wood Resort - 76
Meadowbrook RV Park - 120
Mecca Flat - 95
Medford Oaks Campark - 81
Memaloose State Park - 89
Metzler - 55
Miami Cove RV Park - 22
Mile-Hi Trailer & RV Park - 112
Millpond - 72
Millsite Park & RV Park - 74
Milo McIver State Park - 55
Minam State Park - 118
Mona - 65
Moonshine Park - 28
Mountain Shadow RV Park - 97
Mountain View Holiday - 121
Mountain View Mobile Park - 61
Mountain Vu RV Park - 113
Mt. Home Mobile Village - 76
Mt. Hood RV Village - 90
Mt. View Park RV & Camp - 61
Mud Lake - 121
Mulkey RV Park - 58
Nebo Trailer Park - 74
Nehalem Bay State Park - 21
Nehalem Bay Trailer Park - 21

Nehalem Shores RV Park - 21
Nena Creek - 94
Neptune Park Resort - 110
Nesika Beach RV/Camp - 43
Nesika Park - 39
Neskowin Creek RV Resort -26
Newberry Group Camp - 104
Newport Marina RV Park - 28
Nightingale's Fishing Camp - 34
North Eel Creek - 37
North Lake Resort/Marina - 37
Oak Brook - 92
Oak Fork - 91
Oak Springs - 94
Oakridge RV Park - 69
Oasis Cafe/Motel/RV - 125
Oasis Flat - 93
Oceanside RV Camp - 43
Ochoco Divide - 101
Ochoco Forest Camp - 101
Ochoco Lake State Park - 99
Odell Creek - 107
Ogden Group Camp - 104
Olallie - 65
Old Mill Marina Park - 22
Olde Stone Village RV - 58
Ollokot - 119
Oregon Motel 8 RV Park - 113
Oregon Trails West RV - 122
Oswald West State Park - 21
Outpost RV Park - 119
Overlook - 87
Oxbow - 54
Pacific Campground - 23
Pacific City Trailer Park - 25
Pacific Shores RV Resort - 29
Packard Creek - 70
Page Springs - 126
Paradise - 64
Parker Meadows - 77
Parkway Motel & RV Park - 112
Pass Creek - 71
Patio RV Park - 65
Paul Dennis - 56
Paulina Lake - 104
Pear Tree Center - 82
Pebble Bay - 107
Peninsula - 56
Perry South - 96
Pheasant Ridge RV Park - 53
Pine Cove Motel & Trailer - 19
Pine Hollow Lakeside Res. - 93
Pine Meadows - 71
Pine Point - 91
Pine Rest - 97
Pioneer Ford - 97
Plainview Trailer Park - 39
Point - 103
Poison Butte - 100
Polk County Fairgrounds - 58
Poole Creek - 75
Port Orford RV/Trailer - 42
Port Siuslaw RV/Marina - 33
Portland Meadows RV Park - 52
Portland-Fairview RV Park - 52

Portside RV Park - 46
Post Pile - 100
Powers County Park - 41
Prairie - 104
Princess Creek - 107
Prineville Reservoir Resort - 100
Prineville Reservoir Park - 100
Promontory - 56
Prospector Trailer Park - 124
Puma - 68
Quinn Meadow Horse - 103
Quinn River - 106
Quosatana - 44
R & L Mobile Home Park - 125
Rainbow - 57
Rainies Resort - 26
Rattlesnake - 92
Reeder Beach RV Park - 51
Remote Camp & Cabins - 40
Rhododendron Trailer Park - 34
Richardson Park - 67
Riley Horse Camp - 90
Ripplebrook - 57
River Bend Park - 48
Riveredge - 30
Riverfront RV Trailer Park - 80
RiverPark RV Resort - 77
Riverplace RV Park - 58
Riverside - 57
Riverside - 62
Riverside Lake Resort - 20
Riverview Lodge Camp - 26
Riverview Trailer Park - 106
Roamer's Rest RV Park - 53
Roaring River - 57
Robinhood - 88
Rock Creek - 32
Rock Creek - 41
Rock Creek - 72
Rock Creek - 106
Rock Creek Reservoir - 93
Rocky Point Res./Marina - 114
Rogue Elk Campground - 81
Rogue Valley Overnighters - 78
Rolling Hills Mobile Terrace - 52
Rooke-Higgins Park - 39
Rose Grove RV Park - 54
Rosland - 106
Roundup Travel Trailer - 103
Routson Park - 88
Rujada - 71
RV Park - 118
RV Park at Sandpines - 33
RV Resort @ Cannon Bch. - 20
Saddle Mountain Park - 21
Salem Campground & RV - 59
Salem RV Park - 59
Salmon Creek Falls - 69
Sam Brown - 79
Sam Brown Horse Camp - 79
Sand Bar Mobile & RV - 39
Sand Beach - 26
Sand Creek Station - 109
Sand Prairie - 70
Sands Overnight Trailer - 125

Scandia RV & Mobile Park - 102
Schroeder - 79
Schwarz Park/Dorena Lake - 70
Scipio's Goble Landing - 51
Scout Lake - 98
Sea & Sand RV Park - 28
Sea Bird RV Park - 47
Sea Perch RV & Camp - 32
Sea Port RV Park - 40
Sea Ranch Resort - 20
Seadrift Motel & Camp - 38
Seal Rocks Trailer Cove - 30
Selmac Lake - 45
Shady Acres RV Park - 46
Shady Cove - 60
Shady Dell - 69
Shady Rest RV Park - 117
Shady Trails RV Park - 81
Shamrock Village RV Park - 67
Shaniko Corral & RV Park - 94
Sharps Creek - 71
Sheep Springs Horse Camp - 97
Shelter Cove Resort - 108
Shelton State Park - 94
Sherwood - 88
Sherwood Forest KOA - 67
Shorewood Travel Village - 23
Sid's Fernwood RV Park - 54
Siltcoos Lake Resort - 35
Silver Falls State Park - 59
Simax Group Camp - 108
Sisters KOA - 98
Skookum Lake - 57
Sleepy Hollow RV Park - 40
Slide Creek - 66
Smiling River - 97
Smith Rock State Park - 102
Snowry River RV Park - 103
Snug Harbor - 47
South Beach State Park - 29
South Fork - 77
South Junction - 95
South Shore - 61
South Shore - 98
South Twin - 106
Southgate MH & RV Park - 52
Spaulding Pond - 79
Spinreel - 38
Sportsman's Landing - 27
Sportsman's River Retreat - 111
Sportsman's Trailer Park - 29
Spring - 108
Spring - 123
Spring Creek - 111
Spruce Run - 21
Squaw Lakes - 83
Steens Mt. Resort/Corral - 126
Still Creek - 90
Stillwater - 100
Stringtown - 83
Succor Creek State Park - 124
Sugar Creek - 123
Sugar Pine - 84
Summer Lake Hot Spr. - 109
Sumpter Pine RV Park - 122

Sun Rocks RV/Camp - 100
Sundowner MH Park - 120
Sunny Valley KOA - 78
Sunnyside Park - 63
Sunset - 114
Sunset Bay State Park - 39
Sunset Cove - 108
Sunset Lake RV - 19
Sunstrip - 57
Surfwood Campground - 36
Surprise Valley Mobile Vil.- 76
Susan Creek - 72
Suttle Lake Resort/Camp - 99
Sutton Campground - 34
Tahkenitch Campground - 36
Tahkenitch Landing - 36
Target Meadows - 117
Taylor's Travel Park - 67
Taylors Landing - 31
Terrace Heights MH Park - 89
Thielsen View - 75
Tillamook KOA - 25
Tillicum Beach - 31
Timber River RV Park - 71
Timpanogas Lake - 70
Tin Can - 79
Tingley Lake Estates - 114
Toll Bridge Park - 88
Tollgate - 91
Topsy - 114
Town & Country Mobile - 53
Town & Country RV Park - 46
Trail Bridge - 65
Trailer Park of Portland - 53
Trailer Park Village - 59
Trails End Campground - 46
Trails West RV Park - 95
Trapper Creek - 108
Trask Park - 24
Trask River MH Park - 22
Trees of Oregon RV Park - 73
Trillium Lake - 90
Trout Creek - 64
Trout Creek - 95
Trucke's RV Park - 19
Tucker Park - 88
Tumalo - 102
Twin Lakes Resort - 106
Twin Rivers Vacation Park - 74
Twin Springs - 93
Tyee - 36
Tyee - 73
Ukiah-Dale Forest Park - 120
Umatilla Marina & RV - 117
Umpqua Beach Resort - 37
Umpqua Lighthouse Park - 37
Umpqua Safari RV Park - 74
Union Creek - 77
Union Creek Campground - 122
Unity Lake State Park - 123
Unity Motel & Trailer Park - 123
Valley Falls Store & Camp - 112
Valley of the Rogue Park - 80
Venice RV Park - 20
Viento State Park - 88

Village Green RV Park - 70
Village RV Park - 125
Wahtum Lake - 88
Wallowa Lake State Park - 119
Walt's Cozy Camp - 111
Walton Lake - 101
Wandamere Trailer/Camp - 29
Wapinitia - 94
Water Wheel Campground - 111
Waterloo - 62
Watkins - 83
Waxmyrtle-Siltcoos - 36
Wayside RV & Mobile Park - 33
Webb Park - 26
West Cultus - 106
West Davis Lake - 108
West South Twin - 107
Westerner RV Park - 124
Whaleshead RV Park - 47
Whiskey Springs - 77
Whispering Falls - 62
Whistler's Bend - 74
Whitcomb Creek - 63
White Horse - 79
White River - 93
Whitefish Horse Camp - 109
Whittaker Creek - 32
Wild Mare Horse Camp - 38
Wildcat - 101
William M. Tugman Park - 37
Williamson River - 111
Willow Lake Resort - 77
Willow Point - 84
Willow Prarie Horse Camp - 81
Wilson River RV Fish Park - 24
Wilson's Cottages & Camp - 110
Winchuck - 48
Windy Cove County Park - 37
Wiseman's Mobile Court - 113
Woahink Lake RV Resort - 36
Wolf Creek - 73
Wolf Creek - 123
Woodburn I-5 RV Park - 58
Woodland Echoes Resort - 45
Woods Park - 26
Woodward - 117
Wright's for Camping - 20
Wyeth - 87
Yellowbottom - 63
Yukwah - 64

OR cities - 15-126
Adel - 126
Agncss - 42
Albany - 62
Allegheny - 39
Alsea - 64
Arlington - 89
Ashland - 83-84
Astoria - 19
Aurora - 57
Azalea - 76
Baker City - 121-122
Bandon - 40
Beaver - 24

Bend - 102-103
Blue River - 65-66
Bly - 111
Boardman - 118
Brookings - 46-48
Burns - 125-126
Butte Falls - 77
Camp Sherman - 96-97
Canby - 58
Cannon Beach - 20-21
Canyonville - 76
Cascade Locks - 87
Cave Junction - 45-46
Charleston - 39-40
Chemult - 109
Chiloquin - 110-111
Coburg - 66
Condon - 93
Coos Bay - 38-39
Coquille - 40
Corbett - 54
Corvallis - 62
Cottage Grove - 70-71
Crater Lake - 75
Crescent - 107-109
Creswell - 67
Culp Creek - 71
Culver - 95
Curtin - 71
Dale - 120
Dallas - 58
Depoe Bay - 27-28
Detroit - 60-61
Dexter - 68
Diamond Lake - 74-75
Dodson - 54
Drain - 71
Dufur - 92
Echo - 117
Eddyville - 29
Elgin - 118
Elkton - 71
Elsie - 21
Enterprise - 119
Estacada - 55-57
Eugene - 67
Florence - 32-36
Forest Grove - 54
Fort Klamath - 110
Fossil - 94
Frenchglen - 126
Garibaldi - 21-22
Gearhart - 20
Glide - 73
Gold Beach - 43-44
Gold Hill - 80
Government Camp - 90-91
Grants Pass - 77-79
Gresham - 54
Haines - 120-121
Halfway - 121
Hebo - 25
Heppner - 119
Hermiston - 117
Hood River - 87-88

Huntington - 123
Idanha - 61-62
Idleyld Park - 71-72
Independence - 60
Jacksonville - 82-83
John Day - 122-123
Joseph - 119
Juntura - 125
Keno - 114
Kerby - 45
Kimberly - 122
Klamath Falls - 112-114
La Grande - 120
Lakeside - 37-38
Lakeview - 112
Langlois - 41
LaPine - 103-107
Lebannon - 62
Lincoln City - 27
Logsden - 28
Long Creek - 122
Lowell - 68
Lyons - 60
Madras - 95-96
Manzanita - 21
Mapleton - 32
Maupin - 93-94
McKenzie Bridge - 64-65
McMinnville - 57-58
Medford - 81-82
Mehama - 60
Mill City - 60
Molalla - 58
Mosier - 87
Myrtle Creek - 74
Myrtle Point - 41
Nehalem - 21
Neskowin - 26
Newberg - 55
Newport - 28-29
North Bend - 38
Oakridge - 69-70
Ontario - 124
Pacific City - 25-26
Paisley - 109
Parkdale - 88
Parkrose - 52
Paulina - 123
Pendleton - 118
Philomath - 64
Pilot Rock - 118
Port Orford - 42
Portland - 52-54
Powers - 41
Prairie City - 123
Prineville - 99-101
Prospect - 76-77
Rainier - 51
Redmond - 101-102
Reedsport - 36-37
Remote - 40-41
Rhododendron - 91
Richland - 121
Rickreall - 58
Rogue River - 79-80

Roseburg - 73-74
Rufus - 89
Salem - 59
Sauvie Island - 51
Scappoose - 51
Seaside - 19-20
Selma - 44-45
Shaniko - 94
Sherar's Bridge - 92, 93
Siletz - 28
Silver Lake - 109
Silverton - 59
Sisters - 97-99
Spray - 122
Springfield - 66
Steamboat - 72
Sunriver - 103
Sutherlin - 72-73
Sweet Home - 63-64
The Dalles - 89
Tidewater - 30
Tillamook - 22-25
Tualatin - 53
Tygh Valley - 92-93
Ukiah - 120
Umatilla - 117
Union - 120
Unity - 123
Vale - 124-125
Vernonia - 51
Waldport - 30-31
Wamic - 93
Warm Springs - 95
Warrenton - 19
Waterloo - 62
Welches - 89-90
Weston - 117
White City - 80-81
Winston - 74
Woodburn - 58
Yachats - 32
Yamhill - 54

RV's/trailers over 40' in length -
19, 21, 23, 24, 27, 29, 30, 33, 34,
35, 37, 39, 40, 42, 44, 45, 46, 47,
48, 52, 53, 55, 58, 59, 67, 69, 70,
71, 73, 75, 76, 77, 79, 80, 89, 92,
95, 96, 99, 100, 102, 103, 105,
106, 107, 109, 110, 111, 112, 117,
118, 119, 120, 122, 123, 125, 131,
132, 133, 134, 135, 136, 137, 139,
140, 141, 142, 143, 144, 146, 147,
151, 152, 153, 155, 156, 157, 158,
159, 160, 161, 162, 163, 164, 165,
166, 167, 168, 169, 170, 171, 172,
174, 175, 177, 178, 180, 181, 182,
183, 184, 185, 187, 188, 191, 193,
195, 198, 200, 201, 205, 106, 207,
208, 209, 213, 215, 217, 219, 221,
222, 223, 224, 225, 226, 229, 232,
233, 234, 235, 236

Scuba diving parks - 136, 151,
154, 155, 156, 160, 161, 163, 164,

166, 167, 169, 172, 174, 187, 195, 208, 223

Trailer waste disposal - 19, 21, 22, 23, 24, 25, 26, 27, 28, 29, 30, 31, 32, 33, 34, 35, 36, 37, 38, 39, 40, 41, 42, 43, 44, 45, 46, 47, 51, 52, 53, 54, 55, 56, 57, 58, 59, 60, 62, 64, 65, 66, 67, 68, 69, 70, 71, 72, 73, 74, 75, 76, 77, 78, 80, 81, 83, 84, 87, 88, 89, 92, 93, 94, 95, 96, 97, 98, 99, 100, 101, 102, 103, 104, 105, 107, 108, 109, 111, 112, 113, 114, 117, 118, 119, 120, 121, 122, 123, 124, 125, 126, 131, 132, 133, 134, 135, 136, 137, 138, 139, 140, 141, 142, 143, 144, 145, 146, 147, 151, 152, 153, 155, 156, 157, 158, 159, 160, 161, 162, 163, 164, 165, 166, 167, 168, 169, 170, 171, 172, 173, 174, 175, 176, 177, 178, 179, 180, 181, 182, 183, 184, 185, 186, 187, 188, 191, 192, 193, 194, 195, 196, 197, 198, 199, 200, 201, 202, 204, 205, 206, 207, 208, 209, 213, 214, 215, 216, 217, 218, 219, 220, 221, 222, 223, 224, 225, 226, 227, 228, 229, 230, 231, 232, 233, 234, 235, 236

WA campgrounds - 127-236.
12 West Resort - 204
99 Mobile Lodge/RV - 187
Aberdeen KOA - 140
Adams Fork - 183
Al's Restaurant & RV - 225
Al's RV Park - 132
Alder Lake Park - 179
Alderbrook Estates - 176
Aloha Court - 145
Alpine Motel RV Park - 226
Alta Lake State Park - 196
Altaire - 133
American Adventure Res. - 229
American Heritage Camp - 178
Anacortes RV Park - 156
Andersen's RV Park - 146
Anthony's Home Court - 145
Aqua Barn Ranch - 166
Arrowhead RV Park - 234
Artic RV Park - 140
Ashford Valley RV Park - 180
Atkisson Group Camp - 208
Audrey's RV Park - 220
Backstrom on Tilton River - 182
Badger Lake Resort - 227
Ball Bay View RV Park - 151
Banks Lake Golf - 223
Barbers Resort - 226
Barrier Dam Campground - 181
Battle Ground Lake Park - 187
Bay Center KOA - 144
Bay Shore Resort - 151
Bay View State Park - 160
Bayshore RV Park - 143

Bayview RV Park - 131
Beach RV Park - 235
Beachside RV Park - 151
Beacon Charters & RV - 147
Beacon Rock State Park - 188
Beacon Rock Trailer & RV - 188
Beacon RV Park - 147
Bear Creek RV & Motel - 137
Beaver - 209
Beaver Bay Camp - 185
Beaver Creek - 162
Beaver Lodge RV Park - 215
Beckler River - 195
Beebe Bridge Park - 200
Belair Trailer Court - 151
Belfair State Park - 169
Bells Trailer Park - 224
Bernie's Last Resort - 227
Berthusen Park - 152
Best Western Inn & RV - 231
Beth Lake - 214
Big Creek - 172
Big Fir Campground - 188
Big Foot Park - 209
Big Lake Resort - 159
Big River RV Park - 221
Big Sun Resort & RV Park - 231
Big Twin Lake Camp - 192
Birch Bay State Park - 151
Birch Bay Trailer Park - 151
Black Beach Resort - 216
Black Lake RV Park - 176
Black Pine Lake - 194
Blackpine Creek Horse - 199
Blake Island State Park - 166
Blake's RV Park & Marina - 159
Blue Lake Creek - 183
Blue Lake Resort - 229
Blue Pacific Motel & RV - 139
Blue Shastin Trailer & RV - 199
Blue Sky RV Park - 171
Blueslide Resort - 219
Bogachiel State Park - 137
Bonaparte Lake - 214
Bonaparte Lake Resort - 214
Boulder Creek - 157
Bridge Creek - 199
Bridgeport State Park - 222
Brookhollow RV Park - 185
Brooks Memorial Park - 207
Brown Creek - 173
Browns Lake - 220
Bruceport Park - 144
Bumping Lake - 202
Bunkers Resort - 228
Burlington/Cascade KOA - 159
Bush Point Resort - 161
Camano Island State Park - 161
Camp Benbows Tanwax - 175
Camp Kalama RV Park - 186
Cape Flattery Resort - 131
Cape Motel & RV Park- 131
Captains Landing - 167
Carl Precht Memorial - 218
Carol's Crescent Bch. RV - 133

Carson Hot Springs - 209
Cascade Park Camp - 231
Cedar Grove Shores RV - 161
Cedar Springs - 202
Cedar Village RV Park - 224
Central Ferry State Park - 233
Chalet RV Park - 197
Charbonneau Park - 235
Chatter Creek - 199
Chief Timothy State Park - 233
Chimacum Park - 164
Chinook County Park - 147
Chris's RV & Camp - 144
Circle H RV Ranch - 205
Circle-Up RV Park - 217
City of Pullman RV Park - 233
Clam Tide RV Park - 144
Clark Island - 154
Clark's Skagit River RV - 158
Cle Elum River - 200
Coach Post - 177
Coal Creek Bar - 163
Coho - 140
Coho Resort - 131
Coho RV Park - 141
Collins - 168
Colonial Creek - 191
Columbia Mobile Village - 234
Columbia Park - 235
Columbia Riverfront RV - 187
Columbus Park - 177
Colville Fairgrounds RV - 215
Conconully Lake Park - 191
Conestoga Quarters RV - 135
Connell Park Estates - 233
Connie-Lee's RV Park - 141
Copalis Beach RV Park - 139
Cottage RV Park & Motel - 231
Cottonwood - 197
Cottonwood - 203
Cougar Camp - 185
Cougar Flat - 203
Cougar Inn - 198
Cougar Rock Camp - 179
Cougar RV Park - 185
Coulee City Park - 228
Coulee Lodge Resort - 229
Coulee Playland Res./RV - 222
Country Club Court - 229
Country Estates - 236
County Fairground - 218
County Line Park - 148
Cove Resort - 198
Cove Resort - 204
Cove RV Park - 147
Cove Trailer Park - 168
Cowlitz Falls Park - 182
Cowlitz Resort & RV Park - 184
Cranberry RV & Trailer - 146
Creekside Camping - 157
Cresap Bay Camp - 186
Cresthaven MH Park - 156
Crow Butte State Park - 207
Crystal Springs - 201
Cultus Creek - 208

Curlew Lake State Park - 216
Curley's Resort - 131
Curly's Campground - 222
Daroga State Park - 196
Dash Point State Park - 174
Deception Pass State Park - 160
Deep Lake Resort - 178
Denny Creek - 171
Derry's Resort/Pearrygin - 193
Desert Gold Trailer/Motel - 235
Devil's Park - 191
Diamond Lake Resort - 221
Doe Bay Village Resort - 155
Doe Island - 154
Dosewallips State Park - 168
Douglas Fir - 153
Drew's Trailer Park - 184
Driftwood Acres Ocean - 139
Driftwood RV & Motel - 145
Dunes RV Resort - 139
Dungeness Forks - 136
Dungeness Rec. Area - 136
Eagle Rock Resort - 203
Eagle's Nest Motel & RV - 179
Early Winters - 193
East Crossing - 136
Eightmile - 199
El Rancho RV Park - 224
Elk Meadows RV Park - 208
Elkhorn - 168
Ellensburg KOA - 202
Elma RV Park - 179
Elmer's Trailer Park - 133
Elwha - 133
Entiat City Park - 196
Erland Point MH Park - 168
Esswine Group Camp - 163
Evans - 218
Evergreen Court - 145
Evergreen Manor & RV - 151
Excelsior Group Camp - 153
Fairholm Campground - 133
Falls Creek - 138
Falls Creek - 193
Falls View Campground - 165
Fay Bainbridge State Park - 167
Ferguson Park - 165
Fern Hill Camp & RV - 160
Ferndale Campground - 153
Ferry Lake - 216
Fields Spring State Park - 234
Fir Acres MH/RV Park - 173
Fishhook Park - 235
Fishtrap Lake Resort - 227
Flowing Lake County Park - 165
Forks 101 RV Park - 137
Forks MH & RV Park - 137
Fort Canby State Park - 147
Fort Casey State Park - 160
Fort Ebey State Park - 160
Fort Flagler State Park - 164
Fort Spokane - 223
Fort Walla Walla Camp - 236
Fort Worden State Park - 163
Fortyniner Camp/Motel - 219

Four Seasons Camp - 228
Fox Creek - 197
Frost Road Trailer Park - 184
Game Ridge Motel - 204
Gatton Creek - 138
Gifford - 221
Gig Harbor RV Resort - 174
Glacier View - 198
Glen Ayr RV Park & Motel - 171
Glenoma/Riffe Lake RV - 182
Gold Basin - 163
Golden West Estates - 236
Golden West Mobile - 187
Goodell Creek - 191
Goose Creek - 198
Grandview Inn & RV Park - 217
Granger RV Park - 206
Granite Point Park - 219
Grayland Beach Park - 142
Green Tree RV Park - 235
Guler-Mt. Adams Park - 208
Hamma Hamma - 168
Hammond Trailer Park - 141
Harbor Resort - 141
Harmony Lakeside RV - 181
Harrison Beach - 133
Harrison RV Park - 180
Hause Creek - 204
Heart O' the Hills - 133
Hells Crossing - 203
Henley's Silver Lake Res. - 175
Hidden Village RV Park - 152
Hilltop Mobile Home Park - 233
HoBuck Beach Park - 131
Hoh River - 137
Hoh River Resort & RV - 138
Holand Center RV Park - 141
Home Valley Park - 210
Hood Park - 236
Horseshoe Cove - 157
Horsethief Lake Park - 208
Howard Miller Steelhead - 158
Hunter Hill Vineyard Park - 232
Hunters - 221
Icicle River Ranch - 199
Ida Creek - 199
Ike Kinswa State Park - 181
Illahee RV Park - 140
Illahee State Park - 169
Ilwaco KOA - 147
Indian Creek - 204
Indian Flat - 203
Indian Valley Motel/RV - 134
Ione Motel & RV Park - 215
Ipsut Creek - 176
Iron Creek - 183
Island Country Fair. - 161
Islander RV Park - 141
Issaquah Highlands Club - 171
Issaquah Village RV Park - 171
J R - 194
Jack's RV Park & Motel - 192
James Island - 160
Jarrell Cove State Park - 170
Jarrell's Cove Marina - 173

Jefferson County Fair. - 164
Jerry's Landing RV Park - 221
Johnny Creek - 199
Jolly Rogers - 142
Jones Island - 154
Kachess - 201
Kalaloch - 138
Kamei Resort - 195
Kanaskat-Palmer Park - 175
Kaner Flat - 203
Karwan Village MH/RV - 174
Kayak Point County Park - 162
Keller Ferry - 224
Kenanna RV Park - 142
Keo's Korner - 219
Kettle Falls - 217
Kila Hana Camperland - 142
King's Court RV Park - 222
Kirk's Lodge-Mt. Spokane - 225
Kitsap Memorial Park - 167
Klahowya- 134
Klipchuck - 193
KOA of Spokane - 226
Kopachuck State Park - 174
Kozy Cabins & RV Park - 192
La Wis Wis Campground - 205
Lake Chelan State Park - 195
Lake Creek - 197
Lake Cushman Resort - 172
Lake Cushman State Park - 172
Lake Easton State Park - 201
Lake Gillette - 216
Lake Goodwin Resort - 162
Lake Leland Park - 165
Lake Leo - 216
Lake Mayfield Res./RV - 181
Lake Nahwatzel Resort - 173
Lake Pleasant RV Park - 166
Lake Roesiger Park - 165
Lake Sylvia State Park - 140
Lake Thomas - 216
Lake Wenatchee Park - 198
Lakedale Campground - 155
Lakeshore RV Park - 195
Lakeside RV & Camp - 177
Lakeside RV Park - 165
Lakeview Terrace RV Park - 222
Lamplighter Village RV - 206
LaPush Ocean Park - 136
Larrabee State Park - 157
Last Roundup Motel/RV - 228
Laurents Sun Village Res. - 229
Laze Daze RV Park - 192
Legion Park - 218
Lewis & Clark Camp/RV - 209
Lewis & Clark State Park - 181
Lewis & Clark Trail Park - 234
Lewis River RV Park - 188
Liars Cove Resort - 192
Liberty Lake Park - 226
Lighthouse Marine Park - 152
Lighthouse RV Park - 156
Lincoln Park- 134
Lincoln Rock State Park - 200
Little Naches - 203

Locust Grove - 217
Lodgepole - 203
Lone Fir - 194
Lone Fir Resort - 185
Long Lake - 216
Lost Lake - 214
Louis L. Rasmussen RV - 186
Loup Loup - 194
Lower Falls Rec. Area - 186
Lynden KOA - 152
Lyon's Ferry Marina & RV - 234
Lyons Ferry State Park - 234
Lyre River Park - 134
Majestic Mobile Manor - 174
Manchester State Park - 169
Mar Don Resort - 232
Marcus Island - 218
Marshall Lake Resort - 220
Marten Creek - 163
Martin Way MH & RV - 177
Marv's RV Park - 185
Maryhill State Park - 208
Matia Island - 154
Mauch's Sundown RV - 147
Mayfield Lake Park - 181
McMillan Park - 191
Meridian Terrace Mobile - 175
Mermac RV Park & Store - 184
Methow River KOA - 193
Midway Village & Grocery - 198
Mike's Beach Resort - 172
Mill Village RV Park - 179
Miller River - 195
Millersylvania State Park - 178
Millpond - 214
Mineral Springs - 201
Mineral Springs Res./RV - 201
Minerva Beach - 172
Money Creek - 195
Mora Campground - 136
Moran State Park - 155
Moss Creek - 210
Mossyrock Park - 182
Mount Spokane Park - 225
Mountain Rd. Mobile/RV - 182
Mountain View RV Park - 153
Mountain View Trailer - 159
Mt. Linton RV Park - 215
Mt. St. Helens RV Park - 184
Muralt's Mobile Home RV - 132
Mutiny Bay Resort - 161
Nasalle Trailer Court - 144
Nason Creek - 198
Nassa Point Motel - 148
Newhalem Creek - 191
Nisqually Plaza RV Park - 177
Noisy Creek - 215
Norseland Mobile Est./RV - 169
North Fork - 183
North Fork - 197
North Whidbey RV Park - 160
Northwest Fishing & RV - 188
Oak Bay Park - 164
Oak Harbor City Beach - 160
Oaknoll RV Park - 174

Oaks Trailer & RV Park - 185
Oasis Park - 230
Ocean Aire Trailer Park - 145
Ocean City State Park - 140
Ocean Gate Resort - 143
Ocean Park Resort - 145
Oceanic City Center RV - 145
Odessa Golf & RV Park - 231
Odlin County Park - 155
Offut Lake Resort & RV - 180
Ohanapecosh - 205
Oklahoma - 210
Old Amer. Kampground - 220
Old Chiefs MH Park - 137
Old Fort Townsend Park - 164
Olson's Resort - 131
Olympia Campground - 178
Orchard RV Park - 213
Oriole - 192
Orondo River Park - 196
Osoyoos Lake State Park - 213
Osoyoos RV Park - 213
Overland Station - 224
Pacific Aire RV Park - 142
Pacific Beach State Park - 138
Pacific Motel & RV Park - 142
Pacific Park Trailer Park - 146
Packwood RV & MH Park - 205
Palouse Falls State Park - 234
Panorama Point - 157
Panther Creek - 209
Paradise Creek - 209
Paradise Point State Park - 188
Paradise Resort - 195
Park Creek - 158
Parklane Motel & RV Park - 224
Patos Island - 154
Peabody Creek RV Park - 133
Peaceful Pines RV Park - 227
Peach Beach - 207
Pearrygin Lake State Park - 193
Pedal Inn Campground - 156
Pegg's RV Park- 146
Pend Oreille Park - 221
Penrose Point State Park - 170
Peppertree West Inn/RV - 180
Peterson Group Camp - 208
Peterson Prairie - 209
Pheasant Run RV - 232
Picnic Pines/Silver Lake - 227
Pillar Point - 132
Pine Flat Group Camp - 197
Pine Point Resort - 217
Pine Springs Resort - 207
Pine Village KOA - 197
Pine-Near Trailer Park - 193
Pioneer Park - 220
Pioneer RV Park - 145
Plaza RV & MH Park - 152
Pleasant Valley - 203
Plymouth Park - 236
Point Hudson Resort - 164
Point-No-Point Resort - 168
Ponderosa Hills RV Park - 224
Ponderosa Lodge & RV - 218

Poplar Flat - 194
Porcupine Bay - 223
Port Angeles KOA - 135
Port Ludlow RV Park - 164
Port of Kalama RV Park - 187
Posey Island - 154
Potholes State Park - 232
Potlatch State Park - 172
Quilcene Park - 166
Quincy Valley Golf & RV - 230
R&R Sports Center & RV - 138
Rain Forest Resort Village - 138
Rainbow Cove - 227
Rainbow Falls State Park - 180
Rainbow Resort - 175
Rainbow Resort - 213
Rainbow's End RV Park - 135
Reed Island State Park - 188
Rest A While RV Park - 172
River Bend - 204
River Bend RV Park - 166
River Bend RV Park - 194
River Meadows Park - 162
River Rue RV Park - 224
River's End Campground - 147
Riverbend Campground - 178
Riverbend Park - 159
Riverfront Park RV - 158
Riverside RV Resort - 139
Riverside State Park - 225
Riverview Campground - 202
Riverview Park - 159
Riverview Trailer Court - 213
Roadhouse Inn RV - 182
Robbie's RV Park - 230
Robin Hood Village - 170
Rock Garden RV Park - 221
Rock Island - 199
Rockport State Park - 158
Rocky Point Mobile/RV - 169
Rod's Beach Resort & RV - 139
Rotary Riverside Park - 180
Roy's Motel & RV Park - 182
Royal City Golf & RV Park - 232
RV Resort Four Seasons - 236
RV Town Inc. - 201
Saddle Dam - 186
Saddlebag Island - 156
Salmon Creek Roadside - 144
Salmon La Sac - 200
Salmon Meadows - 192
Salmon Shore Resort - 177
Salt Creek Recreation Area- 134
Saltwater State Park - 174
Sam's Trailer & RV Park- 132
San Juan County Park - 156
Sand Castle RV Park - 146
Sand-Lo Motel & Trailer - 146
Sawmill Flat - 203
Scenic Beach State Park - 169
Schafer State Park - 141
Scotts U-Fish & RV Park- 181
Seal Rock - 168
Seaquest State Park - 184
Seattle South KOA - 166

Sequim Bay Resort - 135
Sequim Bay State Park - 136
Sequim West RV/Inn - 135
Seven Bays Marina - 223
Shades by the Sea - 139
Shadow Mountain- 134
Shadows RV & Camp - 225
Shady Firs Camp & RV - 183
Shady Pines Resort - 192
Shady Tree RV Park - 134
Shady Tree RV Park - 230
Shannon Creek - 158
Shannon's - 213
Shaw Isl. South Beach - 154
Sherwood Hills Adult RV - 169
Shore Acres Resort - 219
Shoreline Resort - 137
Sierra-Rainier RV Park - 175
Silver Beach Resort - 219
Silver Falls - 197
Silver Fir - 153
Silver King Resort - 134
Silver Lake Motel/Res. - 184
Silver Lake Park - 153
Silver Maple RV Park - 140
Silver Shores RV Park - 165
Silver Springs - 176
Skagit County Fair. - 159
Skamokawa Vista Park - 148
Skookum Chinook Camp - 220
Smitty's Island Retreat - 164
Smitty's RV Overnighter - 206
Smokey Point RV Park - 162
Snooz Junction RV Park - 170
Snoqualmie River Camp - 170
Snug Harbor Resort - 156
Soap/Smokiam Camp - 230
Soda Springs - 203
Sol Duc Hot Springs Res. - 135
Soleduck - 135
Sou'wester Lodge/Trailer - 146
South Bend Mobile/RV - 144
South Prairie Creek RV - 176
South Sequim Bay RV - 136
South Skookum Lake - 220
South Whidbey State Park - 161
Spectacle Falls Resort - 213
Spectacle Lake Resort - 214
Spencer Lake Resort & RV - 173
Spencer Spit Park - 155
Sprague Lake Resort - 228
Spring Canyon - 223
Squaw Rock Resort - 204
Squilchuck State Park - 200
Squire Creek Park - 162
Stage Stop at Sully's - 191
Staircase Campground - 173
Stan Hedwall Park - 181
Stars & Stripes RV Park - 230
Steamboat Rock - 223
Stuart Island State Park - 154
Sturgeon Trailer Harbor - 140
Sucia Island State Park - 154
Sullivan Lake - 215
Sumas RV Park - 153

Summertide RV & Marina - 170
Sun Banks Resort - 223
Sun Cove Resort - 214
Sun Crest Resort - 231
Sun Lakes Park Resort - 229
Sun Lakes State Park - 229
Sunset - 187
Sunset RV Park - 207
Sunshine Point - 179
Sunshine RV Park - 136
Surfside Campland - 132
Sutton Bay Resort - 226
Swan Lake - 216
Swift Camp - 186
T-J's RV Park - 175
Taidnapam Park - 182
Takhlakh - 183
Taneum - 201
The Dalles - 176
The Last Resort - 200
The Other Place RV Park - 192
Three Rivers Resort - 137
Thurston County ORV - 178
Tidelands on Beach RV - 139
Tiffany's Resort - 217
Tiffany's River Inn/Boyer - 233
Timberland RV Park - 143
Timberline RV Park - 157
Tinkham - 171
Tolt River/MacDonald - 171
Totem RV Park - 142
Toutle Village RV Park - 184
Tower Rock - 183
Tower Rock U-Fish & RV - 183
Town & Country - 155
Trailer City Park - 235
Trailer Corral RV Park - 201
Trailer Inns RV Park - 167
Trailer Inns RV Park - 205
Trailer Inns RV Park - 225
Trailer Village RV Park - 180
Tranquilcene Trailer Park - 166
Travel Inn Resort - 179
Tretteviks Trailer Park- 132
Tulalip Millsite - 163
Tumwater - 198
Turlo - 163
Turn Island State Park - 154
Twanoh State Park - 170
Twentyfive Mile Creek - 196
Twin Cedars RV Park - 167
Twin Harbors State Park - 142
Twin Spruce RV Park - 143
Tyee Motel & RV Park - 131
Uncle John's RV Park - 176
Valley Cottage Motel - 199
Van Riper's Resort & RV - 132
Vantage KOA - 202
Vasa Park Resort - 167
Verlot - 163
Villager Inn Motel RV - 231
Volcano View Camp - 188
Volcano View Resort - 184
Wallace Falls State Park - 194
Walupt Lake - 205

Wanapum State Park - 202
War Creek - 194
Washington Park - 156
Waterfront Marina - 222
We & You MH/RV Park - 173
Welcome Inn Trailer & RV 133
Wenatchee Con. Park - 200
Wenberg State Park - 162
West Beach Resort - 155
Western Shores Motel - 143
Westgate RV Park & Motel - 145
Whalen's RV Park- 152
Whiskey Creek Beach - 135
Whispering Pines RV Park - 218
White Dove MH Park - 206
White River Campground - 176
Wild Rose RV Park - 225
Wilderness Village - 158
Wilderness West Resort - 215
Wildwood Resort - 157
Wildwood Senior RV Park - 146
Wiley Creek - 163
Willaby - 138
Willapa Harbor Golf & RV - 143
Willapa RV Park - 143
Williams Lake Resort - 228
Willow Bay Resort - 226
Willow Vista MH & RV - 166
Willows - 204
Willows Trailer Village - 232
Wind Ranch - 210
Windmill Inn RV & Trailer - 152
Windust Resort - 236
Windy Point - 202
Winston Creek RV Park - 182
Wish Poosh - 200
Woodland Park - 205
Yakima KOA - 206
Yakima Nation RV Park - 207
Yakima Sportsman Park - 206
Yellow Pine RV Park - 217

WA cities - 127-236
Aberdeen - 140
Acme - 159
Allyn - 169
Anacortes - 156
Ariel - 188
Arlington - 162
Ashford - 180
Asotin - 234
Beaver - 137
Belfair - 169
Bellevue - 167
Bellingham - 156-157
Benton City - 235
Bingen - 210
Blaine - 151-152
Bothell - 166
Bremerton - 168-169
Bridgeport - 221-222
Brinnon - 168
Burlington - 159-160
Carbonado - 176
Carson - 209

Castle Rock - 184
Cathlamet - 148
Centralia - 180
Chattaroy - 225
Chehalis - 180-181
Chelan - 195-196
Cheney - 227-228
Chewelah - 219
Chinook - 147
Clallam Bay - 132
Cle Elum - 201
Colfax - 233
Colville - 215-216
Conconully - 191-192
Concrete - 157-158
Connell - 233
Cook - 210
Copalis Beach - 139-140
Cougar - 185-186
Coulee City - 228-229
Coupeville - 160-161
Dayton - 234
Doty - 180
Dryden - 199
Easton - 201
Eatonville - 179
Elbe - 179
Eldon - 168
Ellensburg - 202
Elma - 179
Entiat - 196-197
Enumclaw - 175-176
Ephrata - 230-231
Everett - 165
Fall City - 170-171
Federal Way - 174
Ferndale - 153
Forks - 137-138
Fort Spokane - 223
Freeland - 161
Gifford - 221
Glacier - 153
Glenoma - 182
Gold Bar - 194
Goldendale - 207-208
Grand Coulee - 222-223
Granger - 206-207
Granite Falls - 162-163
Grayland - 142-143
Harrington - 229
Hoodsport - 171-173
Hunters - 221
Ilwaco - 147
Index - 194
Ione - 215
Issaquah - 171
Jasper - 236
Joyce - 133
Kalama - 186-187
Kelso - 185
Kennewick - 234, 235
Kettle Falls - 217-218
Klipsan Beach - 145
Langley - 161
LaPush - 136-137

Leavenworth - 197-199
Lilliwaup - 172
Long Beach - 145-146
Longview - 185
Loomis - 191
Lynden - 152-153
Lynnwood - 167
Marblemount - 191
Marys Corner - 181
Medical Lake - 227
Metaline Falls - 214-215
Montesano - 140-141
Morton - 182
Moses Lake - 231-232
Mossyrock - 181-182
Mt. Vernon - 159
Naches - 202-204
Nasalle - 144
Neah Bay - 131
Newhalem - 191
Newport - 220-221
Nine Mile Falls - 226
North Bend - 171
Oak Harbor - 160, 161
O'Brien - 135
Ocean City - 140
Ocean Park - 144-145
Ocean Shores - 140
Odessa - 231
Okanogan - 218
Olympia - 176-178
Omak - 218
Oroville - 213, 214
Othello - 232
Pacific Beach - 138
Packwood - 205
Pasco - 234
Point Roberts - 152
Pomeroy - 233-234
Port Angeles - 132-135
Port Orchard - 169
Port Townsend - 163-164
Pullman - 233
Puyallup - 174-175
Queets - 138
Quilcene - 165-166
Quinault - 138
Quincy - 230, 231
Randle - 182-183
Raymond - 143-144
Republic - 216-217
Richland - 234-236
Rimrock - 204
Ritzville - 231
Rockport - 158
Roslyn - 200
Royal City - 232
San Juans - 154-156, 160-161
Seattle - 166-167
Seaview - 145, 146
Sedro Woolley - 158-159
Seiku - 131-132
Sequim - 135-136
Shelton - 173
Skamania - 186

Skamokawa - 148
Skykomish - 195
Snohomish - 165
Soap Lake - 229-230
South Bend - 144
South Prarie - 176
Spokane - 224-227
Sprague - 228
Stanwood - 161-162
Sumas - 153
Tacoma - 173-174
Tokeland - 143
Toledo - 184
Tonasket - 213-214
Toutle - 184
Trout Lake - 208-209
Twisp - 194
Union Gap - 206
Usk - 219-220
Vancouver - 187-188
Vantage - 202
Walla Walla - 236
Washougal - 188
Wenatchee - 200
Westport - 141-142
Wilbur - 224
Winslow - 167-168
Winthrop - 192-194
Woodland - 187
Yacolt - 187
Yakima - 205-206
Yale - 186

Water skiing - 61, 65, 66, 69, 70,
75, 84, 96, 98, 105, 106, 107, 108,
122, 157, 162, 170, 185, 186, 195,
198, 200, 201, 202, 207, 208, 213,
215, 216, 223, 229, 232, 233

Waterfalls - 23, 59, 62, 64, 65, 69,
73, 165, 171, 180, 182, 186, 193,
194, 197, 213, 234

Wheelchair/disabled access - 13,
19, 20, 21, 22, 23, 24, 25, 26, 27,
28, 29, 30, 32, 33, 34, 35, 37, 39,
40, 42, 43, 44, 46, 47, 48, 52, 53,
54, 55, 56, 57, 58, 59, 60, 61, 62,
63, 64, 65, 66, 67, 68, 69, 70, 71,
72, 73, 74, 75, 76, 78, 79, 80, 81,
82, 84, 87, 88, 89, 90, 91, 92, 93,
94, 95, 96, 97, 99, 100, 101, 102,
103, 105, 107, 109, 110, 111, 112,
113, 114, 117, 118, 119, 120, 121,
122, 123, 125, 126, 131, 132, 133,
134, 135, 136, 137, 138, 139, 140,
141, 142, 143, 144, 145, 146, 147,
148, 151, 152, 153, 155, 156, 157,
158, 159, 160, 161, 162, 163, 164,
165, 166, 167, 168, 169, 170, 171,
172, 173, 174, 175, 176, 177, 178,
179, 180, 181, 182, 183, 184, 185,
186, 187, 188, 191, 192, 193, 194,
195, 196, 197, 198, 199, 200, 201,
202, 203, 204, 205, 206, 207, 208,
209, 210, 213, 214, 215, 216, 217,
218, 219, 220, 221, 222, 223, 224,
225, 226, 227, 228, 229, 230, 231,
232, 233, 234, 235, 236

Wilderness area - 64, 72, 98, 101,
108, 113, 119, 191, 200, 205, 209

Windsurfing - 41, 51, 87, 105,
107, 108, 196, 208, 210

253

Books by KiKi Canniff

FREE CAMPGROUNDS OF WASHINGTON & OREGON
This lightweight guide details the region's hundreds of cost free campgrounds. A terrific book for folks who enjoy camping close to nature. *"...very well done, easy to read and to understand ... the cost of this book is saved with the first campground used!"* **This Week Magazine.** ($8.95)

THE BEST FREE HISTORIC ATTRACTIONS IN OREGON & WASHINGTON - FAVORITE FREEBIES - Volume 1
Includes the region's best ghost towns, covered bridges, aging lighthouses, museums, pioneer wagon trails, historic towns, archeological digs, Indian artifact collections, railroad memorabilia and more! *"KiKi Canniff is an expert on freebies"* **Woman's World Magazine.** ($10.95)

UNFORGETTABLE PACIFIC NORTHWEST CAMPING VACATIONS; Your guide to Oregon & Washington's most spectacular camping regions. Each vacation covers a variety of things to see and do as well as campgrounds for both RV and tent campers. *"There's a whole world of natural beauty to explore on the byways and backroads of Oregon and Washington. Nowadays, following those pathways is easier, thanks to the efforts of KiKi Canniff."* **The News-Times.** ($10.95)

A CAMPER'S GUIDE TO OREGON & WASHINGTON; The only complete guide to the region's non-membership RV parks and improved tent campgrounds. Perfect for campers who want showers, hookups or other civilized facilities. Each campground listing includes facilities available, trailer length, activities, and easy to follow directions. *This handy guide belongs on every Northwest camper's 'must have' list."* **The Chronicle.** ($13.95)

ABOUT THE AUTHOR

KiKi Canniff is a Pacific Northwest writer who specializes in books about Oregon & Washington. She is the Portland Oregonian's campground columnist, and an avid camper. KiKi also enjoys hiking, travel, history, nature and exploring Pacific Northwest backroads.

ORDER COUPON

Please send:

___FREE CAMPGROUNDS OF WA /OR @ $8.95 ea. _____

___BEST FREE HISTORIC ATTRACTIONS IN OR/WA;
    FAVORITE FREEBIES - Vol. 1 @ $10.95 ea.   _____

___UNFORGETTABLE PACIFIC NORTHWEST

    CAMPING VACATIONS - Vol. 1 @ $10.95 ea.   _____

___A CAMPER'S GUIDE TO OR/WA @ $13.95 ea.   _____

Shipping   <u>2.00</u>

TOTAL ENCLOSED   _____

Name _____

Address _____

City/State/Zip Code _____

Send this order coupon to Ki² Enterprises, P.O. Box 186,
Willamina, Oregon 97396

C95

✂---✂

Please send:

___FREE CAMPGROUNDS OF WA /OR @ $8.95 ea. _____

___BEST FREE HISTORIC ATTRACTIONS IN OR/WA;
    FAVORITE FREEBIES - Vol. 1 @ $10.95 ea.   _____

___UNFORGETTABLE PACIFIC NORTHWEST

    CAMPING VACATIONS - Vol. 1 @ $10.95 ea.   _____

___A CAMPER'S GUIDE TO OR/WA @ $13.95 ea.   _____

Shipping   <u>2.00</u>

TOTAL ENCLOSED   _____

Name _____

Address _____

City/State/Zip Code _____

Send this order coupon to Ki² Enterprises, P.O. Box 186,
Willamina, Oregon 97396

C95